Ethi

Contemporary World

This is a superb collection of 25 short chapters on current ethical issues. The pieces included are accessible, brisk and often arresting, ensuring that the book will have an important role to play in both philosophical and public discussion.

– Philip Pettit, Princeton University, USA,
and Australian National University

Arguments about ethics often centre on traditional questions of, for instance, euthanasia and abortion. Whilst these questions are still in the foreground, recent years have seen an explosion of new moral problems. Moral and political clashes are now as likely to be about sexuality and gender and the status of refugees, immigrants and borders, or the ethics of social media, safe spaces, disability and robo-ethics.

How should we approach these debates? What are the issues at stake? What are the most persuasive arguments? Edited by best-selling philosophy author David Edmonds, *Ethics and the Contemporary World* assembles a star-studded line-up of philosophers to explore twenty-five of the most important ethical problems confronting us today. They engage with moral problems in race and gender, the environment, war and international relations, global poverty, ethics and social media, democracy, rights and moral status, and science and technology.

Whether you want to learn more about the ethics of poverty, food, extremism, or artificial intelligence and enhancement, this book will help you understand the issues, sharpen your perspective and, hopefully, make up your own mind.

David Edmonds is Distinguished Research Fellow at the Oxford Uehiro Centre for Practical Ethics, University of Oxford, UK, and a BBC journalist. His books include *Would You Kill the Fat Man?* and (with John Eidinow) *Rousseau's Dog* and *Wittgenstein's Poker*. With Nigel Warburton, he runs the popular 'Philosophy Bites' podcast series, which has had 38 million downloads. @DavidEdmonds100

EDITED BY
DAVID EDMONDS

Ethics and the Contemporary World

Routledge
Taylor & Francis Group

LONDON AND NEW YORK

First published 2019
by Routledge
2 Park Square, Milton Park, Abingdon, Oxon OX14 4RN

and by Routledge
52 Vanderbilt Avenue, New York, NY 10017

Routledge is an imprint of the Taylor & Francis Group, an informa business

British Library Cataloguing-in-Publication Data
A catalogue record for this book is available from the British Library

Library of Congress Cataloging-in-Publication Data
Names: Edmonds, David, 1964– editor.
Title: Ethics and the contemporary world / edited by David Edmonds.
Description: Abingdon, Oxon ; New York : Routledge, 2019. | Includes
    bibliographical references and index.
Identifiers: LCCN 2019000843 | ISBN 9781138092013 (hardback :
    alk. paper) | ISBN 9781138092051 (pbk. : alk. paper) | ISBN
    9781315107752 (ebk.)
Subjects: LCSH: Ethics, Modern—21st century.
Classification: LCC BJ320 .E85 2019 | DDC 170—dc23
LC record available at https://lccn.loc.gov/2019000843

ISBN: 978-1-138-09201-3 (hbk)
ISBN: 978-1-138-09205-1 (pbk)
ISBN: 978-1-315-10775-2 (ebk)

Typeset in Joanna and DIN
by Apex CoVantage, LLC

Printed in the United Kingdom
by Henry Ling Limited

Contents

vii **Contents**

Gulzaar Barn is Lecturer in the Department of Philosophy at the University of Birmingham, UK.

Gillian Brock is Professor of Philosophy at the University of Auckland, New Zealand. She is currently also a fellow at the Edmond J. Safra Center for Ethics, Harvard University, USA.

Allen Buchanan is Professor of Philosophy in the Department of Philosophy and Freedom Center at the University of Arizona.

Steve Clarke is Senior Research Fellow in the Wellcome Centre for Ethics and Humanities, and the Oxford Uehiro Centre for Practical Ethics at the University of Oxford, UK, as well as Associate Professor of Philosophy at Charles Sturt University, Australia.

Tony Coady is Emeritus Professor of Philosophy at the University of Melbourne and one of Australia's best-known philosophers. He has an outstanding international reputation for his writings on epistemology and on political violence and political ethics.

Roger Crisp is Uehiro Fellow and Tutor in Philosophy at St. Anne's College, University of Oxford, UK, Professor of Moral Philosophy at the University of Oxford, and Professorial Fellow at the Australian Catholic University.

Katrien Devolder is Senior Research Fellow at the Oxford Uehiro Centre for Practical Ethics and a Research Fellow at Wolfson College, University of Oxford, UK.

Thomas Douglas is Senior Research Fellow in the Oxford Uehiro Centre for Practical Ethics and the Faculty of Philosophy, University of Oxford, UK, and a Hugh Price Fellow at Jesus College, Oxford.

Brian D. Earp is Associate Director of the Yale-Hastings Program in Ethics and Health Policy at Yale University and The Hastings Center, USA, and a Research Fellow in the Oxford Uehiro Centre for Practical Ethics at the University of Oxford, UK.

David Edmonds is Distinguished Research Fellow at the Oxford Uehiro Centre for Practical Ethics, University of Oxford, UK, and a BBC journalist.

Helen Frowe is Professor of Practical Philosophy and Wallenberg Academy Research Fellow in the Department of Philosophy at Stockholm University, Sweden, and Director of the Stockholm Centre for the Ethics of War and Peace.

Stephen M. Gardiner is Professor of Philosophy and Ben Rabinowitz Endowed Professor of Human Dimensions of the Environment at the University of Washington, USA.

Hilary Greaves is Professor of Philosophy and Director of the Global Priorities Institute at the University of Oxford, UK.

Guy Kahane is Associate Professor of Philosophy and a Fellow and Tutor in Philosophy at Pembroke College, UK, and Director of Studies and Research Fellow at the Oxford Uehiro Centre for Practical Ethics, University of Oxford.

Neil Levy is Professor of Philosophy at Macquarie University, Australia, and a Senior Research Fellow at the Oxford Uehiro Centre for Practical Ethics, University of Oxford, UK.

Jeff McMahan is the White's Professor of Moral Philosophy at the University of Oxford, UK, and a Distinguished Research Fellow with the Oxford Uehiro Centre for Practical Ethics.

Seumas Miller is Senior Research Fellow in the Oxford Uehiro Centre for Practical Ethics, University of Oxford, UK. He also has research appointments at TU Delft, the Netherlands, and Charles Sturt University, Australia – in the Cooperative Research Centre in Cybersecurity.

Francesca Minerva is a FWO Post-Doctoral Fellow at the University of Ghent, Belgium.

Theron Pummer is Senior Lecturer in Philosophy at the University of St Andrews, UK, and Director of the Centre for Ethics, Philosophy and Public Affairs.

Regina Rini teaches in the Philosophy Department at York University, Canada, where she holds the Canada Research Chair in Philosophy of Moral and Social Cognition.

Rebecca Roache is Senior Lecturer in Philosophy at Royal Holloway, University of London, UK.

Julian Savulescu is Uehiro Chair in Practical Ethics at the University of Oxford, UK, and a Fellow of St Cross College, Director of the Oxford Uehiro Centre for Practical Ethics, and the Wellcome Centre for Ethics and Humanities. He is also Visiting Professorial Fellow in Biomedical Ethics at the Murdoch Children's Research Institute, Melbourne, Australia, and

Melbourne University as Distinguished International Visiting Professor in Law.

John Tasioulas is the inaugural Yeoh Professor of Politics, Philosophy and Law at the Dickson Poon School of Law, King's College London, UK, and Director of the Yeoh Tiong Lay Centre for Politics, Philosophy, and Law at King's College.

Carissa Véliz is Research Fellow at the Oxford Uehiro Centre for Practical Ethics and the Wellcome Centre for Ethics and Humanities at the University of Oxford, UK, and a Postdoctoral Research Fellow at Christ Church, Oxford.

Heather Widdows is the John Ferguson Professor of Global Ethics and the Deputy Pro-Vice Chancellor for Research Impact at the University of Birmingham, UK.

Dominic Wilkinson is Director of Medical Ethics and Professor of Medical Ethics at the Oxford Uehiro Centre for Practical Ethics, University of Oxford, UK. He is a consultant in newborn intensive care at John Radcliffe Hospital, Oxford, holds a health practitioner research fellowship with the Wellcome Trust, and is a senior research fellow at Jesus College Oxford.

Preface and acknowledgements

Philosophers do not have an obligation to engage with the world – to be public philosophers. This is true not least because many philosophers specialize in areas of philosophy which have little to contribute to contemporary political or moral matters.

But the University of Oxford's Oxford Uehiro Centre for Practical Ethics does what it says on the tin – it focuses on applied morality. That is to say, it encourages reflection and debate about ethical matters. And it specifically aims to guide the choices humans have to make – on everything from climate change, to terrorism, to genetic engineering, to poverty and inequality, to population size, to artificial intelligence.

The Uehiro Centre is now an acknowledged leader in the academic study of applied ethics with an international reputation. And almost all the contributors to this book have some kind of relationship with the Centre. The Uehiro Centre is generously supported by The Uehiro Foundation on Ethics and Education.

This book is aimed at students at the beginning of their philosophical studies. It covers a range of topics that I have grouped under broad headings: race and gender, the environment, war and international relations, global poverty, ethics and social media, democracy, rights and moral status, and science and technology.

Obviously, this is only a snapshot of the wide range of issues which practical ethics can cover. But I hope it is a reasonably representative snapshot nonetheless.

I have several people to thank. First of all, of course, my wonderful contributors. I straddle the worlds of academia and broadcasting. Whilst some of my philosophers may have adopted a slightly more elastic approach to deadlines than the typical journalist is accustomed to, with a little prodding they all delivered their chapters and together have, I hope, created a lovely volume.

I would like to acknowledge the good people of Routledge and Apex CoVantage, especially Tony Bruce, Adam Johnson and Jennifer Bonnar.

I am also indebted to the director of the Oxford Uehiro Centre for Practical Ethics, Julian Savulescu, whose idea this book was, as well as to the administrative staff, Deborah Sheehan, Rachel Gaminiratne, Rocci Wilkinson and especially Miriam Wood, who made the initial contact with the philosophers featured in the book and persuaded them to contribute.

David Edmonds
@DavidEdmonds100

Preface and acknowledgements

Race and gender

Part One

Profiling and discrimination

One

David Edmonds

Here is a story about queue-rage, injustice, and profiling.

Each week, I spend a day or two in the British Library. For as long as I can remember, there has been some sort of security in operation at the main doors. It used to operate like this. The security staff would allow the vast majority of people to walk through unmolested. But occasionally they would stop someone and ask to check their bag. This very rarely happened to me (I have a strikingly innocent face) and, when it did, it was only a minor inconvenience, delaying me by just a few minutes. Still, it would annoy me, and meant that I was pipped to my favourite library seat. The Library has now changed its policy – with an interesting psychological consequence, to which I will return later.

In London, as in many parts of the world, we have had to become accustomed to living with the threat of terrorism. The British Library security guards are presumably on the lookout for would-be terrorists, although the Library is not the most obvious of targets.

Readers, I expect, will find it easy to sympathise with my irritation at having someone rummage through my stuff, and slowing me down. We've all experienced this sort of situation – at public buildings or events, at airports. But now shift the perspective. Imagine not that somebody is searching you, but that you are doing the searching. Imagine that you are one of those guards. Whom would you choose to stop, and why?

Suppose the next two people entering the building were an octogenarian woman and a young male of Middle Eastern appearance. Would it make more sense for you to inspect the young man than the old woman?

Would that be rational? Would it be fair? Would it be racist?

*

The example of targeting specific groups of people for additional security checks is just one instance of profiling. Profiling – attempting to extrapolate information about a person based on a trait or characteristic they possess – is a deeply contentious topic. It is also ubiquitous. We could hardly make our way through the world without making generalisations. Profiling occurs at many levels. When you meet someone new, you make assumptions about them based on how they look or sound. Much of this takes place at a subconscious level. You are processing information, their accent, their clothes, their race, their smile. You use this information to make judgements about them. When an insurance company asks you questions, where you live, what you do, your age, your gender, they are using this information to assess risk.

In our Brave New World, in which decisions are increasingly subcontracted to artificial intelligence, profiling is only going to become more common. Algorithms run by companies will dictate what kind of advertisements you see, what loans you'll be able to access, what utility tariffs you have to pay.

Sometimes you may benefit from profiling and other times you may lose out. If I put down 'journalist' on a car insurance form, I will be asked to pay a higher premium than if I enter 'academic'. Journalists appear to be more prone to accidents than academics. The box I tick won't affect the safety of my driving or the likelihood of my being in a collision. But it does impact how I'm profiled. Profiling relies on there being groups, or categories of people.

Let me talk a little about the logic of groups.

THE LOGIC OF GROUPS

In the loose way in which I use the term, each of us can be categorised into an infinite number of groups. Male or female? American or British or Nigerian or Nepalese? Christian or Buddhist or Jewish or Muslim? They need not be exclusive: I can be American and British.

The school soccer team is a sort of group. You may be a member of the group of people above six foot, or the group of people below six foot. You may be a conservative, a liberal or a socialist. These are all types of groups. In the standard case, members of a group share at least one characteristic in common – e.g. males have a Y-chromosome.

Normally we talk about particular groups only if there's a purpose in doing so. It would be weird to categorise together people above six foot unless there was some reason why this height was pertinent. One could imagine circumstances in which this might make sense. Perhaps a particular disease was prevalent among the tall – or perhaps a clothing company categorised people by height after deciding to specialise in catering to the needs of the tall.

Most groups will have fuzzy borders. It may not be entirely clear whether a person does belong into a particular category. For example, most of us are a tiny bit taller in the morning than the evening – consequently, some people will be above six foot only at certain times of the day. There are some categories, such as sex, which were once regarded as essentially binary: either you were male, or you were female. These days, there's an acknowledgement that it's not as straight-forward as that. Some people, for example, have both male and female physical characteristics. A few people have the Y chromosome but female genitalia.

There are a few more points to make about groups. First, the individuals within some groups will have voluntarily chosen to belong (the soccer club) but in other groups there has been no choice (a person born biologically male did not *choose* his sex). Second, in my expansive understanding of 'groups', it is not necessary to *know* that you are a member of a group to *be* a member of it. If you have never measured yourself, you may not be certain whether you belong to the group of humans who are taller than six foot. Third, groups differ in their structure. Some groups are constituted in a formal sense – a soccer club might have written rules for membership – whilst others don't have anything like this (there is no written constitution governing the male group).

Finally, and importantly, groups can be more or less broad and can be subdivided. For example, as well as the group of men, there are subsections of this group, such as the group of men aged between 25 and 40. This narrowing process can continue indefinitely – for example, the group of men aged between 25 and 40, who live in London, are married, and in a job earning less than £35,000 a year etc.

As I have mentioned, at some level generality and categorisation is inevitable: to identify someone as a human is already to categorise them. But why is it useful to categorise humans into sub-groups? Well, one obvious reason is that we can use membership of groups to make predictions. That is to say, if I know that you are a member of a particular group, I can use this information to assess the likelihood that you will have another characteristic or that you will behave in various ways. That could save me a huge amount of time and a huge investment of resources. If a medical test for a disease is expensive, it would be costly to give it to everyone, when instead it could be targeted at those who are most prone to have the disease.

In general, knowing about your membership of some groups will be more useful than knowing about your membership of others. Knowing that you belong to the group of people whose first name has only one syllable conveys little of use to me. Knowing your sex is much more useful. Sex is correlated with all sorts of other things. On average, women live longer than men. Women are safer drivers than men. Women still earn less than men.

Would it ever be wrong to make use of these statistical links?

THE PROFILER

We should begin on a cautionary note. Often people believe that there is a correlation between a proxy such as race or sex and something else, when there really isn't. There might be a deeply ingrained belief that individuals in a particular group are less friendly or more violent or more corrupt than others. And this might be completely untrue. There might be no such statistical relationship. Sometimes there might be an innocent reason for why people believe something that is untrue. But the explanation for the belief in an unfounded correlation can usually be summed up in one word – bigotry. There is a caricature that Scots are mean. As far as I know, there is no evidence at all to back that claim up. The belief that Scots are mean is pure prejudice.[1] Many of our assumptions about individuals based on their membership of groups will be of this form.

But suppose there is a statistical relationship? What then?

Even so, there are reasons for the would-be profiler to be wary. Why? Well, the relationship might be very weak indeed. It might be the case that there's a link between 49.9% of women and some other characteristic, X, and 50.1% of men and the same characteristic. For most purposes, that's hardly a wide enough statistical gap to justify treating men and women differently.

What's more, even if there were a more statistically significant correlation, we would still need to worry about false negatives and false positives. If we were using a proxy like religion to determine whom to search in a security operation, then a false positive would involve stopping someone who was innocent, and a false negative would be failing to stop somebody of a different religion who posed a danger. Suppose that almost all terrorists in the past have emerged from one religious group X. Still, these terrorists would represent only a miniscule percentage of total X. So if all members of X are searched by the security forces, the vast majority of people targeted in this way would be innocent. And if a few members of other religious groups were would-be terrorists, ignoring this possibility could prove extremely costly.

Numbers, and statistical relationships, are not fixed forever. Correlations are not carved in stone. Society evolves. So another problem with profiling is that the very practice of profiling might itself alter the statistics about the world and in ways we should regret. There are at least two routes this might take.

First, human beings are adaptable. If a terrorist organisation is determined to blow up a plane, but realises that everyone with a certain profile – a particular age, race, sex, nationality – is closely questioned at airports, they will shift their tactics and try to recruit bomb carriers from another demographic group. Using profiling to combat terrorists would then be self-defeating. Because institutions tend to be sluggish about reforming their methods and policies, the statistics on which they base their policies may be out of date.

Second, and conversely, profiling might entrench a statistical difference between two groups and so cement divisions in society. Imagine that one racial group was disproportionately responsible for street crime. If, consequently, the police chose to target members of this racial group, there is a strong possibility that individuals would feel harassed and oppressed. They would resent being suspected. They might feel under a constant threat of being stopped. They might become hostile to the police, unwilling to cooperate in the battle against crime and increasingly alienated from the wider community. Narrowing in on one racial group might contribute to driving members of that group into crime, which in turn might encourage profiling – a vicious circle.

THE PROFILED

All of these are reasons why, from the point of view of the profiler, we should be cautious about profiling. What about the perspective of those being profiled?

The benefits and the costs of profiling are not distributed among the population evenly. This generates a further asymmetry. Those who benefit from profiling are likely to take their privileged status for granted. If you belong to, let's say, the wealthy majority community, you probably won't even notice how favourable assumptions are constantly being made about you.

By contrast, those who bear the brunt of profiling are likely to be acutely conscious of it. Their justified belief that they have been searched, or might be searched, because of, say, their ethnicity, will make that search a humiliating and alienating experience. Profiling often works to the disadvantage of already disadvantaged groups. This is not always the case – medical profiling, allowing doctors to identify our medical risks, may benefit everyone and benefit those most at risk most of all. But it is because profiling often harms the disadvantaged that it is usually divisive and can be destabilising for society as a whole.

THE FUTURE

The practice of profiling appears to be riddled with drawbacks and risks. Is there any way in which it can be salvaged?

Let us begin by noting that not all forms of profiling cause the same damage.

One reason why those stopped by the security forces because of – they suspect – their ethnicity, feel so hurt and resentful is because ethnicity is powerfully linked to identity. So is religion, gender, nationality, perhaps even class. By identity, I mean the sense of attachment, or belonging, or loyalty one feels to particular groups. Not all members of, say, an ethnic minority, will feel a strong sense of identity with it, but many will. Often, people will marry within their ethnic group and their values, their social and their work lives will be fundamentally shaped by their background, as perhaps will their choice of neighbourhood in which to live.

For this reason, knowing somebody's ethnicity can be usefully predictive. If you discover someone was born on a Monday, that tells you almost nothing useful. People born on Mondays share nothing beyond this trivial fact in common. By contrast, ethnicity will be correlated with many important aspects of life – including income, educational attainment, health, the likelihood of being a victim of a crime, the likelihood of living in a particular part of town, and so on.

The groups to which people feel the strongest sense of attachment or belonging are usually the groups that are also most predictive about their lives. This is not always the case. For example, Manchester United supporters might feel very strongly about their group, yet their support of Manchester United might not be very predictive. However, on the whole, identity and predictability are linked. People born on a Monday don't feel a sense of affinity to others born on a Monday. And it is no coincidence that knowing that a person is born on a Monday is a useless piece of information for a policy maker or insurance broker.

Now, there may be some groups to which people belong without having a strong sense of identity which, nonetheless, are usefully predictive about their lives. Take height. We know that tall men on average earn a bit more than short men. Suppose, as a short man, you discovered that a bank was using your shortness as a factor in calculating the probability of your being able to repay a mortgage. You might be upset. But, I contend, not as upset as you would be if you thought they were profiling you by race or ethnicity. Why? Because, for most of us (even us short men), height is not an identity marker. We do not feel a strong bond with people of the same height.

And this is where the future of profiling holds opportunities and dangers.

The data revolution – the huge explosion of data tracking our lives – combined with the artificial intelligence revolution, means that profiling is going to become easier and more ubiquitous, and will increasingly be done by machine. The optimistic scenario is this. Sophisticated profiling algorithms, which do not simply rely on crude correlations involving emotive identity groups such as race, will be both more effective and may possibly arouse less resentment. Time will tell; but if our insurance comes to be based on 50 characteristics (rather than just a few blunt ones), we may take less umbrage when it occurs. And profiling will increasingly offer real benefits in, say, identifying health risks for patients or targeting educational techniques to different children, or solving crime. A criminologist experiment in Florida points the way. Burglaries there were subdivided into several categories – such as those which were clearly premeditated, those which were opportunistic (taking advantage, say, of an open window), those which were disorderly (in which graffiti might be scrawled on the walls). By creating profiles of what sort of person committed these different categories of crime, police departments were able to solve many more crimes. For example, it was useful to know that the sophisticated and premeditated burglaries tended to be committed by older white males with long criminal records but few arrests. Racial profiling has long been controversial: but at least here race is reduced to only one factor among many.

But there are dangers for the future of profiling, particularly around artificial intelligence. Machines are progressing through a process of deep learning. That is, they are learning themselves. But their 'learning' may involve absorbing existing human biases. Thus, if women are less likely to be promoted because of ingrained sexism in society, then the machine may 'learn' that women are less qualified than men and treat them accordingly. Dating websites, based on past preferences, could predominantly match individuals of the same ethnicity. This could have destructive societal consequences.

Profiling is potentially beneficial to almost everyone, to doctors, teachers, social workers, the police, businesses. However, to guard against the costs of profiling, it will be vital to ensure that the algorithms that machines use to determine, for example, who gets a job interview or a loan from a bank, are made transparent. If I am rejected for a job interview following a computer profile of my application, I will want an explanation. But transparency is easier demanded than achieved – it will not be information that organisations will wish to reveal. What is more, even if regulators do successfully manage to ban 'black boxes' – allowing the scrutiny of algorithms – humans may increasingly find it difficult to understand them. As machines become more sophisticated, their decisions will become more opaque. Here's an analogy. Several chess software programmes can now beat the best players in the world – we know that the moves of these programmes are successful (they win games), but often even chess grandmasters don't fully understand them, and being handed the computer code does not help.

So there are reasons to be pessimistic. Perhaps the greatest risk for our profiling future is this. Profiling already disproportionately impacts the least well off in society. Left unchecked, profiling inequality will surely grow. Again, think of the insurance industry. In the past, those who are most at risk, of illness, or burglary, say, have in effect had their insurance subsidised by those who are less vulnerable. But once insurance companies are able to far more accurately identify people who carry the highest risk, these people will face rising premiums or be shut out of opportunities altogether. The most vulnerable in society will become more vulnerable still.

*

Profiling in multiple forms is here to stay. It is simply too useful to be jettisoned. But my hope is that we – individuals, organisations, and government – will also acknowledge the possible costs and do our best to mitigate them.

I should end by telling you about the new British Library security practice. I began by mentioning that in the old days they only stopped a few people. They have since introduced a new system, in which they stop everyone. The upshot is that the queues are much longer. We are all delayed; there is more inconvenience for everyone.

And yet, I at least now feel less annoyed and frustrated than I did on the occasions when I was singled out alone.

NOTE

1 It has been suggested that the origin of this silly prejudice is grounded in the attitude to Scottish churches which insisted on contributions from the congregation.

Feminism and the demands of beauty

Two

Heather Widdows and Gulzaar Barn

BETH'S CASE

Beth is 22 years old. She has wanted fuller lips for as long as she can remember, believing that her own are too thin, and therefore unattractive. She has heard about celebrities having filler injected into their lips to increase their fullness, and decides that this is something she would also like done. She proceeds to search online for a local lip filler practitioner, managing to find one that she likes the look of. She reads reviews of the practice online, feels satisfied with her choice, and books an appointment with the salon. On the day of her appointment, Beth is nervous. The practitioner applies numbing cream to her lips so that the injection containing the filler does not hurt too much when it pierces her skin. After the procedure, Beth is told to come back one month later for a top-up injection. Her lips have swollen and feel painful. This is Beth's first cosmetic procedure, and she doesn't know what to expect, so she treats this as normal. She returns in a month to have the top-up filler. After this, her lips become lumpy, distorted, and more painful still. Again, she presumes this is normal, and hopes that they will settle down with time. When this does not happen, however, Beth visits a doctor. The doctor carries out a medical examination and tells Beth that her lip procedure has been botched. The filler has been injected into the wrong place, with some too close to the surface, and some too deep. This has resulted in an uneven lip shape and a number of lumps. The doctor sets out to correct the damage by injecting a product that will dissolve the previous filler. After this, the doctor injects Beth's lips with higher quality lip filler. Beth's lips are better, and begin to look natural again. However, a small lump remains, which she may have to live with forever.

This case is based on true events.[1]

The number of botched operations in the UK is on the rise, and doctors and campaigners are calling for better legislation to protect clients. Is the only thing wrong about this case that the procedure went badly and that Beth's lips were damaged? If the procedure had been carried out successfully by a competent and qualified practitioner, would there be anything to object to? Or should we be concerned with the practice itself, along with the idea that Beth felt the desire to alter the appearance of her lips?

There are different ways to respond to what happened to Beth. At one end of the spectrum, you might think that as long as Beth wasn't forced into modifying her lips, no one has done anything wrong. At the other end, you might think that dangerous practices like these (especially without health benefit) should be prohibited by law, and anyone who offers them penalised.

You will find ethicists defending both of these extreme positions, as well as many views in between. In the UK, and globally, there is currently no consensus on what is ethical when it comes to cosmetic procedures, or on how to regulate them.

Exact data on the number of people who are having cosmetic surgery or having non-surgical procedures is not available, but numbers are rising (Table 2.1). Going 'under

Table 2.1 Examples of cosmetic procedures

Surgical procedures	Non-surgical procedures
Implants (breasts, buttocks, cheeks)	Botox
Facial reshaping and lifting	Dermal fillers (to plump
Blepharoplasty (double eye-lid surgery)	lips or reduce wrinkles)
Liposuction	Laser hair removal
Genital surgery	Microneedling

the knife' or 'under the needle' is no longer restricted to Hollywood celebrities. While only some of us do it, very many of us say we would not rule it out, would consider it, or would do it if we had the money. Growth in non-surgical procedures, such as Botox and lip-pumping injections, is even greater. In some places, not to have had Botox is unusual, and it is the wrinkled rather than the frozen face that looks abnormal. Likewise, among some groups in the UK and US particularly, full lips that have been injected with fillers are the norm. But, as Beth's story tells us, there are serious risks which attach to these procedures. Currently, what happened to Beth was not illegal. In fact, in the UK, there is little regulation of non-surgical procedures, other than Botox, which is only available on prescription (though it can be ordered online). Worries about this lack of regulation were highlighted in a 2013 UK Government review which famously stated that:

> Dermal fillers are a particular cause for concern as anyone can set themselves up as a practitioner, with no requirement for knowledge, training or previous experience. Nor are there sufficient checks in place with

regard to product quality – most dermal fillers have no more controls than a bottle of floor cleaner.[2]

In this chapter, we will explore two opposing feminist perspectives on how we should ethically address cosmetic procedures. The first argues that women should be able to choose to have any cosmetic procedure they want, and to interfere with this choice is to undermine their autonomy. The second argues that the 'choice' to have cosmetic procedures is not free or individual, but one which women are effectively forced to make, as a result of social structures and pressure.

Before we begin, a quick note about the breadth of feminist philosophy and feminism in general. There is no single and agreed definition of feminism and there are all kinds of feminisms: liberal feminisms, radical feminisms, social feminisms, libertarian feminisms and Marxist feminisms. Some popular definitions of feminism are a commitment to the 'equality between genders', or 'the promotion of women's rights'. But even these very general definitions are complex. What does equality mean? Is it about equal pay or radically transforming society? Some feminists would argue that equality is not about treating women the same as men, but about respecting the difference between the genders. In this chapter, we simply understand feminism and feminist philosophy as positions which centre women's experiences and use gender as a category of philosophical analysis.

IT'S ALL ABOUT CHOICE

Some feminists would argue that any and all use of cosmetic surgery and non-surgical procedures is ethically permissible as long as the person choosing to have the procedure has met the standards of 'informed consent'. What is required by 'informed consent' is very clear in a medical setting. A person needs to know about what the procedure involves, what the risks are (including possible side effects), and have a good understanding of the outcome. Surgeons are required to obtain formal consent from cosmetic surgery clients. Those performing non-surgical procedures are not governed by such rules, but beauty practitioners often regard it as good practice to make sure that clients are informed of side effects and risks. Similarly, it is also standard practice for hairdressers and beauticians to do 'strand tests' 24 hours before applying hair dye, to be sure that the client won't have an allergic reaction.

So-called liberal feminists may think that some regulation is required to make sure that clients really are properly informed – that they really know what they are getting into – and to ensure that they are not deceived, duped, or cheated. They might even think that some groups of people – vulnerable groups – should be protected by regulation on the grounds that they don't have the capacity to make an informed choice about decisions with such high risks. Typically, they might think it is right to restrict young people's access to cosmetic surgery and/or non-surgical procedures. So, while predominantly thinking that individuals should be allowed to do whatever they want with their own bodies, they might support a ban on allowing under-18s to have cosmetic surgery. In general, though, the liberal feminist holds that it is morally permissible for individuals to be able to choose to have lip fillers – or Botox or surgery or anything else – as long as they have been properly informed of the risks and chosen to accept them.

Where does this leave Beth? On this view, what happened was unfortunate, but not necessarily an instance of wrong-doing, or something unethical. Assuming the beautician acted in good faith, no one here did anything immoral. Further, it was all within the law. On the liberal view, regulation might be implemented to ensure that non-surgical procedures, such as lip fillers, require informed consent, and to require practitioners to have obtained the relevant qualifications and gone through proper training. However, to regulate to stop Beth from making the choice to get the look she wants, would be unethical. It would curtail her autonomy. It would limit her choice unjustly. On this view, as long as Beth's actions are not harming another person, then she is at liberty to make as many risky choices as she likes. To seek to limit or reduce those choices is unreasonably paternalistic. It is effectively telling Beth what she can and can't do with her own life. On this view, Beth is best placed to know what Beth wants, and if Beth knows and understands that there are risks, then no one should prevent her from acting as she chooses. After all, the liberal will point out, many things we do in life are risky, and far riskier than having non-surgical cosmetic procedures. We do very risky things every day – from driving to drinking. We don't prohibit these activities, and there are no legitimate grounds to single cosmetic procedures out for special treatment.

IT'S NOT A *REAL* CHOICE

Other feminists argue that Beth's choice to have lip fillers wasn't wholly 'free'. Rather, it was a choice made within a context in which there is great social pressure for Beth to look a certain way. Such pressure influenced Beth to conform to the dominant beauty standard, which currently places value on having full lips.

This type of feminist view holds that our choices are often shaped by circumstance and are socially constructed. As individuals living in a society, we are subject to various outside influences. Even a decision as innocent as buying a chocolate bar can be influenced by factors such as whether that chocolate has been advertised heavily, and the amount we have available on us to spend. Research also shows that placing confectionary at checkout tills in supermarkets encourages 'impulse buys', causing people to purchase such items even though they may have had no previous intention to. This feminist approach, therefore, is alert to all the ways that our so-called free choices can be swayed.

In the context of beauty, some feminists have argued that women's choices to participate in beauty practices are formed under conditions of oppression. That is, under conditions of gender inequality, where women, on the whole, have less power and influence than men. One feature of this inequitable world is the importance that is placed on women's appearance, compared to men's. Women are typically valued and judged more on their appearance than men. There is pressure on women to meet the dominant standard of beauty, and there are significant costs to not conforming to these norms. This pressure results in women adopting beauty practices such as routinely wearing make-up, removing body hair, and even undergoing cosmetic procedures. The prevailing standard of beauty has historically been Eurocentric, excluding non-white women. This has resulted in dangerous practices in some communities such as skin bleaching.

Some feminists argue, therefore, that we need to look beyond the idea that Beth has *chosen* to have lip fillers. An individual's choice is not the end of the matter if what they are choosing is problematic or has stemmed from unjust social circumstances. Rather, we need to examine the social context that causes people to adopt certain preferences and practices in the first place, especially when such practices can be harmful, or affect one group of people more than any other. Although male beauty practices are on the rise, women are still choosing to undergo practices such as cosmetic surgery at a much higher rate than men. Crucial to the ethical examination of Beth's case, therefore, is the question of why she chose to undergo such a procedure in the first place.

It is important to consider how this social influence can take hold. Factors such as advertising and social media play a key role in transmitting the beauty ideal and creating the environment that fostered Beth's decision to have lip fillers. From scrolling on her smartphone, watching TV, to walking past billboards, Beth is immersed in a world of images, many of which are digitally manipulated, and perpetuate an unrealistic and unattainable ideal.

While lip fillers are an appealing choice for Beth, their appeal is the result of a social context that places considerable importance on appearance, and dictates that fuller lips are more attractive. Beth's choice, many feminists argue, is the result of a problematic context, which itself needs remedying so that women like Beth don't even consider such a procedure.

On this perspective, we need to change the social context and dismantle the beauty standard. The state has a key role to play here, as sometimes, protecting someone's autonomy and freedom requires preventing them from making choices that disadvantage or harm them. For example, someone might want, out of necessity or choice, to undertake more shifts at their company, and work dangerously long hours, in order to gain as much income as possible. However, we have labour laws in place that protect people from making decisions like these, which may harm them, no matter how much they may believe that working excessively to earn more money is in their best interests. Similarly, we might seek to protect Beth from making a choice that is disadvantaging to her or which may harm her, even if she believes it is in her best interests. One such way to do this would be to ban cosmetic procedures altogether, due to their roots and role in perpetuating gender inequality.[3]

JUST A WOMAN'S ISSUE?

The two feminist arguments are very different, and result in very different practical recommendations. The liberal feminist believes that what matters is protecting women's freedom to choose and empowering women to make the choices they want. In contrast, other feminists believe that this is to fail to protect women and, even worse, regarding such choices as free and individual reinforces an unjust system and structures. Yet both arguments have women at their centre.

There are two key issues which feminist philosophy always has to address, and which sometimes can be difficult. First, is feminist philosophy and ethics really just philosophy about women's concerns? Second, is gender a useful category for analysis?

Is feminist philosophy simply about women's issues? At first glance, perhaps. Much of feminist philosophy, especially feminist ethics, has focused on distinctively women's concerns, such as reproductive rights and autonomy, equal economic and social rights, and issues of interpersonal gender justice (such as rape and domestic violence). But feminist philosophy does not just apply philosophy to women's issues. By bringing in a women-focused perspective, it brings new tools of analysis and methodologies which are applicable to philosophy as a whole. For instance, the claims of social construction do not only apply to women. How would the arguments be different if Beth were Ben? While Beth might feel she needed big lips to be beautiful – or just to be normal in a culture where big lips are needed to fit in – Ben might feel he needs to bulk up his chest and shoulders. Feminist analysis of this type provides a way to critique social norms which cross genders or apply to other groups. In this way, feminist philosophy offers a standpoint which challenges and enriches philosophy as a whole.

Whether gender is a useful category for analysis has been a deeply troubling issue for feminist philosophy and one which has destabilised the whole feminist project. Feminist philosophy has been criticised for presenting gender as the most important category and presenting the position of all women under patriarchy as the same. Critics charge feminism and feminist philosophy with ignoring or playing down difference, especially differences of race, class, and sexuality. Rather than being a way to call out injustice, feminism has been accused of being part of the problem – by pretending that the problems of white, privileged women are all women's problems. Feminism has struggled to address these criticisms and to find a way forward which is properly inclusive and yet can still make gendered claims about the ways in which women as a group or class suffer. One approach that has risen to prominence is 'intersectional'. This treats the interaction of characteristics – such as gender and race – as key to addressing injustice. These cannot be separated or aggregated. The injustice of gender can't simply be added to the injustice of race. Specific injustices fall within the intersections. Black women experience forms of discrimination faced by neither black men nor white women.

Differing feminist approaches, therefore, offer distinct solutions to Beth's story. If Beth had not been deceived or duped but, rather, had been 'fully informed' of the risks of lip fillers, then the liberal feminist may be unlikely to intervene. Indeed, the liberal feminist might defend Beth's freedom to choose whichever procedure she sees fit. Other feminists might wish to regulate in some way, either to improve conditions to reduce the likelihood of adverse actions, or to ban such practices altogether. They may come to this decision by focusing on the wider social context and considering why it is that women like Beth choose risky practices such as these in the first place. Such feminists might seek to reduce the pressures that influence Beth's desire to look a certain way, by regulating the advertising of, or even banning, certain procedures. What these views have in common is that they use gender as a lens of analysis. While the liberal position would seek to defend Beth's equal rights and freedom to make choices as a woman, other perspectives might point to the way in which Beth's position in gender hierarchies makes her vulnerable in particular ways, and that this can intersect with Beth's place in other hierarchies, such as race and class. Feminists agree that if we are to properly address the issues discussed in this chapter, we cannot ignore the role that gender plays.

NOTES

1 http://neconnected.co.uk/ae-doctor-calls-tighter-regulations-aesthetic-practices/

2 B. Keogh, *Review of the Regulation of Cosmetic Interventions* (Keogh Review). London: Department of Health, 2013. www.gov.uk/government/uploads/system/uploads/attachment_data/file/192028/Review_of_the_Regulation_of_Cosmetic_Interventions.pdf, accessed 9 April, 2017.

3 Clare Chambers, *Sex, Culture and Justice: The Limits of Choice*. University Park, PA: The Pennsylvania State University Press, 2008.

The environment

Part Two

Part Two

Climate engineering

Three

Stephen M. Gardiner[1]

Consider the following scenario:

> *Virtue Incarnate:* In the second half of the twenty-first
> century, the newly elected President of the Earth, Her
> Eminence *Virtue Incarnate*, faces a major decision. In the
> wake of many decades of political inertia on climate
> action, impacts on the ground have turned from worry-
> ing, to serious, to severe. Moreover, there is little doubt
> that continuing to allow climate change to accelerate
> unchecked risks imminent catastrophe, and constitutes
> a clear and present danger for humanity and other spe-
> cies. In light of this threat, the world's leading scientists
> unanimously declare that the Earth President should
> attempt a massive, planetary-scale technological inter-
> vention ("geoengineering"), in the hope of dampen-
> ing down global temperatures and so holding off the
> worst. Such an intervention poses countless risks, many
> underexplored, some unknown. Nevertheless, the sci-
> entists are confident that the perils of geoengineering
> are moderate in comparison to the threat of climate
> catastrophe. Prompt action, they say, is "the lesser evil" –
> and so is overwhelmingly justified.

Reflecting on a scenario like this, some in the present day argue that we – you, me, our governments, humanity as a whole – have strong moral reasons to advocate *now* for the technologies that would make geoengineering feasible. As much as we may lament the ongoing failures of conventional climate policy in cutting carbon emissions, taking measures to adapt to climate change, and so on, we should not let this get in the way of "arming the future" with geoengineering so that humanity can defend itself against the threat of catastrophe.

Exactly which interventions count as "geoengineering" is contentious. So, to fix ideas, let us consider a paradigm case. Stratospheric sulphate injection (SSI) involves spraying sulphate aerosols into the higher reaches of the atmosphere to deflect incoming sunlight ("planetary sunscreen"). It has a natural analogue. Large volcanic eruptions also spew ash into the stratosphere, reflecting some incoming sunlight away and thereby cooling the Earth's surface. Proposals to "geoengineer" using SSI involve artificially mimicking this process, but over a much longer timescale, of at least many decades and perhaps centuries.

CHEAP AND EASY?

Not much is yet known about how to do SSI and what the precise consequences would be. However, early discussions offer some insight into the potential pros and cons. On the positive side, the technical aspects of deploying SSI – such as figuring out how to spray sulphates into the atmosphere – may not be too difficult. For instance, some say that, within a decade and for a couple of hundred million dollars, one could refit a small fleet of aircraft to deliver sulphates to the stratosphere, gather the needed materials, and train the personnel. Moreover, this makes it tempting to infer that SSI is administratively easier than conventional climate action. In theory, a small country could manage it, or a wealthy individual (perhaps a billionaire "greenfinger"). Thus, this kind of climate engineering seems much easier to bring about than a robust international treaty that effectively reduces emissions, funds adaptation and compensates for climate losses. Indeed, some hope that a push for geoengineering might help to break the current international gridlock on climate action.

Unfortunately, such optimism is premature, and probably naïve. Saying that SSI is cheap because it does not cost much to spray particles into the stratosphere is a little like saying "brain surgery is cheap" because it would not cost much for me to buy a scalpel and start cutting into your head. While true in one sense, the point is largely irrelevant. What we care about in the brain surgery case is much wider, such as what the consequences of my digging will be, whether I am qualified, whether I have the right to do it, and what will happen if things go wrong. The same is true of climate engineering. To say that SSI is "cheap" is to ignore the most relevant "costs".

It is also naïve to think that SSI would be "administratively easy" because a small country or a motivated billionaire could "go it alone". Just as you have strong reasons for resisting my attempts to cut into your skull, it seems likely that individual countries will have strong objections to others deploying SSI. In particular, SSI potentially has huge implications for lots of issues right at the heart of human life, such as well-being, rights, justice, political legitimacy, and humanity's relationship to nature. Consider just two examples.

First, those who deploy SSI are likely to hold substantial global political power, of an unprecedented kind. They could make choices that influence climate across whole regions of the Earth, including, for example, by affecting where it rains, how strong the monsoon is, and so on. As a result, the decisions of climate engineers would pose clear threats to those affected by them. Here it is important to remember that SSI is not one unique thing. There are different ways to do it, and many targets that one could aim at. Thus, the choices made by a geoengineering power could have profound implications for the impacts of SSI and how they are distributed. For example, suppose SSI at level 1 is good for region X and region Y, but level 2 is good for X and bad for Y. If the climate engineers are in region X, they could threaten region Y with level 2 geoengineering, and gain concessions for choosing level 1.

Second, implementing SSI may serve to perpetuate problematic attitudes that are at the heart of many environmental problems, including indifference to marginalized communities and alienation from nature. For instance, arguably, asymmetries in power make it likely that SSI will be deployed by the rich and in their interests, rather than in the interests of the poor and most vulnerable, exacerbating environmental injustice. Similarly, some argue that embracing a grand "techno-fix" both creates new risks and prolongs the dangerous illusion that we can continue to put off the need to confront the deeper issues that drive the climate and other environmental problems, such as overconsumption and overpopulation.

In light of these points, we can conclude that, rather than being "cheap and easy", SSI raises fundamental questions in global politics, including in political philosophy and ethics. In particular, we should ask: what would justify geoengineering interventions? And, what effect would taking the right justifications seriously have on the kind of interventions that might be considered, how they might be implemented, and how we should think about research now?

Questions such as these deserve to be at the centre of any serious discussion of geoengineering. However, here I want to consider a way in which they are marginalized in much contemporary discussion. In our original scenario, some argue that *Virtue Incarnate* does not have the luxury of reflecting on how to justify geoengineering. Instead, she has no real choice but to set any scruples to one side and get on with saving the planet. She must, they say, avert the great evil of climate catastrophe, even if lesser evils are involved. Given this, we should aid her by investing in research now.

This kind of reasoning is made vivid in what I call the "arm the future argument" (AFA). It runs as follows:

AFA1: Reducing global emissions is by far the best way to address climate change.

AFA2: Over the last twenty-five years or so, there has been limited progress on reducing emissions.

AFA3: There is little reason to think that this will change in the near future, especially on the scale needed to avert dangerous climate change.

AFA4: If very substantial progress on emissions reduction is not made soon, then at some point (probably in the second half of this century or beyond) we may face a choice between allowing catastrophic impacts to occur or engaging in some form of geoengineering to hold off the worst impacts (e.g., SSI).

AFA5: Both SSI and allowing climate catastrophe to unfold are bad options (i.e., "evils" that we would otherwise like to avoid).

AFA6: But SSI is less bad (i.e., of the two, it is the "lesser evil").

AFA7: Therefore, if we are forced to choose, we should choose SSI.

AFA8: But if we do not start to do serious scientific research now, then we will not be in a position to choose SSI should the above scenario arise.

AFA9: Therefore, we need to start doing SSI research now.

At first glance, both the *Virtue Incarnate* scenario and the "arm the future" argument seem compelling. Nevertheless, I will now argue that we should be suspicious of "lesser evil" arguments for geoengineering. This is not so much because ultimately they fail. (They might; they might not. Perhaps you can amuse yourself by thinking of ways the AFA can be challenged.) Instead, we should be suspicious because of what the most basic lesser evil arguments obscure, especially from the ethical point of view. I'll briefly sketch some general ways in which the obscuring occurs, before commenting on the central idea of "choosing the lesser evil".

WHICH NIGHTMARE?

Let us begin by revisiting the original choice scenario. This involves the President of the Earth being presented with the unanimous scientific consensus that intervention is warranted, in part because catastrophe is imminent and geoengineering is the only way out. However, notice that this scenario is a highly unusual one and it is not clear how likely it is to arise. One obvious issue is that its vision of global politics looks deeply unrealistic: the prospect of an "Earth President" seems remote, and the idea of a global leader who is "virtue incarnate" even more so. A second issue is that the level of knowledge assumed looks optimistic. The thought experiment envisions a unanimous scientific consensus and a high level of confidence that the risks of SSI are modest in relation to the climate threat averted. This is in spite of the fact that we will only really know the true implications of SSI after actually doing it, and even then probably not for many decades. Given these uncertainties, it is difficult to rule out in advance the prospect that intervention may make things (much) worse. Perhaps the whole idea of geoengineering our way out of a climate catastrophe is, as one prominent scientist puts it, "barking mad".[2]

This brings us to our first fundamental point. Perhaps the whole *Virtue Incarnate* scenario is so unrealistic that it is not worth preparing for. Perhaps there are more salient scenarios that deserve our attention. Consider two possibilities that might be more plausible.

The first involves a different scientific situation:

> Hidden Threshold: Due to accelerating climate change, the Earth system hits a tipping point which causes a major change in how fundamental systems operate (e.g., flipping ocean cycles), radically shifting the distribution of factors that matter a great deal to humans and nonhuman life (e.g., temperature, rainfall). Hitting this tipping point was not predicted in advance by scientists. Moreover, there is no clear way to reverse the change, and some reasons for believing that attempting to do so would provoke additional forms of climate disruption that would make matters worse than trying to adapt to the new order.

The second scenario involves a different geopolitical situation:

> Corruption Incarnate: A longstanding dictator and leader of a global superpower is told by his favorite scientists that

there are many ways in which SSI may be attempted, some of which would be especially beneficial to his own interests while also threatening those of his major geopolitical rivals. He announces to the world that his country will intervene "on behalf of the most vulnerable, and in the interests of all the Earth's creatures". However, in fact his primary motivation is that SSI enables him to project power over various regions in a way that extends his influence over the global political and economic order. For instance, he can now threaten one region of the world with a type of SSI that is bad for it (e.g., because it reduces rainfall in its major agricultural areas), and so make extortionate demands of it, turning its countries into little more than vassal states.

The important thought here is that it is not obvious that research on SSI is the best response to either scenario. For instance, SSI looks unlikely to be of any help in Hidden Threshold, and the most important response to Corruption Incarnate is probably to avoid the kind of global political system that makes that scenario likely in the first place. In both cases, the lesson for what we should do now may be that our most central duty is to prepare a much better political system, including one capable of delivering a more just and legitimate kind of climate policy, whether or not that includes geoengineering. SSI is at best a side issue, rather than the centre of moral concern.

WHOSE NIGHTMARE?

The second fundamental point is related. Virtue Incarnate's choice is not one we – the current generation – actually face. In the scenario presented, current decision-makers are considering whether to prepare the future for the possibility of a climate emergency. We are not actually in it. (If we were, we would be asking about "arming the present", not the future.)

The fact that it is not our emergency makes at least two crucial differences. First, the people facing the toughest choices won't be us. If we are thinking of the threat of runaway climate change emerging late in this century, the toughest choices will confront future decision-makers. This is important because in my view, one cause of political inertia on climate change – and a big part of the moral problem more generally – is that climate change constitutes what I call a "tyranny of the contemporary": it allows the current generation of decision-makers to pass on the costs of its failures to the future, and in grossly unethical (e.g., unfair, extortionate) ways. For example, those over 50 can indulge in high emissions activities that bring modest benefits to themselves but impose severe risks on the young and future generations.

The second crucial difference is that we are anticipating an emergency. One of the usual effects of actually being in an emergency is to make considerations of how the situation arose much less salient. For example, if you see a small child drowning in a pond, it is not usually appropriate for you to stop to ponder how it came to be there. The relevant question is what to do here and now. However, this is not the case if one is *anticipating* an emergency. Then it is perfectly appropriate to consider how the emergency might arise.

One reason for this is that the best way to plan for an emergency may be to *prevent* its arising (e.g., put a fence around the pond when it is being built). In such cases, the fact that we would choose a (lesser) evil if the nightmare scenario did arise is not of much relevance to what to do now. More broadly, the fact that we can prepare allows us to put other options on the table. The *Virtue Incarnate* example implicitly suggests that the best we can do now to help future people faced with catastrophic climate change is to research geoengineering. However, presumably this is not the only possibility. For instance, we could radically step up mitigation efforts (to reduce climate change) and adaptation efforts (to adapt society to climate change). We could also institute additional or alternative emergency measures, such as by establishing a massive international climate assistance and refugee program, or investing in alternative energy in order to prepare future people for, say, a massive emergency deployment of a "Strategic Solar Panel Reserve" in case they approach a relevant tipping point. Indeed, perhaps we could do all of these things, together with any number of other alternatives.

A further reason why all of this matters is that there seems to be an important difference between preparing for an emergency and preparing for an emergency that is to be brought on by one's own moral failure. The idea that usually lurks behind the "arm the future" argument is that we ought to pursue mitigation and adaptation, but we probably won't; therefore, we should research geoengineering. But, if we put someone in a very bad situation through our own bad actions, we don't usually think it enough to respond merely by offering them an evil way out. Instead, the natural conclusion is that we have substantial obligations not only to help them to find better alternatives, but also, if none are to be found, to find a way of compensating them for our failure. If this is right, then even if the argument that we should prepare the future for SSI were correct in other respects, we should not conclude from it that we only owe future generations research on geoengineering. Much more seems to be required (e.g., a very substantial compensation fund).

This leads us to the third fundamental point. Given the background problem of political inertia, it seems likely that the same forces that oppose substantial mitigation and adaptation measures would also oppose other serious efforts to aid the future, including substantial compensation proposals, climate refugee programs, and perhaps huge investments in geoengineering too. This brings a larger issue into focus. It is often claimed that research on geoengineering acts as a kind of insurance policy. However, there are many policies that might help us combat climate change. This gives rise to the concern that what is implicitly being promoted in most discussions of arming the future is a very narrow and complacent one – "modest geoengineering research only" – and that this gains prominence just because it is the one that seems most congenial to a very narrow group of "us", the current generation of affluent decision-makers, as a way of facilitating an ongoing tyranny of the contemporary. Perhaps "we" would be happy to spend a few million dollars researching technology our generation won't have to bear the risks of implementing, and even happier to think that in doing so we are making a morally serious choice in favour of protecting future generations. But this may merely reflect a deeper moral corruption. Perhaps we are attracted to the "arm the future" argument primarily because it provides helpful cover for yet another attempt to shirk our climate responsibilities.

CONFRONTING EVILS

Let me close with some more general concerns about the "lesser evil" framing. This framing may appear innocuous enough if we understand "evil" in a minimal way, as referring to "something that we have serious reason to avoid". It seems highly plausible that SSI is "an evil" in this minimal sense: it is something that most people would pursue only very reluctantly, given (for instance) the risks, the concentration of geopolitical power involved, and what it would mean for our relationship to nature.

Nevertheless, there are other ways of understanding "evil" which suggest that the principle that we should pick the lesser evil is more controversial than it appears. One takes an evil to be "something that should not be done (period)". On this meaning, lesser evil arguments fail: evils are not to be done, even if they are in some sense "lesser" (e.g., torture to save lives perhaps). Another understanding of "evil" is more complex. It allows that evils should sometimes be done, but emphasizes that doing "necessary" evils comes with a further moral cost for those who do them. In particular, choosing a lesser evil in some sense mars or blights the lives of those called upon to do it. On this kind of view, choosing the "lesser evil" of SSI may involve the best of the bad options, but it remains no small thing for those called upon to carry out the choice. Perhaps this is because those implementing SSI will make themselves responsible for deaths and suffering which would otherwise not occur, or occur in other parts of the world, to different people (e.g., if one "side effect" of SSI were weakening of the Asian monsoon, causing serious crop failures). Or perhaps it is because choosing geoengineering under such circumstances would show that humanity had failed a basic evolutionary test (e.g., by "fouling its own nest"). Whatever the reasons, the point is that taking the language of "lesser evils" seriously shows that there is far more at stake in the ethics of geoengineering than the *Virtue Incarnate* scenario might initially suggest. Again, even if we should prepare to geoengineer, that scenario should not be treated lightly.

CONCLUSION

We have briefly explored one popular argument for pursuing geoengineering. In doing so, we have not demonstrated that something like SSI is not worth pursuing. (This is an issue you should explore further.) Instead, we have shown that any debate about the pursuit of geoengineering must take seriously some complex ethical and political issues. Still, perhaps that is itself one small way of "arming the future".

NOTES

1 This chapter summarizes and extends concerns raised in Gardiner (2011).
2 Pierrehumbert (2015). Pierrehumbert was then Louis Block professor in geophysical sciences at the University of Chicago and is now Halley Professor of Physics, University of Oxford.

REFERENCES

Gardiner, Stephen M. 2011. *A Perfect Moral Storm: The Ethical Tragedy of Climate Change*. Oxford: Oxford University Press.
Pierrehumbert, Raymond. 2015. "Climate Hacking Is Barking Mad", Slate, February 10:https://slate.com/technology/2015/02/nrc-geoengineering-report-climate-hacking-is-dangerous-and-barking-mad

Four

Hilary Greaves

INTRODUCTION

Elaine is in her old age. But she's still in excellent health. She enjoys walks and garden bowls, going out to eat, and meeting up with her old college friends, and she's recently got into local history and traditional woodworking. Not bad for a woman of 373.

This example is, of course, fictional. But the world has been going in this direction. In the Stone Age, those who reached 15 years old could expect to live only about another 30 years. Thanks to improvements in nutrition, medicine, and general living conditions, developed-world children can now expect to live to 80, or longer.

Eighty is, of course, a far cry from 373. Some people think that life expectancy is now approaching biological limits, so that cases like Elaine's will remain forever fictional. But not everyone agrees. "Life extensionists" don't: they believe that future progress in regenerative medicine (for instance) will enable humans to have ever-increasing lifespans, certainly well into the hundreds of years, and perhaps eventually indefinite lifespans. While the technology to achieve this does not presently exist, some have conjectured that it isn't far off, and even that the first person who will live to 1,000 has already been born.

Supposing this is indeed a technological possibility, should we welcome it, or shrink from it? Should we encourage, or try to prevent, the research that might turn it into a reality? Would it make the world better?

Two questions about the value of life extension

To organise our thoughts, it helps to start by distinguishing between two senses of the word "better". Suppose we change the world in some way. One type of question we might ask is whether that change made things better *for a particular person*. A quite different question is whether the change made things better *overall* – "from the point of view of the Universe", as we might say – once *everyone's* interests have been adequately taken into account. These questions can receive different answers. Imagine a brilliant author called Jo. Suppose her writing brings joy and inspiration to millions. But suppose further that Jo hates her work, and would have been much happier as a mediocre engineer. Then it might well be that Jo's choice to become an author made things better *overall*, while (as it turned out) making things worse *for Jo*.

Returning to the issue of life extension, we can now distinguish between two questions. The first is whether life extension makes things better for the individual whose life length is at stake – whether it made things better for Elaine, for instance. The second is whether it would follow, from the fact (if it is a fact) that the answer to the first question is "yes", that significant further life extension, leading to the existence of cases like Elaine's, would make things better overall.

THE POINT OF VIEW OF THE INDIVIDUAL

I for one am glad to be a child of the late 20th century, rather than of (say) the Stone Age. To be sure, this is partly a matter of quality of life, rather than quantity of life. But I am also glad to have a modern rather than a Stone Age quantity of life. I am guessing that like me, you also prefer to live for 80 years, rather than, say, 45. The lesson seems to be that if life is good, and will continue to be good, then more life is better.

But are there limits to this lesson? It's one thing to say that an 80-year life is better for the individual than a 45-year life. It's quite another to say that a 400-year life is better for the individual than an 80-year life. Should we envy Elaine, or pity her?

There are at least three reasons you might think there are limits. The first two reasons apply only to particular versions of the life-extension scenario, and are easy to set aside. The third concern runs deeper.

The poor health concern

First, you might worry that the most likely scenario in which you live to (say) 400, rather than 80, is one in which, like the status quo, your health starts to decline around age 70 or 75, and what you then get is an extra 320 years (past the age of 80) in increasingly poor health. You might well feel that, if that was the offer, you'd rather not take it. Better to die at the end of your span of reasonably good health than to drag on in an extended state of old age, perhaps unable to do many of the things that make life fun, and increasingly in pain.

This is, of course, a reasonable concern, if the offer on the table was the one described in the previous paragraph. But the concern does not apply to a different version of the offer. Suppose instead that what we hold fixed, when we lengthen your life, is the number of years lived in ill health, rather than the number of years lived in good health. Suppose, in other words, that the choice is between an 80-year life with good health up to around 70 or 75 on the one hand, and a 400-year life with good health up to around 390 or 395 on the other. Elaine was in good health at 373. Clearly, the understandable aversion to having a state of poor health drag on and on gives no reasons for thinking that this kind of life extension is undesirable. And regenerative medicine, if it came into being, would be likely to increase health span at the same time as increasing lifespan.

The loneliness concern

Second, you might worry that if the offer of life extension was open only to you, and not to your family and friends, then you'd get lonely. If you lived to 400 while your family and friends lived only to 80, typically your school and college friends and your "life partner" would all die a mere 20% of the way through your life; by the end of your life, you'd have no-one left to hang out with except your great-great-great-great-great-great-great-great-great-great-grandchildren, and some friends 320+ years your junior that you made towards the end of your life. You might well worry that purely in social terms, the later parts of a life like this would not be worth living.

This concern, too, though, is easy to set aside. The scenario in which life extension is only available to you, and not also to your family and friends, is anyway not the most likely one. That might in effect be the scenario if you alone, among your family and friends, happened to be interested in taking up the various hypothesised future technologies that would offer life extension. But if such technologies became mainstream, that seems unlikely – no more likely than family and friends resisting medical treatment for cancer. Elaine, recall, was still hanging out with her college friends at 373. In any case, we can still ask the question of whether you would be interested in life extension if the deal was a group one that would bring your family and friends along with you.

The boredom concern

This brings us to the third concern. You might worry that if your life became long enough (at any rate), you would simply get bored. Plausibly, what we like about life depends in significant part on novelty. We enjoy a hobby or career or relationship for a while, but maybe we would tire of it after a few centuries, if not decades. Maybe what's fun about a hobby or career is the learning process, so that once you reach the top of the learning curve, it's time to move on. Maybe if the same relationship continued indefinitely, you'd reach a point at which you'd had all the conversations there were to have, shared all the experiences there were to share, and it would be time, in the interests of both parties, to move on. But there are only so many hobbies and careers and potential partners – at some point, you would have exhausted the supply. Similarly for pieces of music you could listen to again and again, novels you could read and re-read, countries you could explore and re-explore. Maybe once you'd sampled literally all that life had to offer enough times, the prospect of carrying on living simply to do more of the same would nauseate rather than inspire. Many people think that, for this reason, living forever (at least) would be more of a curse than a blessing.

Maybe it would; maybe it wouldn't. If it would, let's simply assume that, while we're talking about radical life extension, we're not talking about life extension as radical as all that. I take it that while a lifespan of billions of years might lead to concerns of boredom, a modest increase in life expectancy, perhaps from 80 years to 400, would not be enough to trigger those concerns. Elaine was enjoying taking up new hobbies at 373. At any rate, suppose we accept this for the sake of the argument. (If you think the number 400 is too high, simply change the numbers in the examples that follow – how would you feel about, say, a 140-year life?)

THE POINT OF VIEW OF THE UNIVERSE

This takes us to the second question. Does it follow that relatively moderate life extension – from, say, 80 years to 400, and assuming that it applied equally to everyone and was accompanied by a corresponding extension in the span of good health – would be a good thing overall? That is, *supposing we accept* that their relatively moderate life extension was a good thing from the point of view of Elaine and each of her friends, does consistency then force us also to accept that moderate life extension is a good thing overall, or "from the point of view of the Universe"? To use religious metaphor, is it something that a benevolent god should welcome? In more prosaic terms, is it a cause on which a well-advised philanthropist might spend her precious dollars, assuming she thought there was a reasonable chance that her dollars could bring it about? The rest of this chapter will concentrate on the second question.

Sharing space on a finite planet

What would happen to population size if everyone lived to 400 rather than 80? Or to 1,000, or 1 million?

Clearly, the answer depends on what happens to the birth rate. But if life lengths continued increasing *and there was no corresponding reduction in the birth rate*, at some point planet Earth would run out of space. For a given level of technology and set of lifestyle habits, there is a finite number of people that the Earth can support at any one time. This number is sometimes called the Earth's "carrying capacity", relative to the technology level and lifestyle patterns in question. It's hard to estimate precisely what the carrying capacity is, and even harder to decide what are the right predictions for future carrying capacity, given that both technology and lifestyles evolve. Scholars who have tried to estimate upper limits to possible carrying capacity have come up with figures anywhere between 2 billion (i.e. several times lower than the current population size – these estimates were made in the past!) and several hundred billion. But few people deny that there is *some* finite limit to the number of people the Earth could sustain, even under the most optimistic assumptions about future technological progress.

This means that at least eventually, we would face a trade-off. Beyond a certain point, lives could be further lengthened only at the cost of reducing the rate at which new people get to be born.

To make things vivid, consider the period of time between the years 2200 and 2600 CE. Suppose the choice is between 80-year lives and 400-year lives, and suppose that the Earth's carrying capacity is 30 billion. (The precise number one picks for the carrying capacity doesn't matter.) Then, during the period 2200–2600 CE, we can have either:

- *Scenario 1*: 30 billion people, each living for 400 years, or
- *Scenario 2*: 150 billion people, each living for 80 years.

The crucial question is: which of these two scenarios would be better?

This is not obvious. There are at least three types of argument we might use to try to resolve the question. But in all three cases, it will turn out that an argument of roughly that type could support choosing Scenario 1, and could also support choosing Scenario 2. In each of the three cases, the resolution will depend on some thorny details.

Argument-type 1: the veil of ignorance

A "veil of ignorance" argument tries to establish which of two scenarios is better via asking which you would prefer *from a purely selfish point of view, if you had an equal chance* of being any of the people involved in the scenarios.

It might initially seem obvious that this type of argument will favour Scenario 1. If we've granted the assumption that a 400-year life is better for the individual living it than an 80-year life, then, at least from a selfish point of view, we should prefer to live in the scenario in which everyone gets that better outcome.

The question "which scenario would you rather live in?", though, might not be the right question to ask. That question *assumes that you get to exist either way.* But five times as many people get to exist in the second situation than in the first. This suggests that a more relevant question might be: would you rather have a 20% chance of getting a 400-year life (and an 80% chance of never being born at all), or a 100% chance of getting an 80-year life? Here the answer is much less clear; if anything, my guess is that more people would prefer the second option.

Argument-type 2: the Pareto Principle

The Pareto Principle is a widely accepted principle of welfare economics and moral philosophy. It says that if one scenario is better *for each individual person* than a second scenario, then the first scenario is also better than the second *overall*, or *from the point of view of the universe*. This principle seems hard to deny: difficult questions of trade-offs arise when we can make things better for some people only at the expense of making things worse for other people, but when everyone's interests point in the same direction, the decision is an easy one.

Again, it might initially seem obvious that the Pareto Principle will favour Scenario 1. That is because if we choose Scenario 1 rather than Scenario 2, then each person in existence – all 30 billion of them – has a 400-year life rather than (at most) an 80-year life; remember again that we are assuming that the longer life is better for the individual.

But this argument, too, might be too quick. Here is a counterargument that could be offered without denying the spirit (at least) of the Pareto Principle. Suppose again that we choose Scenario 1. Then, *as a result of that choice*, there do not in fact exist any people for whom Scenario 2 would have been better. However, *if we had chosen Scenario 2*, then there would have existed many people – at least 120 billion of them – for whom, arguably, Scenario 2 is better than Scenario 1. "Arguably": Scenario 2 is better than Scenario 1 for these people if existing (with a good life) is better for a person than never getting born at all. If we do think that Scenario 2 would be better than Scenario 1 for the people who would get to exist in Scenario 2 but not in Scenario 1, then it would be very odd to think that we don't have to take this into account, just because we chose not to let those people have a chance at life. If we interpret the Pareto Principle to include the interests of all possible people, not just the interests of the people we happened to bring into existence, then it's not at all clear we have any grounds for preferring Scenario 1 over Scenario 2.

Some people doubt that it makes sense to say that existing (with a good life) is better for the person concerned than not existing, somewhat similarly to the sense in which asking which of two objects is bigger presupposes that both objects exist. On the other hand, it seems natural, if you have a good life, to be very glad of all the massive coincidences that led to your parents both meeting, and then (further) deciding or happening to conceive a child at precisely the time they conceived you. It seems natural, in other words, for you to be glad, from a purely selfish point of view, that you exist. And that very natural thought is hard to make sense of unless existing, with a good life, is indeed better for you than never being born in the first place.

Argument-type 3: what to maximise?

We might take a mathematical approach to comparing Scenarios 1 and 2. To implement this approach, we would decide on some quantity that we want to maximise, so that each scenario generates a number, with higher numbers corresponding to scenarios we regard as being better. For instance, we might start by attaching a number to each person who ever lives, measuring how well their life goes for them, and then try to maximise the average of these numbers. That procedure would clearly favour Scenario 1 over Scenario 2, since, we are assuming, living a 400-year life corresponds to things going better for that individual than living only an 80-year life. However, alternatively, we might try to maximise the sum of these numbers, rather than their average. Which scenario this second procedure would recommend is less clear, but it might well favour Scenario 2 over Scenario 1. That would happen if (as seems plausible, although not inevitable) the 80 years in the shorter life tend to be happier than the average 80-year period in a life that is five times as long, or otherwise would tend to judge that Scenarios 1 and 2 are about equally as good as one another.

So the two mathematical formulae we have considered disagree with one another about which scenario is better. The point now is that while mathematics can help us to work out which scenario is better *after* we have decided which quantity to maximise, mathematics alone cannot tell us which quantity gives the right criterion (or tell us which is the more reasonable or sensible criterion, or guide our judgment about which criterion maps on to the things we actually care about, or help us to decide which things to care about). The choice of criterion is essentially a value judgment. That does not mean that the choice is arbitrary, but it does mean that neither mathematics nor experiment can directly dictate the choice.

SUMMARY

According to life extensionism, it will be possible in the future to extend human lifespans far beyond the current limits of 80–120 years. This raises questions about whether such life extension would be desirable, either from the point of view of the individuals whose lives are extended, or from an impartial point of view – what we might call "the point of view of the Universe" – that weighs all people's interests equally.

Radical life extension could be undesirable from the individual's point of view if it involved poor health and/or loneliness. But in at least some plausible versions of the life extension scenario, neither of those concerns applies. Considerations of boredom could place some limit on the length of life that could be desirable for the individual, but this limit would anyway be significantly higher than the current life expectancy.

Perhaps more interesting is the question of whether, even if fairly radical life extension would be a good thing for the individual whose life gets extended, it follows that widespread life extension would be a good thing *overall*. Here there are reasonable arguments in both directions, from a variety of different points of view. A "veil of ignorance" argument supports life extension if we assume that the person deciding behind the veil already knows that she will get to exist, but not if we assume that her chance of existing depends on how many people get to exist. An appeal to the Pareto Principle might support life extension if we count only the interests of actual people, but not if we also count the interests of merely possible people (and we think that having a good life is better than never being born). A mathematical approach, similarly, can either support life extension or not, depending on which mathematical quantity is chosen.

Radical life extension could be one of humanity's greatest achievements, on a par with the eradication of ignorance, persecution, and material need all rolled into one. Or it could simply be a monstrous piece of selfishness under which one generation clings onto existence, refusing to make way for the descendants who would have come after.

War and international relations

Part Three

Part Three

Five

Who should be allowed in?

Gillian Brock

SOME CASES

Consider the following cases of applicants wishing to enter the United Kingdom.

Two refugee cases

Abdul is from Afghanistan. He worked with the British Army as a translator on its peacekeeping missions for ten years. Because of his perceived "collaboration with infidels", he is now being shunned by many in his village, which is largely made up of Taliban members. Few wish to buy his crops, now his main source of income, and he is often refused service in shops. He fears for his ongoing safety and that of his family. Should Abdul and his family be allowed to resettle in the United Kingdom?

Bashir recently left Syria after his home and his entire village were bombed in the civil war raging in the nation, destroying everything of material value that he owned. With his few remaining resources, he paid human traffickers for safe passage to UK shores for himself and his wife and children. He now presents himself to authorities in the north-eastern port city of Hull seeking asylum. Does the United Kingdom have an obligation to grant Bashir's request?

Two economic migrant cases

Christine wants to work in the United Kingdom as a care-worker. She is from the Philippines and the salary she could earn in the United Kingdom far exceeds the wages she could possibly earn over a lifetime if she remains in her native Philippines, even though she has a nursing degree from a good university in her country. There is much demand for her services looking after young children and older adults who live in nursing homes. Because of migrant visa constraints, she would be coming alone, though would be intending to visit her family once a year for three weeks and would send back a significant percentage of her salary for them to enjoy a very comfortable standard of living compared with others in her village. Should Christine be permitted to work in the United Kingdom?

Chandra is a very successful businesswoman from India, and she would like to gain entry into the United Kingdom in virtue of a policy in operation called "the Tier 1 Investor Category". To be eligible for citizenship on this program, a person must invest £1 million in a United Kingdom business. She plans to invest this amount and gain citizenship, which would also entitle her family to admission. Are policies such as the Tier I Investor Category Program defensible?

Two family unification cases

David is a British citizen. He wishes to bring his elderly mother to the United Kingdom. She lives alone in Jamaica and, because of a disability, has frequent falls. He would be able to assist her better with any needed recovery if she lives with him. He has ample funds to take care of her and she would not be a burden on the state. Should David's mother be permitted to enter the UK as a permanent resident?

Eddie lives in Britain. His fiancée, Delia, lives in Costa Rica and they would like to begin their married life together in Britain. Delia, an experienced, award-winning teacher, has recently been offered employment in a remote, rural school desperately in need of teachers. She has a son who, because of a congenital handicap, has expensive medical needs, which neither Eddie nor Delia could afford to pay. The medical costs are covered in Costa Rica and it is hoped that continued coverage by the National Health Service would be permitted. Should Delia relocate, she would need to bring her son; she cannot imagine leaving him alone in Costa Rica. Should Delia and her son be allowed in?

DISCUSSION OF CASES

All of these cases raise difficult issues, and comparing them brings many salient considerations to prominence. The cases of Abdul and Bashir invite questions about our responsibilities to assist where there is urgent need and people are in peril. Abdul has become vulnerable to significantly increased danger because of his long association with the British army. The army would not have been able to complete its mission without the help of translators, and so Abdul's assistance was vital to British success. Does this not give Britain a fairly strong obligation to assist now, given their significant previous relationship?

What should we make of Bashir's situation? Arguably, Bashir is in a worse predicament. With everything he has worked for destroyed and many killed from his community, he feels he now has no choice but to leave and apply for asylum in another country. He has no previous direct relationship with Britain, but believes he and his family will be able to settle in there relatively easily because of the high number of Afghans already resident in the UK.

There is a pressing need for care-workers in the United Kingdom. Given demographic trends and an aging population, someone like Christine will have no problem finding work and will no doubt be of valuable service. Christine clearly judges that she will greatly benefit both herself and her family – that's why she is willing to be separated from them for such long periods of time. Contrasting her situation with that of Chandra prompts further questions. Is Chandra's contribution to British society worth so much more than Christine's potential contribution in virtue of her vast wealth? It would seem that the UK has decided that this is indeed the case. Chandra is granted almost automatic entry into the UK because of her £1 million investment. She will also be able to bring her family, unlike Christine. Christine would be offering her many care-related services for much of her productive life, yet her admission is at the discretion of UK authorities. Should her contribution be valued more highly?

Family reunification is frequently protected in immigration law. Certain close family relationships, such as between spouses or parents and children, are widely thought to have high importance in human well-being, and rightly so. The ability of a citizen to sponsor a close family member would therefore seem to be entailed by our respect for the value of these close relationships. But what if family members would place high costs on the state? Should the state be willing to absorb them, just as it would for current citizens? Or is it perfectly justified in weeding out those applicants it judges too burdensome?

In considering these questions, we must confront several basic issues that are in the background.

What gives states the authority to control admission onto their territory? States assume that they have rights to self-determination and to make decisions about who should be permitted to enter. But is there a defensible argument for such a right? And if so, how might it go?

Another salient issue is massive inequality and injustice in the global sphere, especially concerning vast disparities in life prospects. High unemployment, high levels of violence, and civil war frequently prompt people to want to leave their countries of origin and seek a better life elsewhere. So much of how one's life will go is influenced by the state one happens to have been born into. States vary considerably over the kind of opportunities they provide for earning income, educational advancement, interesting careers, levels of crime, and opportunities to live healthy lives. Even life expectancy can vary considerably by state. In some countries such as Sierra Leone it is around 40 years, whereas if one is lucky enough to be born into Japan or New Zealand, this is roughly double and one can expect to live about 80 years.

Most states – in particular, high-income states – adopt very restrictive admissions policies. They allow only a small number of those who apply to reside permanently on their territories. Should they be more generous in their admissions policies?

Two authors have been especially influential in analyzing these issues in the philosophical literature, and their arguments often set the terms of the debate. Michael Walzer and Joseph Carens take different positions on how we should think about justice in relation to migration. They shed light on our main question for analysis here: as a matter of justice, should high-income states admit more immigrants, given the tremendous opportunities high-income states afford?

One kind of argument that might be appealed to in presenting a negative answer begins with the idea that states are (or should be) self-determining communities. Their ability to control borders is an important right, if they are to continue to be self-determining. The thought is that if they are unable to restrict immigration, this might have important implications for those who are already members of the state. Perhaps it will undermine the community's ability to provide education, healthcare or other necessary goods to current citizens. If too many enter, this might even affect the ability of states to secure justice for its citizens, so the argument goes. A defender of a strong right to control borders might also appeal to the community's current cultural identity and indicate that it could change considerably, perhaps even be threatened entirely, should enough newcomers from other cultures settle on the territory. Michael Walzer is someone who has prominently defended these views (Walzer, 1981).

However, even though he defends strong rights to restrict entry, Walzer also acknowledges that states have obligations of mutual aid (or good Samaritanism) which require states to admit the desperately needy in certain cases, such as when strangers are seeking refuge. On his account, positive assistance is morally required if there is urgent need and the costs or risks to the would-be helper are low. Parallel reasoning applies to groups. Political communities must take in needy strangers under certain conditions.

What does this imply? What are our obligations to strangers in need? Well, for some, we can supply resources where they are. In the case of refugees, however, what they need is access to our territory; for instance, when they are victims of political or religious persecution. There will be cases when there is a causal connection between our actions and their status as refugees now. An example would be the refugee crisis created by US involvement in the Vietnam War. Following Walzer's line of argument, the United States had a stronger obligation to admit refugees from this conflict than nations which were not involved. The US did in fact resettle a large number of refugees from Laos, Cambodia, and Vietnam in the wake of that war, suggesting that this idea has had force in the past.

Another interesting feature of Walzer's arguments is that he believes that if a state allows guest or migrant workers to work in the country, they must also be offered a pathway to citizenship. Not to allow access to citizenship would be highly exploitative. What is more, it would mean that the ideal of self-determination was not being properly followed. The processes of self-determination through which a state shapes its internal life must be equally open to all who live in the territory, work in the local economy and are subject to its local laws.

Joseph Carens takes a completely different stance on many of these issues and famously argues for a position known as the open borders position. In his view, there is little justification for keeping out the many poor and oppressed people who wish to move to high-income countries. He believes that "borders should generally be open . . . people should normally be free to leave their country of origin and settle in another" (Carens, 1987, 251). He invokes a provocative analogy by comparing citizenship in Western liberal democracies to feudal privilege in being "an inherited status that greatly enhances one's life chances. Like feudal birthright privileges, restrictive citizenship is hard to justify when one thinks about it closely" (Carens, 1987, 252).

Carens takes the dominant philosophical theories and claims to show that they would all offer the same conclusion: namely, that open borders are justified. He concludes that this is strong evidence for the claim that open borders is the position that we should endorse. In what follows, I pick out just a few of his ideas, using two of the most accessible theories to which he appeals.

On a libertarian theory, in which freedom is paramount, individuals have the right to enter into voluntary activities and exchanges with other individuals. The state may not obstruct such liberty-enhancing exchanges and activities, provided such activities do not violate others' rights. So, if a farmer from the United States wishes to hire a worker from Mexico, the government should not interfere and has no right to prohibit this transaction. Indeed, the government's restricting such an exchange would violate the rights of both the US farmer and the Mexican worker to engage in mutually beneficial voluntary transactions.

On a utilitarian account, in which we aim to maximize good consequences, Carens argues that an open borders position is again justified. If we considered the economic gains and losses for all affected and thought especially about the approximately 1 billion people who currently live in poverty, or in a situation precariously close to poverty, it is plausible to see that the well-being of more people would be enhanced were we to allow more of the disadvantaged from low-income countries to move to higher-income ones.

Michael Walzer and Joseph Carens represent two important positions. As we have seen, Walzer starts from existing communities and from the idea that self-determination deserves special weighting. His argument supports restriction, though he has made the case for important limits on state's rights to restrict. Carens also allows for some restrictions, for instance, insofar as large numbers of entrants might threaten public order, safety, and security. Generally, however, while Walzer asserts relatively strong rights to control borders and to exclude, Carens proposes much weaker rights to control borders, and for us to take much more seriously the interests of the global disadvantaged. Many who choose to leave their communities have very good reasons to want to exit, such as poverty, persecution, and oppression. Carens believes that we need to give those reasons more weight than we currently do in our admissions policies.

Issues concerning who has the authority to control borders invite questions about the justification for our system of states. The world is carved up into states and, in this system, each person is assigned to one of these states that is supposedly responsible for its occupants' well-being. When a state fails to provide what citizens need at the most basic level – either by being unable or unwilling to do so – it is not clear why those citizens should feel obligated to remain where they are, given that the justification for the state system would have failed.

So consideration of these broader issues lends itself to analysis of justice in the global sphere. There is an important and lively discussion on these issues. Some (such as this author) believe that it is difficult to talk about migration without engaging in this broader conversation. So let's do some of that here.

What responsibilities do we have to people around the world who do not have good prospects for decent lives in their home countries? Central to answering that question will be views about what people need to live good lives and views about the mechanisms available to facilitate such opportunities. On my account, there is much we can and should do to help strengthen the possibilities of resilient states capable of providing key goods, services, and opportunities (see Brock, 2009). One example can be found in the area of defective tax and accounting regimes that allow so many corporations and wealthy citizens to escape paying vast amounts of taxes owed to their governments and to the governments of nations in which they do business. Let me explain how this one example works.

By supporting reforms to international tax and accounting regimes, we help strengthen the hand of governments in being able to collect more of the revenue they are owed. With this money they could do much to provide their citizens with the goods, services, and environment conducive to opportunities for good lives. Helping societies (that many citizens currently want to leave) to become great places to live will provide an option many migrants would like: to stay and live a good life in the place they currently call home. Most people do not relish the thought of leaving their home, family, and everything familiar to them. While there will always be people who will want to migrate for any number of perfectly valid reasons (be it to do with religion, lifestyle, employment or culture), the genuine opportunity to stay is important as well. Some of our global justice obligations should focus on helping to provide this much-desired option (Brock, 2009; Brock and Blake, 2015).

REFERENCES AND FURTHER READING

Brock, Gillian. *Global Justice: A Cosmopolitan Account* (Oxford: Oxford University Press, 2009).

Brock, Gillian and Michael Blake. *Debating Brain Drain: May Governments Restrict Emigration?* (Oxford: Oxford University Press, 2015).

Carens, Joseph. "Aliens and Citizens: The Case for Open Borders", *Review of Politics* 49 (1987): 251–273.

Carens, Joseph. *The Ethics of Immigration* (Oxford: Oxford University Press, 2013).

Miller, David. "Immigration: The Case for Limits", in Andrew I. Cohen and Christopher Heath Wellman (eds.), *Contemporary Debates in Applied Ethics* (Oxford: Blackwell, 2005), 193–206.

Miller, David. *Strangers in Our Midst: The Political Philosophy of Immigration* (Boston, MA: Harvard University Press, 2016).

Risse, Mathias. "On the Morality of Immigration", *Ethics and International Affairs* 22 (2008): 25–33.

Seglow, Jonathan. "The Ethics of Immigration", *Political Studies Review* 3 (2005): 317–334.

Walzer, Michael. "The Distribution of Membership", in Peter G. Brown and Henry Shue (eds.), *Boundaries: National Autonomy and Its Limits* (Totowa: Rowman and Littlefield, 1981), 1–35.

Wellman, Christopher Heath and Phillip Cole. *Debating the Ethics of Immigration: Is There a Right to Exclude?* (New York: Oxford University Press, 2011).

Six

Helen Frowe

THE ETHICS OF WAR

Consider the following case, *Break-In*:

> *Break-In*: Burglar breaks into Owner's house to steal some
> of Owner's things. Owner tries to defend her things by
> punching Burglar. Burglar tries to kill Owner. Owner
> can save her own life only by killing Burglar.

Most people are likely to describe Burglar as a wrongdoer – a
culpable attacker – and Owner as his innocent victim.

Plausibly, this moral asymmetry is explained by the fact that
Burglar is responsible for an unjust threat to Owner and thereby
forfeits his usual right not to be harmed. Thus, if Owner harms
Burglar, she doesn't violate his rights. Owner, in contrast, does
nothing to forfeit her usual right not to be harmed. Burglar
will violate Owner's rights if he kills her.

This analysis of *Break-In* is unlikely to be controversial. But
now consider *Aggression*:

> *Aggression*: The combatants of State A invade State B, as
> part of an unjust aggressive war aimed at stealing some
> of State B's legitimate resources. State B's combatants are
> guarding the border. State A's combatants try to kill State

B's combatants. State B's combatants can save their own lives, and prevent the invasion, only by killing State A's combatants.

Aggression is similar to *Break-In* in various respects. And yet, the moral status of State A's combatants, and the killings they inflict, is very controversial indeed.

What I will call the *traditional* account of the ethics of war endorses two core principles:

1   It is permissible to intentionally harm combatants, irrespective of whether their country is fighting a just or unjust war (*combatant non-immunity*).
2   It is impermissible to intentionally harm civilians in war, irrespective of whether their country is fighting a just or an unjust war (*civilian immunity*).

In modern times, this traditional view is most closely associated with the political scientist Michael Walzer, and is defended in his influential *Just and Unjust Wars*.[1] It is also reflected in international law, which grants lawful combatants a "privilege" to fight and kill, and prohibits intentionally harming civilians.[2]

This traditional view implies that the combatants in *Aggression* are on a moral par: that members of both groups are legitimate targets. This thesis is known as the *moral equality of combatants*. Walzer's defence of this equality rests on two main claims. First, he argues that combatants are not responsible for the justness of the wars they fight, and thus for the justness of the threats they pose. Second, combatants on both sides have "allowed themselves to be turned into dangerous men".[3] In war, Walzer argues, it's posing a threat that makes someone a legitimate target. Once State A has attacked State B, State B's combatants pose threats to State A's combatants – and so they may be killed. And this also explains why civilians may not be killed: unlike combatants, they do not pose threats.

REDUCTIVE INDIVIDUALISM

Both combatant non-immunity and civilian immunity have been subjected to sustained criticism by what I will call *reductive individualist* philosophers of war. Reductivists reject the popular belief that war is a morally distinctive enterprise, with its own moral rules. On the contrary, actions in war are to be judged by reference to the same moral principles that we use to judge our actions in the rest of our lives. In particular, we can understand harming in war by thinking about the ethics of harming more broadly. War is certainly an especially complex and dangerous endeavour, but these facts do not generate special moral principles, any more than natural disasters or outbreaks of disease generate special moral principles.

Individualists hold that moral evaluations and prescriptions are properly directed towards individuals, addressing their rights and duties. It is a rejection of the idea that our moral evaluation of war should approach war as primarily a relationship between states or other collectives.

According to reductive individualists, the facts that generate moral asymmetry between Burglar and Owner in *Break-In* also generate moral asymmetry between the combatants in *Aggression*.[4] State A's combatants (who are "unjust combatants") pose unjust threats to State B's combatants (who are "just combatants").

Reductivists typically reject Walzer's claim that combatants are not morally responsible for the justness of the threats they pose, or that they might not act wrongly in killing enemy combatants.[5] For example, Jeff McMahan argues that, given that wars cannot be just on both sides, we can know *a priori* that at least half of wars are unjust. And, since wars are often unjust on both sides – for example, one side might wrongly commit an act of aggression, to which the other might respond with disproportionate or unnecessary force – we know that, of actual wars, the majority are unjust. So a combatant already has good reason to be sceptical that any particular war she is ordered to fight is just. If she is being deployed overseas, this too is often evidence that the war is more likely to be aggressive than defensive. And, particularly in the age of the internet, combatants are often aware that a war is controversial. Note that it's not enough to justify killing that one isn't sure whether one's war is unjust. One needs, at least, very good evidence that the killing is positively *justified*, since we are under stringent moral duties not to unjustly kill people. And it is unlikely that, for example, American soldiers who fought in the 2003 Iraq war had very good evidence that their war was just. At best, unjust combatants might be *excused* for their wrongdoing if they fight under significant duress, but this would not make them the moral equals of just combatants, who do not act wrongly in fighting, and would not apply to combatants who fight voluntarily.

According to reductivists, insofar as they are morally responsible for the unjust threats they pose, State A's combatants are legitimate targets for defensive killing. They, like Burglar, forfeit their usual rights against being harmed. But insofar as State B's combatants pose only proportionate, necessary defensive threats, they retain their usual rights not to be harmed. They do nothing wrong, and are not legitimate targets. In our original case, in which State A was an unjustified aggressor, when State A's combatants kill State B's combatants, they violate the State B combatants' rights.

Some writers have defended the permissibility of combatants' fighting in unjust wars against the reductivists' challenge. It has been argued that combatants are justified in fighting provided that they are confident that their country has a morally sound procedure for deciding to go to war.[6] Even if, on occasion, the procedure yields an unjust result, it would be wrong for a combatant to substitute her own judgement for that of the citizenry. Note, though, that this argument does not hold that just combatants lack rights not be killed. Rather, it holds that unjust combatants are justified in killing just combatants *despite* the fact that the just combatants have rights not to be killed. Even if this argument is sound, then, it does not vindicate the moral equality thesis.

Similarly, several writers have tried to show that even if it's wrong for unjust combatants to kill just combatants, it's *less* wrong to kill just combatants than kill civilians on the just side.[7] For example, we might think that just combatants in some way consent to being targeted, or (more plausibly) ask that they be targeted rather than their country's civilians.[8] One philosopher suggests that in targeting just combatants, unjust combatants at least show "some small measure of respect" for the preferences of the people they kill.[9]

Importantly, these arguments apply only to the actions of unjust combatants, identifying how they might act less wrongly in light of the fact that nobody whom they target is liable to be killed. They don't apply to the killings perpetrated by just combatants. Of course, we might think that since only the combatants on the unjust side will be liable to attack, it's just obvious that killing them is less wrongful than killing civilians. But, as we'll now explore, the reductivist view also challenges the moral immunity of civilians whose country is engaged in an unjust war.

CIVILIAN IMMUNITY

Consider *Helpful Break-In*:

> *Helpful Break-In*: Burglar wants to break into Owner's house. He needs a gun, in case Owner disturbs him. Friend offers to lend him a gun, knowing it will be used to kill Owner if necessary.

Friend does not pose a direct threat to Owner. But he does knowingly contribute to the threat to Owner's life. Both Friend and Burglar seem to be morally responsible for the unjust threat that Burglar poses. The same goes for someone who drives the getaway car for the burglary, or for the ringleader who orders Burglar to rob the house. The general point is that moral responsibility for threats extends beyond people like Burglar who pose a direct threat. And if indirectly contributing people can be morally responsible for unjust threats, that suggests that they can be liable to defensive harm.

Civilians make many indirect contributions to the unjust threats posed by the members of their armed forces. They provide, amongst other things, weapons, vehicles, specialist clothing, food, medical supplies and money. They may also contribute politically, by voting for or otherwise endorsing warmongering leaders. If it seems plausible that Friend in *Helpful Break-In* might be liable to defensive force to save Victim, it seems plausible that civilians who contribute to unjust wars might be similarly liable to defensive force.

Given these implications, we might be tempted to revise our view of *Helpful Break-In*. Perhaps, as merely an indirect threat, Friend is not liable to defensive harm. But the difficulty for proponents of civilian immunity is that a large proportion of *combatants* also pose only indirect threats. Even amongst those on the frontline, there will be people who, for example, drive the tanks or run communications rather than directly kill people. And many combatants work behind the frontline, providing training and logistical support, gathering intelligence, fixing equipment, planning offensives, and so on. If we think that all or even most members of the armed forces are liable to attack – at least when they are fighting in an unjust war – then we must grant that indirect contributions to an unjust threat can ground liability to defensive harm.[10] If so, the claim that it is nonetheless impermissible to target contributing civilians in war stands in need of defence.

DEFENDING CIVILIAN IMMUNITY

Several reductivists have tried to show that even if civilians contribute to unjust wars, they are not legitimate targets. These defences typically focus on the nature of civilians' causal contributions. We've seen earlier that merely citing the indirect nature of civilian contributions won't work. Alternative suggestions include the claim that civilians don't contribute *enough* to the war to render themselves liable to defensive harm,[11] and that only those whose contributions are *distinctively warlike* can be liable to defensive harm.[12]

We can explore these claims in the context of the following (rather stylised) example:

> Munitions: During World War Two, Albert works in a munitions factory in Germany. The factory supplies anti-aircraft guns for the German armed forces, who are waging an unjust, aggressive war against several European countries. Albert knows that the guns he helps to build are part of

his country's war effort. One day, a British pilot is shot down behind enemy lines by one of the guns that Albert helped to build. Albert stumbles across the pilot as the pilot is waiting to be rescued. Only by killing Albert can the pilot stop Albert from raising the alarm and save his own life.

Our example includes some stipulations to help us answer the theoretical question of whether, by working in the munitions factory, Albert might render himself liable to defensive killing. First, we've stipulated that Albert knows that he's making guns for the war. Second, Albert has made a causal contribution to the threat to the pilot. Third, the pilot must kill Albert to save his own life.

Trivial contributions

Jeff McMahan and Cécile Fabre argue that even if civilians contribute to unjust wars, their contributions are typically too small or insignificant to render lethal force a proportionate response. For example, Fabre's account holds that contributions to unjust threats ground liability only if they pass a certain "threshold of causal significance".[13] If Albert merely tightens screws on the guns, he does not do enough to render himself liable to attack. But a civilian who plays a more significant role, such as "taking overall responsibility for negotiating and drafting sales contracts between one's factory and the army [or] driving a truckload of munitions or protective clothing to an armory division" might be so liable.

One worry about this view is that it enables people to evade liability to defensive harm simply by distributing causal responsibility for a threat across a sufficient number of people. For example, it suggests that if Albert runs his own factory, (slowly) making guns on his own, drafting his own sales contracts and so on, then he is liable to defensive harm. But once he realises his mistake, Albert can protect himself from liability simply by hiring enough employees to ensure that everyone's contribution lies below the liability threshold. It seems implausible that we can escape liability to defensive harm in this way.

It's also unclear what makes a causal contribution trivial or significant. For example, consider a security guard whose only role in a robbery is to turn off the alarm in the bank. In terms of what the guard does – flipping a switch – her causal contribution might be considered small. But it could also be necessary: perhaps the robbery can succeed only if the alarm is switched off, or is much more likely to succeed if the alarm is switched off. Is the guard's causal contribution trivial or significant? Now consider a variation in which two of the bank's guards are on the robbers' payroll. If one does not turn off the alarm, the other will do so. It might be necessary that *someone* turn off the alarm if the robbery is to succeed, but it's not necessary that it be one guard rather than the other. Is the contribution of the guard who switches off the alarm significant or trivial? These are difficult questions to answer, but this strategy of defending civilian immunity depends on answering them.[14]

Welfare contributions and military contributions

Some writers have defended a limited form of civilian immunity by drawing a distinction between welfare contributions – such as food and medical supplies – and military contributions, and arguing that only the latter can ground liability to defensive harm. Michael Walzer argues that those who provide the armed forces with food and medical supplies are not really supporting the war effort, because these are things that the combatants need as human beings, rather than as fighters.[15] Farmers, for example, are not doing anything special or different in light of the war: by providing food, they simply do what they normally do, even if some of that food goes to the armed forces. In contrast, contributions that specifically enable combatants to fight, rather than live, can ground liability, and render a civilian a legitimate target. On this account, Albert in *Munitions* will be liable to defensive harm, since his contribution is distinctively warlike.

However, it seems unlikely that this approach will provide the kind of widespread immunity that Walzer envisages. It's not as if members of the armed forces fight in their regular clothes, or eat normal food. Rather, they require specialist clothing and rations – for example, camouflaged and protective clothing, and food that can be stored, rehydrated, and easily transported, and with high nutritional value.[16] Providing these "welfare" items is not to provide something that the combatants require as ordinary, non-fighting human beings. Rather, they are tailored to their role as combatants and help them to fight.

Moreover, even if we could draw a plausible distinction between welfare and military contributions, it's not clear why this distinction has the kind of moral significance Walzer alleges. As Fabre argues, both welfare and military contributions are necessary for enabling combatants to fight:

> combatants are not able to kill if hunger or untreated wounds make it impossible for them to lift their arms and train those guns on the enemy. Generally, meeting

combatants' material need for food, shelter, appropriate clothing, and medical care goes a long way toward enabling them to kill in war, even if the resources in question do not in themselves constitute a threat.[17]

Without some further argument for why only some types of necessary contributions to unjust killing ground liability, this defence of civilian immunity looks unpromising.

Contingent protections

Some reductivists believe that civilians who contribute to unjust wars are, often, liable to defensive killing, but that there are nonetheless contingent moral reasons to retain a wide-spread prohibition on targeting civilians.[18] For example, even if we know that some civilians contribute to unjust threats, it will often be difficult to identify those civilians. Whereas combatants are easily identified by their uniforms, contributing civilians are often indistinguishable from non-contributing civilians. Contributing civilians are also typically located in populated areas, which means that it will be hard to target them without also causing harm to innocent civilians (which includes, for example, all children, who cannot be morally responsible for contributing to the war effort, even if they do contribute). In contrast, combatants are often physically isolated from the rest of the population, living in camps or on bases. The risk of collaterally killing a non-liable person are thus much smaller when one attacks combatants compared to civilians. Perhaps most importantly, we should be mindful that the laws of war do not distinguish between just and unjust wars. A more permissive stance towards the range of legitimate targets for just combatants will be taken to apply to unjust combatants as well. Thus, even if we have reason to doubt that civilians who contribute to unjust wars retain their usual rights not to be harmed, we also have reason to retain a prohibition on targeting them.

CONCLUSION

The principles of civilian immunity and combatant non-immunity are ingrained in popular culture and international law and, until recently, dominated scholarship on the ethics of war. And yet both principles seem unstable. It's hardly plausible that combatants fighting just wars lack rights not to be killed, and that unjust combatants do nothing wrong in killing them. Nor is it plausible that those who indirectly contribute to unjust killings cannot be liable to defensive harm. We may find, then, that the permissions and prohibitions of war are best understood as reflecting contingent, instrumental considerations, rather than some deep moral distinction between combatants and civilians.

NOTES

1 Michael Walzer, *Just and Unjust Wars* (New York: Basic Books, 1977).
2 Although legal scholars disagree about whether the law permits soldiers to kill each other, or merely grants them legal immunity from prosecution for killing each other. See Adil Ahmad Haque, *Law and Morality at War* (Oxford: OUP, 2017), 23.
3 Walzer, *Just and Unjust Wars*, 145.
4 Jeff McMahan, *Killing in War* (Oxford: OUP, 2009).
5 E.g. Jeff McMahan, 'On the Moral Equality of Combatants', *Journal of Political Philosophy*, 14/4 (2006): 377–393.
6 David Estlund, 'On Following Orders in an Unjust War', *Journal of Political Philosophy*, 15/2 (2007): 213–234: 215.
7 Seth Lazar, *Sparing Civilians* (Oxford: OUP, 2015); Haque, *Law and Morality at War*.
8 See e.g. Haque, *Law and Morality at War*, 82; Lazar, *Sparing Civilians*, 127.

Helen Frowe

9 Haque, *Law and Morality at War*, 82.

10 Some writers deny that all these combatants are legitimate targets. See e.g. Haque, *Law and Morality at War*.

11 Jeff McMahan, *Killing in War*; Cecile Fabre, 'Guns, Food and Liability to Attack in War', *Ethics*, 120/1 (2009): 36–63.

12 Walzer, *Just and Unjust Wars*, 146.

13 Fabre, 'Guns, Food and Liability to Attack in War', 61.

14 See e.g. Victor Tadros, 'Causal Contributions and Liability', *Ethics*, 128/2 (2018): 402–431.

15 Walzer, *Just and Unjust Wars*, 146.

16 Fabre, 'Guns, Food and Liability to Attack in War', 44.

17 Fabre, 'Guns, Food and Liability to Attack in War', 43–44.

18 E.g. Helen Frowe, *Defensive Killing* (Oxford: OUP, 2014).

Seven

Seumas Miller

In the context of a well-ordered, liberal, democratic state, such as the US or the UK, terrorist acts should be treated as ordinary, albeit very serious, crimes. Nonetheless, they have additional destabilising features that might reasonably call for different applications of the use of lethal force in response. Here I discuss the ethics of using lethal force in two real-life counter-terrorism scenarios: (1) The 9/11 attack on the Twin Towers in New York; (2) The killing in London by UK police officers in 2005 of a suspected suicide bomber who turned out to be an innocent Brazilian electrician, Jean Charles de Menezes. The political, economic, and moral significance of a large-scale attack on an iconic institution, such as the Twin Towers, is obvious. While an individual suicide bomber cannot wreak havoc in the manner of the Twin Towers attack, the cumulative impact of multiple individual suicide bomber attacks can be destabilising, as has been shown in Iraq, Afghanistan, and elsewhere. As we shall see, both kinds of terrorist attacks give rise to acute moral dilemmas for the security agencies.

In what follows I define terrorism[1] as a political strategy that:

1   Consists in intentionally killing, maiming, torturing, or otherwise seriously harming, or threatening to seriously harm, innocent civilians;

2   Is a means of terrorising, individually and/or collectively, the members of some social or political group in order to achieve political or military purposes;

3   Relies on the killings – or other serious harms – receiving a high degree of publicity, at least to the extent necessary to engender widespread fear in the target political group.

CASE STUDY 1: 9/11

At 8:46 on the morning of 11 September 2001, the United States became a nation transformed. An airliner traveling at hundreds of miles per hour and carrying some 10,000 gallons of jet fuel ploughed into the North Tower of the World Trade Center in Lower Manhattan. At 9:03, a second airliner hit the South Tower. Fire and smoke billowed upward. Steel, glass, ash, and bodies fell below. The Twin Towers, where up to 50,000 people worked each day, both collapsed less than 90 minutes later.

At 9:37 that same morning, a third airliner slammed into the western face of the Pentagon. At 10:03, a fourth airliner crashed in a field in southern Pennsylvania. It had been aimed at the United States Capitol or the White House, and was forced down by heroic passengers armed with the knowledge that America was under attack.

More than 2,600 people died at the World Trade Center; 125 died on the four planes. The death toll surpassed that at Pearl Harbor in December 1941 (when a US naval base in Hawaii was attacked by Japanese planes).

This immeasurable pain was inflicted by 19 young Arabs acting at the behest of Islamist extremists headquartered in distant Afghanistan. Some had been in the United States for more than a year, mixing with the rest of the population. Though four had training as pilots, most were not well-educated. Most spoke English poorly, some hardly at all. In groups of four or five, carrying with them only small knives, box cutters, and cans of mace or pepper spray, they had hijacked the four planes and turned them into deadly guided missiles.

(Extract from Executive Summary of 9/11
Commission of Inquiry)[2]

ANALYSIS

Large-scale terrorist attacks on well-ordered liberal democracies perpetrated in peacetime are more likely than other criminal acts perpetrated in peacetime to give rise to one-off, acute moral dilemmas of a kind more routinely confronted in wartime. In the light of the 9/11 case study, consider, for example, the notional possibility that the US Air Force might have been called upon to shoot down a US domestic airplane in order to prevent it crashing into the World Trade Center.

Here the dilemma is whether intentionally to refrain from protecting the lives of the innocent many (those in the building and its surrounds) or intentionally to kill the innocent, relatively few, passengers to protect the lives of the innocent many (and given the passengers were almost certain to be killed in any case).

Some argue that this dilemma is easy to resolve. Governments, including liberal democratic governments, are not, and cannot be, legitimately authorised to (in effect) execute some of their own citizens in order to save the lives of other people (whether they're their own citizens or not) – or indeed for any other 'larger' purpose. The reason for this is simply that the moral legitimacy of governments – liberal democratic governments in particular – derives in large part from, and crucially depends on, respecting the human rights of autonomous human persons considered individually, and not simply in aggregate. Put simply, individual citizens in liberal democratic societies have not relinquished their right to life to governments, and the only conditions under which it is permissible for governments intentionally to take the lives of their citizens are ones in which the rights to life of the citizens in question have been suspended by virtue of their own rights violations, e.g., these citizens are themselves unjustifiably attacking other citizens.

Scenarios like this one have given rise to philosophical debates between so-called consequentialists and deontologists. Roughly speaking, consequentialists hold that actions are morally right or wrong depending on their consequences and, since it is better for a larger number of innocent persons to live than a smaller number, then it may well be morally justified to shoot down the plane. By contrast, deontologists stress the inherent moral rightness or wrongness of particular actions and, typically, argue along the lines mentioned earlier that it would be wrong to shoot down the plane. Pluralists, by contrast with both consequentialists and deontologists, have a bet both ways. They may partially agree with deontologists that shooting down the plane would not be morally justifiable. However, they might also partially agree with consequentialists in accepting that at some point the numbers will be such as to override the moral principle that prohibits deliberate killing of an innocent in order to save another innocent, e.g., if I have to murder one ageing innocent person in order to save the entire human race. In these debates, little attention is paid to the prior question of who (if anyone) is morally entitled to make such a decision and, if so, under what circumstances. In liberal democracies, arguably the citizenry – via their democratically elected legislators – ought to be the ones to decide the general policy in such cases. This is consistent with the executive or perhaps in some cases, senior members of the relevant security agencies making the actual decision in any specific set of circumstances. However, in doing so they would need to comply with the agreed policy.

In respect of our plane scenario, there may, of course, be other softer options, such as impeding the further progress of the domestic airplane by disabling one of its engines (perhaps by means of small arms fire) and, thereby, causing it to make a crash landing. Under these circumstances, the terrorists might seek to ensure that the plane did not land safely, but rather crashed, killing all on board. However, this would be an outcome deliberately caused by the terrorists, not the state. The state would have put the passengers' lives at risk by disabling the engine, but it would not be guilty of intentionally killing them.

CASE STUDY 2: THE JEAN CHARLES DE MENEZES SHOOTING

In London in July 2005, a day after a failed bomb attack, police shot dead a terrorist suspect who turned out to be an innocent, defenceless Brazilian electrician, Jean Charles de Menezes, going about his day-to-day business. Jean Charles de Menezes was killed by police at an underground station in the belief that he was a mortal threat to the passengers.

The events that terminated in Mr de Menezes' death involved a number of mistakes or errors of judgement on the part of police. Notably:

1   The failure of the surveillance team located in the London road from where Mr de Menezes emerged to determine whether or not Mr de Menezes was the terrorist suspect Hussain Osman. The failure, too, to communicate to their

commanding officer, Commander Dick, that they were uncertain of their subject's identity;

2   Commander Dick's failure to see to it that Mr de Menezes was challenged and stopped prior to his entering the underground station, and in a manner that would not have required killing him (he being at most a threat to himself, the arresting officers and, perhaps, one or two passers-by);

3   The failure of each of the two officers who shot Mr de Menezes to provide adequate grounds for believing that they were shooting dead a suicide bomber who was at the time in question a mortal threat to train passengers. After all, the person shot was merely a suspected suicide bomber and the firearms officers had no clear evidence that he was carrying a bomb. Nor, at any point, did they see a bomb or be otherwise provided with good evidence that the suspect was carrying a bomb. Commander Dick had not declared this a Kratos operation.[3] A Kratos operation involves someone known to be a suicide bomber, and allows for the use of lethal force to prevent the bomber killing innocent people by detonating a bomb.

(Case study derived from Miller (2016: Chap. 5))

ANALYSIS

In the case of suspected suicide bombers, police are not usually able to issue a warning since, typically, this will alert the bomber to their presence and he or she will immediately detonate the bomb.[4] Moreover, in the case of suicide bombers, the harm to be done is both potentially very great, e.g. dozens or even hundreds of innocent lives, and perpetrated by a single action – unlike, for example, in the case of serial murderers. Finally, there is often the problem of uncertainty – is the suspect a suicide bomber about to set off a bomb? In this respect, suicide bombers are unlike lone gunmen shooting at passers-by. Moreover, when police are confronted by a suspected suicide bomber there is likely to be a problematic division of labour; the firearms officer (the shooter) relies on intelligence provided by other police officers that the person he or she is contemplating shooting is in fact a suicide bomber. That can lead to mistaken identity, as in the de Menezes tragedy.

In this case study, and similar cases, the police actions are often described as failings or errors of judgment. This does not necessarily imply any specific *moral* failing on the part of the police; whether or not there was a moral failure is a further matter to be determined. There was no intention to kill an innocent person; indeed, police actions were carried out with the intention to save innocent lives.

In this case study, we need to distinguish between any moral failures on the part of the police officers to comply with the Kratos operational police and the possible moral deficiencies of the policy itself. Is Kratos a morally justified operational policy? If it is not justified – perhaps because it puts the lives of innocent persons at too great a risk – then who should be held morally responsible for this? The answer to the latter question is presumably that senior police and, perhaps, the politicians to whom they answer, should be held morally responsible. But let us assume that the policy is morally justified, say because it is effective in protecting the lives of innocent persons. Does this imply that if the police shot dead a person under the same circumstances as they shot Mr de Menezes, except that the person turned out to be Mr Osman, then their actions would have been justified? What if Mr Osman was planning a bomb attack but, as it turned out, was not carrying a bomb with him at the time?

Is it morally justifiable for police to shoot dead a suspect without warning, when the suspect is in a crowded location and they have good evidence that he is a suicide bomber, i.e. intends at some point in the future to blow up himself and others, but they do not know whether he has a bomb on him at this time? In other words, is it acceptable for police to shoot a suspect if they are unsure whether his intended murderous act is imminent?

The dilemma for the firearms officers in such situations is acute. The suspect they shoot dead may turn out to be innocent. On the other hand, if they do not shoot and he turns out to be a suicide bomber, then they will have failed to prevent the death of innocent civilians.

One important moral issue that arises in this case study is that of individual versus collective moral responsibility. If a police firearms officer shoots dead a suspected suicide bomber on the basis of intelligence provided by other police officers, and the suspect turns out not to be a suicide bomber who, if anyone, is to be held morally responsible? Is it only the firearms officer who fired the fatal rounds? Is it the firearms officer but also the members of the surveillance team who provided the incorrect intelligence with respect to the identity of the suspect? Is no-one morally responsible? Or should we employ some notion of collective responsibility? After all, in the de Menezes case, arguably, no single person was fully responsible, albeit the failure of several individuals was a necessary condition for the tragic outcome.

CONCLUSION

The two case studies in this chapter illustrate some acute moral dilemmas faced by members of security agencies engaged in counter-terrorist operations. In each case study, police and other security personnel confront situations in which the loss of innocent life is likely whatever decision is made; they are between a rock and a hard place. In the first case study, loss of innocent life is highly likely even if security agencies manage successfully to disable a plane hijacked by terrorists. In the second case study loss of innocent life is likely, given that the firearms officers have not been provided with clear and correct instructions. In the Twin Towers attack, the specific lesson to be learned was the need for better intelligence collection and dissemination processes among law enforcement agencies. In the case of the de Menezes shooting the lesson to be learned was the need to ensure accurate information collection and better command and control processes in relation to lethal actions based on information. But surely the broader lesson is the importance of avoiding outcomes in which such moral dilemmas have to be confronted.

NOTES

1 See Coady (2007); Miller (2009); Primoratz (2012).
2 https://govinfo.library.unt.edu/911/report/911Report_Exec.pdf
3 Kratos (a demi-God in Greek mythology) was the name originally used to refer to the London Metropolitan Police's lethal force policy against suicide bombers. The name is no longer used, albeit the essential policy is still in force.
4 An earlier version of the material in this section appeared in Miller (2016: Chap. 5).

REFERENCES

Coady, C. A. J. 2007: *Morality and Political Violence* (Cambridge: Cambridge University Press).

Miller, Seumas. 2009: *Terrorism and Counter-Terrorism: Ethics and Liberal Democracy* (Oxford: Blackwell).

Miller, Seumas. 2016: *Shooting to Kill: The Ethics of Police and Military Use of Lethal Force* (Oxford: Oxford University Press).

Primoratz, Igor. 2012: *Terrorism: A Philosophical Investigation* (London: Polity Press).

Part Four

Part Four

Eight

Allen Buchanan

HUMANITARIAN MILITARY INTERVENTION

Tens of thousands of people, members of an ethnic minority, are being brutally killed in a foreign country by their own government. Your country or an alliance to which it belongs has the military capacity to stop the killing. If there is no intervention, the killing will continue. What could possibly be wrong with intervening? Far from being wrong, isn't intervention morally mandatory? Isn't that obvious?

This is not a purely "academic" matter of interest only to moral philosophers. Over a period of three months in 1994, a genocide occurred in Rwanda. Approximately 800,000 people, mainly members of the Tutsi ethnic group, were brutally murdered by members of another ethnic group, the Hutus, aided by government forces. The world stood by, although military experts largely agreed that the violence could have been stopped quickly and at relatively low costs. And as I write this chapter, there are other countries where massive violence against innocent people is occurring as a result of internal conflicts. Shouldn't we all, and especially our leaders, feel deeply ashamed that such violence goes unchecked?

In this chapter, I want to convince you that what seems obvious isn't so obvious – that the morality of humanitarian military intervention is a bit more complicated than that.[1]

But first we need to clarify terminology. Humanitarian military intervention (henceforth "intervention" for short) can be defined as the use of military force by one country or a group of countries to intervene in another country, without the consent of that country's government, to prevent or stop large-scale violence in that country. The violence could be perpetrated by the government or by non-governmental groups (insurgents, separatists, revolutionaries).

If you are a pacifist, you'll have no sympathy with intervention because you reject all military action. There are two kinds of pacifists: those who reject all uses of military force in principle (because they think that it is always wrong to kill) and those who concede that though the use of military force might be justifiable in principle, it is never permissible in our world, due to certain facts about the conditions under which it would actually be employed. The first fact is that, under modern conditions at least, war always involves the taking of innocent lives, even when combatants conscientiously try to avoid doing so. If you think there is an absolute moral prohibition on taking innocent lives, then – if you are consistent – you will be a pacifist; you will reject all uses of deadly violence, even in the name of protecting the innocent. The second is a fact about history: too often, perhaps in the majority of cases, when countries have gone to war, they have done so without sufficient justification. Intervention carries its own special moral risk: governments may claim to be acting out of concern for the well-being of the victims of violence in another country, but they may simply be using this as a pretext for pursuing their own geopolitical aims, which may be anything but moral.[2]

For the rest of this chapter, I will simply ignore the first kind of pacifism; one has to do so to even get the moral debate about intervention going. I will address the second kind of pacifism by examining the special moral risks that intervention poses, without weighing in on the larger question of whether all other types of military actions are so liable to abuse as to be ruled out.

THE CASE IN FAVOUR OF HUMANITARIAN MILITARY INTERVENTION

There are two main arguments in favour of intervention. First, and most straightforwardly, if all human beings count, morally speaking – and especially if all have certain human rights, including the right to physical security – then surely those who have the ability to prevent or stop the massive killing of innocent people ought to intervene. In other words, a proper recognition of the basic equal moral status of all human beings requires those who can undertake humanitarian military action, with a good prospect of success, to do so. This last statement may require a proviso: if they can do so without excessive costs to themselves. In other words, the idea that there is a moral duty to intervene is most plausible if it is understood to be a limited duty – a duty to help others but not a duty to engage in self-sacrificial actions. Most advocates of intervention acknowledge this proviso.

Second, quite apart from the fact that intervention in a particular case shows proper respect and regard for the current innocent victims, intervention can deter future wrongful mass violence. In other words, a predictable pattern of intervention may have morally important effects beyond the particular case, reducing the risk that future cases of massive violence against innocents will occur.

Morally mandatory or merely morally permissible?

One also has to consider the possibility that intervention, though not morally mandatory (not a moral duty), is nonetheless morally permissible – that is, that a country can engage in it without acting wrongly. Most of the debate about the morality of intervention focuses on the question of whether it is ever permissible and, if so, under what conditions.

The focus on permissibility rather than duty is understandable, for two reasons. First, the permissibility question is prior in the sense that if something is not permissible, it can't be mandatory. So the first order of business is to determine whether it is morally permissible.

The second reason for the focus on permissibility is more subtle: it has to do with the nature of the international system. The latter is a system of states, understood as equal in their possession of *sovereignty*. The concept of sovereignty is much contested, but the basic idea is that sovereign entities have certain rights and privileges, including a right against interference in their internal affairs. To say that all countries are equal regarding sovereignty simply means that these rights and privileges are the same for all. These rights and privileges are specified in international law. From the standpoint of the international legal status quo, the question is whether intervention is legally permissible – whether it can be engaged in without committing a legal offense – because existing international law does not recognize any duty of intervention. The point can be put in this way: in the existing international system, the rights of sovereignty are so robust that international law is mainly a matter of what countries agree to, and in fact they have not agreed to a rule stating that they have a duty to intervene. It is another question, of course, as to whether the system ought – morally ought – to be changed so as to recognize a legal duty of intervention on the part of countries. But before engaging that question, another must first be answered: is humanitarian military intervention even permissible under existing international law?

The answer to the latter question is "yes", though only if the intervention is authorized by the UN Security Council. The difficulty – which motivates the current debate about the permissibility of intervention – is that the Security Council has not authorized intervention in several cases, including that of Rwanda, in which the moral case for intervention looked strong. So, one key question is whether, and if so under exactly what conditions, is it morally permissible for states to do what it is legally impermissible for them to do under existing international law: namely, engage in intervention without Security Council authorization.

It is wholly predictable that the Security Council will not authorize intervention in some cases in which, morally speaking, intervention appears to be a no-brainer. That is because of the nature of the Security Council, as it is specified in the UN Charter. The Council has five permanent members: China, Russia, the U.S., the U.K., and France. Each permanent member has the right to veto any proposed Council resolution, including resolutions authorizing (that is, permitting) intervention. But here is the catch: permanent members are not held accountable for using the veto in a principled way. They often use it to further their own interests rather than in ways that take seriously one of the UN's professed aims: the protection of human rights. China and Russia, in particular, have tended to oppose any kind of intervention in the internal affairs of countries and their use of the veto reflects this. They have been advocates of a very strong understanding of sovereignty, one that erects formidable obstacles to intervention, in the name of the freedom and independence of countries from external "interference".

But even if a proposed intervention is impermissible under international law because it does not receive Security Council authorization, the question of whether it would be morally permissible remains. After all, there are other cases in which it is morally permissible – or even morally mandatory – to act illegally; justified civil disobedience being a case in point. Especially if one thinks that there is no good reason for giving the permanent members the veto right, then one will reject the idea that the international legal impermissibility of a case of intervention settles the question of its moral permissibility.

THE CASE AGAINST HUMAN MILITARY INTERVENTION

The most common objection to intervention is that it violates sovereignty – and in particular the right against interference in a country's internal affairs. To evaluate this objection, one needs to get beyond the ambiguous term "country" and distinguish between the state, the government, and the people. The state is a persisting institutional structure specified in a particular constitution (whether a written constitution, which most countries have, or an unwritten one, as with the U.K.). The government is a group of officials who occupy various roles in the institutional structure specified by the constitution. The people are the citizens of the state. Most political theorists now agree that the government ought to be the servant of the people (not the other way around) and that sovereignty is possessed by the people as a collective, with the government merely being the agent through which the rights and privileges that comprise sovereignty are to be exercised on behalf of the people.

If this picture is correct, then one can readily see how acting against a government need not be a violation of sovereignty. If the government is failing to exercise agency on behalf of the people – but instead is using its power to persecute some of the people – then resisting it, even with armed force, need not be a violation of the people's sovereignty.

Suppose, however, that the massive violence against innocents is not being perpetrated by the government (or by some group acting as the government's agents), but by some group within the country. If the government fails to stop their murderous acts, one might conclude that it is no longer the legitimate agent through which the people's sovereignty is exercised and consequently that acting against it (e.g., overcoming its efforts to keep an intervening force from crossing its borders) need not be wrong.

What if the objection to intervention is that it violates the *people's* sovereignty if the people do not give permission for the intervention? The sort of massive violence that raises the issue of humanitarian military intervention does not typically occur nowadays within democratic states – states in which the people have a significant, institutionalized voice in what their government does. In non-democratic states, there is no provision for the people, as a collective comprised of individuals with equal rights of political participation, to authorize or refuse to authorize intervention. In democratic states, the people have the ability, through their political institutions, to authorize intervention or to allow their representatives to authorize it or to refuse to do so. But it doesn't follow that if the people of a democracy were to refuse to consent to intervention, that is the end of the matter. If a democracy is a form of political organization in which the majority determines what's to be done, it is important to remember that majorities sometimes persecute minorities. When this occurs, the power of the government is not being used to protect all the citizens, but only the majority. So, the fact that the majority of the people have not consented to intervention does not show that intervention is morally impermissible.

Sometimes this point is put by saying that sovereignty, or at least those elements of it that prohibit intervention without consent, is conditional – that it only exists if the sovereign (i.e., the people as a collective) behaves within certain moral limits. Killing innocent fellow citizens transgresses those limits. To summarize: although proper respect for sovereignty may create a presumption against intervention (or other forms of interference in a country's internal affairs), that presumption can be defeated if the country's government is engaged in massive violence against innocents or is failing to prevent some groups from perpetrating such violence against others. So, respect for sovereignty does not rule out intervention. At most, respect for sovereignty entails a strong presumption against intervention, meaning that there must be very powerful reasons in favour of intervention if it is to be permissible.

A different and more cogent objection to intervention is that it is simply too liable to abuse and/or error. There are many instances in which a state has embarked on conquest while "justifying" it as humanitarian intervention. Hitler used humanitarian intervention to protect ethnic Germans as a pretext for his invasions of Czechoslovakia and Poland.

Even if the intervener's motives are pure and the appeal to humanitarianism is not a mere cover, there is a serious risk of errors, including disastrous ones, due to the limitations of the ability to predict the consequences of intervening. Potential interveners may not understand the history and traditions of the country in which they are to intervene. This ignorance may lead them wrongly to predict that the people will greet them as liberators, underestimating the hostility that many people feel toward any foreign troops taking control of their country, no matter how bad or ineffective their government is. Or the interveners may overestimate their ability to stop or prevent the violence; indeed, they may exacerbate tensions, cause additional casualties and fail to solve the problem. Finally, the interveners may underestimate the risk that some other country or group of countries may engage in counter-intervention, sparking a wider conflict with even greater violence. The history of warfare is rife with examples of disastrously wrong predictions. There are very few examples of successful humanitarian military interventions.

WHY INSTITUTIONS MATTER

The risks of abuse and error are real. Unless they can be mitigated, the most responsible course of action would be to adopt a general rule against intervention. Indeed, many people who think seriously about intervention have drawn this conclusion. But that only makes sense if the risks of error and abuse cannot be effectively mitigated. There are many cases in which one of the key functions of institutions is to reduce such risks. So, we have to consider the possibility that institutional innovation could make intervention justifiable.

We have already seen that the one international institution that is designed to regulate intervention, the UN Security Council, does not reliably perform this function. I would also argue that no country today has domestic institutions that one should trust to make the right decisions about intervention, given the serious risks of error and abuse. Democratic countries are presumably more reliable as potential interveners than authoritarian ones, because they generally show greater respect for human rights. But democratic processes are designed to hold the government to account to their own people, not to foreigners. So, there is the risk that a democratic intervener will not take the interests of the supposed beneficiaries of the intervention seriously, or that they will underestimate the negative effects of their actions on those people or other foreigners.

The risks might be sufficiently mitigated if new multilateral institutions were created: institutions involving multiple states, with well-designed procedures for holding interveners accountable for the consequences of their actions and for ensuring that they make decisions in the light of the best information available.[3] Whether or not such institutional innovation is feasible, or feasible at present, is a difficult question. My point is simply this: if the strongest case against intervention is that it involves unacceptably high risks of error and abuse, then the question is whether measures to mitigate those risks can be developed. After all, ruling out intervention because of the risk of error and abuse comes at a high moral price: standing idly by while thousands of innocent people are brutally killed.

Improving the decision-making of potential interveners is only one type of institutional response to the risks of errors and abuse. Another is what has been called a "precommitment regime".[4] This is a contractual arrangement whereby the legitimate government of a country could authorize future intervention by a specified country or coalition, if a grave humanitarian crisis were to occur. A country that only recently had managed to become democratic or one that had just emerged from violent ethno-national conflict might find such an arrangement a good insurance policy and it might also serve to deter violence within its borders. Because this arrangement would be authorized by the legitimate government – and revocable by it at will – it would not be a violation of sovereignty but rather an exercise of sovereign rights.

To think clearly about the morality of humanitarian intervention, one must first specify the institutional context: where there are no domestic or international institutions capable of adequately reducing the risk of error and abuse, a general rule against intervention may be the best course. But if better institutions can be developed, then there is a strong moral case for doing so. In the meantime – in the absence of adequate institutions – the conclusion that the best general rule is one prohibiting intervention, does not get us off the moral hook: we must consider the possibility that some cases are exceptions to even the most sensible rules. In my judgment, the case of Rwanda was such an exception. Rwanda was not strategically important for any of the powers that contemplated but refrained from intervention, so the risk that intervention would have been a cover for domination was insignificant. There was also little prospect that intervention would have provoked counter-intervention and lead to a wider conflict. Finally, the probability that intervention would succeed was very high.

I want to conclude with a note of scepticism. Perhaps too much energy is devoted to wrestling with the morality of humanitarian *military* intervention. Many more people die of malnutrition and lack of access to health care every year than die as a result of violence. Moreover, some measures for reducing these non-violent deaths (e.g., vaccination programs) are much less morally problematic than the use of military force. Could it be the case that the fact that most of us respond more indignantly to deliberate violence than to the larger toll that disease and poverty exact is simply a reflection of our irrationality or moral obtuseness? Do we have our priorities straight?

NOTES

1 For a good sampling of rival positions on the morality of intervention see *Humanitarian Intervention: Ethical, Legal, and Political Dilemmas* (Cambridge: Cambridge University Press, 2003).
2 Larry May, *Contingent Pacifism: Revisiting Just War Theory: Revisiting Just War Theory* (Cambridge: Cambridge University Press, 2015).
3 For an account of the importance of the institutional environment for just war theory, see Allen Buchanan, *Institutionalizing the Just War* (Oxford: Oxford University Press, 2018).
4 Allen Buchanan and Robert O. Keohane, "Precommitment Regimes for Intervention: Supplementing the Security Council", *Ethics & International Affairs*, Vol. 25, Issue 1, Spring 2011, pp. 41–63.

Nine

Tony Coady

> I have a dream that one day every valley shall be exalted, every
> hill and mountain shall be made low, the rough places will be
> made plain, and the crooked places will be made straight, and
> the glory of the Lord shall be revealed, and all flesh shall see
> it together.
>
> (Martin Luther King Jr.)

No history of the US Civil Rights movement would be complete without citing Martin Luther King Jr.'s famous speech
from the steps of the Lincoln Memorial in Washington DC on
August 28, 1963. Its moral and political influence is widely
applauded. Yet the flavour of some central elements in his
speech seems to pose a philosophical and ethical problem.

King was a Baptist minister. Using the very words of the
Old Testament prophet Isaiah, his appeal to a religious source
for the project of racial equality constitutes a direct, though
seldom acknowledged, challenge to a widely accepted sceptical view amongst both philosophers and broader public opinion about the role of religion in liberal democratic politics.

King, it is true, also employed appeals to values commonly
accepted by many of his listeners whether religious or not. He
appealed to the American Constitution's promise to all of "the
inalienable rights of life, liberty, and the pursuit of happiness",
to the value of freedom, a concept much honoured, at least

nominally, by most Americans, and to "citizens' rights". But he also underpinned much of this "secular" appeal with distinctive religious notes such as "faith", stressing, for instance, that the striving for justice should continue "with the faith that unearned suffering is redemptive".

This might suggest, as I intend it to, that religious reasoning can have a powerful place in the political arena. There is, however, an opposing position. What might be called an exclusionist view, though it is really a loose family of views, was captured vividly on Australian television some years ago in a debate about abortion laws when a feminist journalist responded to a Catholic clergyman's criticism of abortion with the cry: "Keep your rosaries off my ovaries!" The idea behind this dramatic metaphor is that there is something profoundly wrong with religious thinking having any significant role in democratic debate about policy questions involving potential coercion of citizens.

Exclusionists are influenced by three things.

The first is the belief that religion is a private matter that should be protected by a state guarantee of religious freedom but should not intrude into the public sphere.

The second is a fear of the divisive and even violent potentiality of religious adherence for the peace and contentment of the civic order.

The third is the conviction that liberal democracy rests upon a respect for the equal dignity of all citizens, and that attempts to support public policies by religious reasoning are an affront to the standing of non-religious citizens.

These views of the place of religion in the public arena are implicit and sometimes explicit in widespread attitudes to religion across the Western world and even beyond. They surface in debates about legalising abortion, same-sex marriage, sex education in schools, euthanasia, and infanticide. Moreover, philosophers have developed sophisticated versions of exclusionism. Two of the most influential philosophical treatments are those of John Rawls and Robert Audi, but, as we shall see, they differ in important respects.

An initial cautionary note, however, is that the exclusionist claim about religious reasons should not be confused with the claim that liberal democracy requires the separation of Church and State. That separation is primarily concerned with institutional relations not limitations on individual reasoning and behaviour. It also stipulates that religious organisations not exert control over that state. And it requires that the democratic state should not endorse or favour one religion exclusively, nor interfere in matters properly the concern of religion (though difficult issues can arise about the limits of proper concern).

The fact that the separation claim is distinct from the exclusionist claim does not imply that there are no connections between the two; separation and exclusionist reasons may sometimes overlap. It is also worth noting a couple more significant points. First, that the separation of Church and State, most pronounced in the constitutions of the United States and France, is not universally respected in all states usually regarded as liberal democratic: England, Scotland, Norway, Denmark, and Finland, for instance, have established churches, and several others have close relations with a particular church short of establishment. Second, that much of the drive for the separation of Church and State has come from religious organisations anxious to maintain freedom from state domination.

JOHN RAWLS AND PUBLIC REASON

John Rawls has been one of the most significant political philosophers of our time and his book *A Theory of Justice* (1971, revised edition 1999a) provides a politically liberal account of justice that dramatically changed the direction and focus of political philosophy. His later books, especially *Political Liberalism* (1993, with new Introduction 2005) and *The Law of Peoples: With the Idea of Public Reason Revisited* (1999b), developed a concept of "public reason" in ways that were exclusionist in design while attempting to remain sympathetic to religious commitment. This sympathy is displayed in three concessions:

1   His concept of public reason excludes not only religious reasons, but any reasons drawn from some comprehensive doctrine that offers principles and some broad insights into how to achieve a good life.

2   Religious and other "comprehensive" reasons are only out of place in debates about constitutional essentials and "matters of basic justice" such as the right to freedom of political speech (to cite an example Rawls gives). This public reason restriction applies to the likes of judges and political actors but also ordinary citizens when, for example, they vote in determining those sort of issues. All other political contexts are unconstrained by public reason.

3   Within non-public arenas, the background culture of civil society, religious, and other comprehensive reasons are allowed to play a part even on constitutional essentials. For Rawls, this includes the media, the universities and other associations. I take this to mean that religious reasons should be excluded directly from the political

domain – voting, political campaigning, judicial decisions and so forth – but not elsewhere.

Regarding 1, Rawls would exclude even comprehensive doctrines like utilitarianism and other ideological outlooks telling us how to conduct our lives. A comprehensive doctrine, Rawls says: "includes conceptions of what is of value in human life, as well as ideals of personal virtue and character, that are to inform much of our non-political conduct (in the limit our life as a whole)" (Rawls, 2005, 175). The utilitarian, for example, says that you should always act so as to maximise happiness or well-being. By contrast, Robert Audi's exclusionism is concerned only to reject religious reasons from public reason-giving about all matters that require coercive measures against liberal democratic citizens. His concept of "secular reason" is therefore much wider in scope than Rawls' public reason though it stems from similar concerns. Significantly, Audi is not hostile to religion; indeed, he is an observant Christian.

As we saw earlier, there are three parts to the concern about "religious reasons" being used in the public arena. Let us consider them in turn:

1 *The privacy claim.* The idea of religion as a purely private affair is not advocated by Rawls (or Audi), though it supports widely held beliefs about religion in secular societies. But it does not bear a moment's examination since virtually all religions contain ethical teachings that have implications for believers in their social and political lives. Religious believers need to worship publicly, and, more significantly, they need to embody their ethical convictions in practice. Business people, for instance, who are Christian but engage in corrupt or shady activities are rightly criticised by

many for restricting their religious beliefs to church-going. Even non-religious people who are normally exclusionist will make this charge when it suits their agenda. What is true about a privacy claim regarding religion is that what religion you can have is rightly no longer determined by public authority but by private conscience.

2 *Tendency to promote divisiveness and violence.* This is more significant for the philosophical debate. It can hardly be denied that religious motivations have played a part in civil unease, strife, and violence. Striking examples are the medieval Crusades, Christian pogroms against Jews, and most recently Islamic terrorist campaigns. Two things, however, need to be noted about the relevance of this to the proper role of religion in liberal democratic politics. First, there is abundant evidence that non-religious outlooks have provided reasons and motives aplenty for civic disruption and resort to often extreme violence. Nazism, communism, nationalism, imperialism, racism, and even elements in liberal democracy itself provide immediately recognizable examples of this. Second, many instances of unjustified violence and disruption commonly claimed to be exclusively based on religious motives and reasons can be seen on closer examination to involve as well, or even primarily, non-religious factors. So the Thirty Years War (1618–1648) in Europe, standardly called a war of religion, and the duration of which was blamed on religious fanaticism, seems on the basis of recent research to have been something quite different. Peter Wilson's recent comprehensive history of that war argues that it was "not primarily a religious war" at all. Contemporary observers "spoke of imperial, Bavarian, Swedish, or Bohemian troops, not Catholic or Protestant" (Wilson,

2009, 9). The war's ferocity and duration, it seems, was not principally due to religious fanaticism but dynastic ambition and political fissure.

3   *The issue of respect for equal dignity of citizens.* Different formulations of this concern are foremost in the philosophical arguments of Rawls, Audi, and several other theorists. The basic idea for Rawls is that, on crucial matters, reasons drawn from sectional religious values disrespect the equal status of one's fellow citizens who find those reasons unacceptable. As Rawls puts it, liberal democracy requires a basis of "fair terms of cooperation" and "reciprocity" (Rawls, 1993, 50–51) and this implies that public reason contains only considerations that are "accessible" to all "reasonable" citizens. Likewise for Audi's secular reason.

Rawls' concept of public reason certainly has its attractions. It is not hostile to people of faith reflecting on their religious commitments and their implications for public life. At the same time, it offers safeguards for the non-religious against what might be seen as undue influence of religious convictions upon significant public debate, especially about controversial matters such as legislation on abortion, euthanasia, and same-sex marriage. Religious people can come to conclusions based on religious premises, but in advocating those conclusions for determining issues of basic justice, they must advance reasons that are accessible or, in a sense, acceptable to non-religious citizens.

WHAT TO MAKE OF "PUBLIC REASON"?

Nonetheless, there are problems with Rawls' concept. A primary one concerns the idea of reasons that are "accessible" or "acceptable". Rawls is clear that the acceptability of a reason doesn't mean that it has to be accepted. We can see the relevance of an argument in favour of Brexit that it restores a proper degree of sovereign control to the United Kingdom while rejecting it on various grounds that can also be seen as a legitimate part of public debate, such as the loss of important trading opportunities. Factual, legal, and common values will be marshalled for and against, and all of these reasons seem "accessible" even where they are rejected and even sometimes silly.

Perhaps we think these reasons accessible because we can all *understand* them even when we reject them, whereas religious reasons are inaccessible to the non-religious because they cannot understand them. But this cannot be a correct reading of accessibility. In any ordinary sense of the word, most non-religious people can understand religious claims and reasoning; indeed, most rejections of them require prior understanding of what is to be rejected. There are atheists and agnostics who teach in university Religious Studies departments and Philosophy of Religion classes, and plainly understand their subject matter.

So if "accessibility" or "acceptability" is not to be scanned as "understandable" or "actually accepted", then perhaps a public reason is one that *could* be accepted in some possible circumstances. But the problem now shifts to understanding such possibilities. Non-religious people are sometimes converted to religion, which makes it is hard to deny wholesale the accessibility of religious reasons. If, however, we dig in and say that we mean something much narrower than that by "could be accepted", we will rule out far too many reasons from the public arena. The environmental movement, for instance, seems legitimately to be a significant player in the politics of liberal democratic societies and that movement contains proponents of deep ecology who see intrinsic value in the natural world, including rainforests and coral reefs. Initially that outlook was viewed by vast numbers of citizens as something they could never accept; even now, many who accept that human benefits support environmental preservation find the deeper ecological reasons beyond acceptance.

Rawls does discuss the environmental issue and treats deep ecology as a comprehensive doctrine, but tries to avoid the weird conclusion that it cannot be a legitimate part of the public debate. He claims it can because it does not concern constitutional essentials or matters of basic justice (see Rawls, 2005, 246). This raises questions about the narrowness of his constitutional essentials, but in any case, if basic justice involves, as Rawls writes in *The Idea of Public Reason Revisited*, "questions of basic economic and social justice" (Rawls, 1999b, 133 fn. 7), then the tenets of deep ecology surely raise such questions for farmers and timber workers, whose livelihoods and much else will be affected by environmental policy. Other comprehensive doctrines such as socialism, libertarianism, and feminism often reach to issues of basic justice and constitutional essentials and their reasonings seem a valid part of public debate even if different sections of the citizenry find them "unacceptable". I don't think Rawls gives a satisfactory solution to this problem.

ROBERT AUDI AND SECULAR REASON

As already mentioned, Robert Audi and Rawls are in the same exclusionist camp when it comes to religion but their differences are important. The two most prominent differences are:

1 Audi's concept of secular reason excludes only religious reasons and not reasons invoking other comprehensive outlooks.

2   Audi does not restrict the exclusion to issues involving only constitutional essentials (or basic justice) but makes it include all political coercive measures such as prohibiting Sunday trading or restricting immigration.

The first difference enables Audi to avoid the implausible sweep of his exclusionism and some puzzles in the idea of "comprehensive doctrine" that we noted as problematic for Rawls. But it raises the complaint that religious reasons are being unfairly singled out from other sweeping outlooks, a complaint that Rawls seeks to meet by his exclusion of all comprehensive doctrine reasons. The second difference makes Audi's exclusionism more sweeping than that of Rawls.

What this suggests for both Rawls and Audi is that there is something debatable in the initially plausible contrast of religious and other reasons.

At one level, there are clear demarcations. If someone argues that abortion is wrong because "God told me so", they have given a religious reason, but if they argue that abortion is wrong because "women always regret it", they have given a secular or public reason (though both are probably false claims). But what if their reason is that abortion is wrong because it is the killing of something that is already a human person? Many who say this have been convinced of its truth by religious teaching. Are they offering a religious reason that would be ruled out by exclusionism?

Another interesting case is provided by the abolition of slavery since many influential 19th-century abolitionists were devout Christians. They offered what seem religious reasons, such as "slaves are children of God just like us" for their opposition. John Rawls considers the slavery case and argues that the Christian abolitionists provided acceptable religious reasons because they could have done so thinking that this was the best way to bring about a just society "in which the ideal of public reason could eventually be honoured" (Rawls 1993 250–251). It is possible, I suppose, that they might have had some such motive, but they might only have wished to remove slavery and thought the appeal to Christian principle would help achieve it. Their idea of a just society need have had no inkling of Rawlsian public reason about it.

Audi, for his part, allows that religious people may have and offer religious reasons for some public policy, but they also must have, and be willing to offer, at least one evidentially adequate and motivationally sufficient secular reason (Audi, 1997, 25; also Audi, 2000, 86 ff.) The abolitionists did indeed use other "secular" reasons such as those countering pro-slavery arguments about the economic importance of the practice, but this doesn't establish that appeal to religious reasons alone would have shown improper disrespect for their fellow citizens. Other examples such as Martin Luther King Jr.'s mentioned earlier and some Christian opposition to South African apartheid also need to be considered. Where religious reasons have been primary in advancing worthy reforms without the backup of Audi's appropriate secular reason and motivation, Audi makes another possible exclusionist response, namely, to insist that the exclusionist restriction is strong but allows for exceptions. In certain dire situations, such as the slavery debate, the appeal to religious reasons may work in favour of abolition where others don't, and hence it would be permissible.

One further problem with a stark contrast between religious and secular (or public) reason is that all societies seem to have had a core of religious belief interacting with other central beliefs over centuries. The modern public discourse of human rights, for instance, can plausibly be traced, at least in part, to the universalist Christian doctrines of human equality before God. The interaction goes both ways so that official Roman Catholic opposition to liberal democracy, persisting well into the 20th century, withered in the face of the democratic benefits experienced by Catholic citizens; where bishops and popes once railed against the horrors of religious freedom, their contemporary successors treat it as a profoundly religious value. In the controversial case of abortion, Catholics and other "pro-lifers" often invoke the sanctity of life, an apparently religious appeal, but the non-religious will have some related commitment requiring a high degree of moral respect for some values: the non-religious philosopher Ronald Dworkin, for example, explicitly uses a concept of the sanctity of life with regard to abortion, though his conclusions are not those of strong "pro-life" religious activists. Nor is it clear that avowedly religious reasons are beyond dispute on their own terms: in the case of abortion, reasons offered from religious tradition have been challenged as misinterpretations of that tradition (see Dombrowski and Deltete, 2000), and the few biblical references often cited by more conservative Christians as condemnations of homosexual acts have been contested by some modern scriptural exegesis.

None of this is to deny that respect for fellow citizens in the complex engagement of liberal democratic politics requires civility and engagement in political debate on terms that are both honest and persuasive. It is rather to keep open the possibilities that religious reasons are capable of expanding political horizons for the better beyond the reliance upon so-called public (or secular) reason.

REFERENCES

Audi, Robert, "Liberal Democracy and the Place of Religion in Politics", in *Religion in the Public Square: The Place of Religious Convictions in Political Debate*, edited by Robert Audi and Nicholas Wolterstorff. London: Rowman and Littlefield, 1997.

Audi, Robert, *Religious Commitment and Secular Reason*. Cambridge: Cambridge University Press, 2000.

Dombrowski, Daniel, and Deltete, Robert, *A Brief, Liberal, Catholic Defense of Abortion*. Champagne: University of Illinois Press, 2000.

Rawls, John, *A Theory of Justice*. Cambridge MA: Harvard University Press, 1971. Revised edition, 1999a.

Rawls, John, *The Law of Peoples: With the Idea of Public Reason Revisited*. Cambridge, MA: Harvard University Press, 1999b.

Rawls, John, *Political Liberalism*. New York: Columbia University Press, 1993, with new Introduction 2005.

Wilson, Peter H., The Thirty Years War: Europe's Tragedy, Cambridge MA: Harvard University Press, 2009. (Published confusingly in Penguin as *Europe's Tragedy: The Thirty Years War*, London: Allen Lane, 2009.)

Ten

Theron Pummer[1]

Many of us give to charities that are close to our hearts rather than those that would use our gifts to do more good, impartially considered. Is such partiality to charities acceptable?

PARTIALITY TO PEOPLE

Nearly all of us have close personal relationships. We have friends and loved ones. We characteristically care deeply about these people in particular. We have rich histories with them that we do not have with strangers. Often those close to us have done kind things for us that they would not do for others, and us for them.

We tend to favour the particular individuals we are close to over strangers. By this I mean that, both in our concerns and in deciding what to do, we tend to give greater priority to their well-being than that of strangers. I favour my mother over strangers. Suppose she and five strangers are trapped inside a burning building. She is in one room, the five strangers together in another. Unfortunately, not all six people can be saved. It's either my mother, or the five. I would prefer my mother be saved over these strangers. If I were brave enough to enter the building myself, I would save her rather than them.

Is my favouring my mother in this way morally defensible? I cannot defend favouring my mother over strangers by pointing to the fact that I and other relatives would be very sad if my mother died, for we can suppose this is equally true of the relatives of the five strangers. Nor can I defend favouring my mother by pointing to the fact that, since I know my mother, I know that she would want to be saved, for we can again suppose that this is equally true of each of the five strangers. We can add that each of the five strangers is no less saintly than my mother, no more responsible for their plight, and so on.

Many philosophers claim that morality is *impartial*, in the sense that each individual's well-being is of equal moral priority. They can nonetheless offer a defence of my favouring my mother. Just as I might take more pleasure in going for a hike if I focus on the trees and birds, rather than on my own pleasure, so I might do what's better from an impartial point of view if I routinely favour my nearest and dearest in deciding how to act, rather than always deciding on the basis of what would be impartially best.[2] This is a contentious claim, since it seems obvious that there are some occasions when it is clearly not best from an impartial point of view to favour my nearest and dearest.[3]

In any case, I here assume the intuitive view that often *partiality to people* is morally acceptable. That is, I assume you are justified in favouring your friends, your loved ones, and indeed yourself, over strangers – even when this is indefensible from the standpoint of what's impartially best. Though it is wrong to save one *stranger* over five strangers, other things being equal, it is not wrong to save *your mother* over five strangers.[4] Some go further, claiming that partiality to people is in some cases not merely justified, but morally required. They might claim that it is wrong to save five strangers over your mother.

I do not assume that you are justified in prioritizing your friends, your loved ones, or yourself, over strangers to *any* degree you wish. It seems unreasonable for me to prefer getting another pair of shoes over preventing a stranger's child from dying a painful death. It does not seem unreasonable for me to prioritize my mother's life over the lives of five strangers. Is it unreasonable for me to prefer that her life be saved over the lives of hundreds, or even millions, of strangers? Many of us will undoubtedly find this a difficult question. Arguably if the number of strangers were sufficiently large, I would be morally required to save the lives of all these strangers over my mother's.

PARTIALITY TO CHARITIES

Different people have different motivations for giving to charity.[5] Some give out of a sense of justice, to help rectify local or global injustices.[6] Some give out of gratitude, to 'give something back' to their communities. Some give to improve public relations or gain other social advantages. Many people give to particular charities that are close to their hearts, based on personal connections. Many give out of a general altruistic desire to help others. Indeed, there is a growing number of so-called *effective altruists*, who use evidence and reason to figure out how to help others most effectively, and take action on that basis.[7]

Recall that partiality to people consists in favouring particular individuals, such as your friends or loved ones, over others. Such favouring departs significantly from what someone with the sole impartial aim of helping others in general would do. Analogously, *partiality to charities* consists in favouring particular charities or charitable causes, such as those that are close to your heart, over others (i.e. giving to them out of proportion with what can be defended impartially).

Partiality to charities departs from fully impartial giving, where the latter would in practice involve being guided by the findings of effective altruist organizations like GiveWell.[8] GiveWell provides scientifically rigorous rankings of charities in terms of how much they help others per dollar donated (for example, how many lives they save, cases of blindness they prevent, illnesses they treat, and so on, per dollar donated).[9] While a perfect effective altruist would not engage in less than fully impartial giving, one needn't be a perfect effective altruist to be an effective altruist.[10] Occasionally running slower than you are able to does not disqualify you from being a fast runner.

Can partiality to charities be justified?

A CASE STUDY: *CANCER VERSUS MALARIA*

Many people – like me – will have lost a loved one to cancer, heart disease, Alzheimer's, diabetes, ALS, or some other dramatically life-shortening disease. Those of us who have suffered this misfortune may in turn have a personal connection to charities that aim to prevent or treat the particular disease that killed the particular person to whom we are partial. Many of us give to these charities on this basis. To examine whether this is acceptable, let us focus on a hypothetical case.

> Cancer Versus Malaria: You lost a loved one to cancer, whose suffering and death you witnessed first-hand. You are now contemplating giving a large sum of money to charity, and are deciding between Cancer Charity and Malaria Charity. You correctly believe all of the following: if you give this sum of money to Cancer Charity, you will prevent one person from dying of cancer; if you instead give this sum of money to Malaria Charity, you will prevent five people from dying of malaria; each of the six people would, if saved, go on

to live equally happy lives; each would, if not saved, die in an equally painful way; each equally wants to be saved; the death of each would equally negatively impact the respective colleagues, friends, and families; each is equally innocent and equally not responsible for their plight; each is an equally morally good person; and you will never meet any of the six, nor learn their identities.

About this case, many would claim both that you are justified in giving the sum of money to Cancer Charity over Malaria Charity, and that this is so because you have lost a loved one to cancer.

Notice that, in this hypothetical example, Malaria Charity saves five times as many lives as Cancer Charity, for a fixed donation size. In the real world, the cost-effectiveness gap is wider still. Both research and care-based cancer charities operating in affluent nations are already well-funded. This dramatically reduces the difference one can expect to make by giving to them. Cancer charities that offer donors the best bets for making a difference focus on preventing cancer in developing nations. The likely best of these on average prevent one death caused by stomach cancer per $19,000 donated. By contrast, GiveWell's top-ranked charity, the Against Malaria Foundation, on average saves one life per $3,000 donated. The best cancer charities are therefore likely to be significantly more than five times less cost-effective than the best malaria charities.[11] However, presumably even if we adjusted the example by making Malaria Charity ten times more cost-effective than Cancer Charity, many would still claim that you are justified in giving to Cancer Charity over Malaria Charity.

But isn't partiality to charities importantly different from partiality to people? After all, the beneficiaries of your donation to Cancer Charity are not your deceased loved one(s), but currently living people who are prevented from dying of cancer. Though cancer victims, these beneficiaries are strangers to you. In the discussion of partiality to people, I assumed that you are justified in favouring your loved ones over strangers, and not that you are justified in favouring some strangers over other strangers.

Can partiality to charities be defended nonetheless? I will continue to focus on the specific form of partiality to charities in which one gives to prevent or treat the particular disease that killed one's loved one, but much of the following discussion applies to many other forms of partiality to charities as well.

SYMPATHY

Having been closely acquainted with the sort of pain and loss cancer brings, you tend to have *greater sympathy* for cancer victims. Could this justify you in favouring cancer victims over the victims of other diseases, and giving to Cancer Charity over Malaria Charity? Assuming you have a choice about which of these charities to give to, and are able to give to either, it is unclear that sympathy alone could provide such a justification.

One might have greater sympathy for one person than another for various reasons. You might have greater sympathy for one child than another because one child is more expressive, or cuter, or because you have seen a video of one child but instead merely read a short description of the other. Even if understandable, it does not seem justifiable, particularly in matters of life and death, to favour more expressive children, or those you have seen via video recording, merely in virtue of your greater sympathy toward them. That would seem unfair and arbitrary.[12]

One response is that, if you have significantly greater sympathy for one person than another, it would be psychologically painful for you not to actively favour the former. So, on the basis of the justifiability of favouring *yourself* over others, we can defend your favouring those to whom you have greater sympathy over others.

But there are at least two problems with this response. First, while it may be justifiable for you to prefer saving your own life over the lives of several others, it is somewhat harder to see how it is justifiable for you to prefer your avoiding psychological pain over saving the lives of several others. For this to be true of *Cancer Versus Malaria*, the psychological pain of giving to Malaria Charity rather than Cancer Charity would have to be very severe. This pain would have to be much more severe than a migraine headache, as avoidance of the latter would not justify you in failing to save several lives, or so it seems to me.

Second, most of those who believe their partiality to charities is justified would resist the idea that the justification rests on their own pain avoidance, however severe their pain might be. This sort of justification lacks something important.

PROJECTS

Can the mere fact that you *want* to give to Cancer Charity rather than Malaria Charity justify you in doing so? Presumably not, as in general merely wanting to save one stranger rather than five would not justify you in doing so. But you might more than weakly desire to give to Cancer Charity. Your desire to give to Cancer Charity might be very strong, as well as very central to your life. Fighting cancer might well be a *ground project* of yours in that it is central to who you are and what you are all about, and gives meaning to your life.[13] It does seem plausible that you would be justified in not abandoning such a project, even if doing so were needed to save the lives of several strangers.

None of this commits us to the implausible thought that you are justified in maintaining your projects, regardless of what they are or how they were acquired. It is wrong to acquire projects that seriously harm, disrespect, or infringe the rights of others, and there is very little if any justification for maintaining such projects once acquired. Fighting cancer through charitable donations is a rather kind thing to do, and is neither harmful nor disrespectful, but it does depart from the fully impartial project of helping others as much as possible.

It seems at least sometimes justifiable, however, for you to acquire and maintain projects that are less than fully impartial in this sense. This may be especially plausible insofar as these projects are linked to particular people whom you are justified in favouring. Suppose, for example, that the very reason you acquired the project of fighting cancer is that it was one of your lost loved one's projects. Indeed, even if your lost loved one did not have fighting cancer as one of their projects, you might have acquired it as one of yours out of respect and concern for them. Moreover, while the projects-based defence of favouring Cancer Charity is still based on the claim that you are justified in favouring yourself (your ground projects), it is less self-centred than the psychological pain-based defence. After all, the project in question is itself altruistic.

But this defence of favouring Cancer Charity, like the psychological pain-based defence, applies in only a relatively narrow range of cases. Very many people would give to Cancer Charity over Malaria Charity, and regard themselves as justified in doing so, even if fighting cancer were not one of their life projects.

HONOUR

There appears to be a wide range of cases in which partiality to charities is not justified by appeals to sympathy, psychological pain, desires, or ground projects. Is there some other type of justification that could fill in the gap?

Perhaps the most widespread justification for giving to Cancer Charity is that it is a way of honouring your lost loved one. This, of course, raises difficult questions about the moral status of dead people, including whether we have reasons to honour them.[14] There are further difficult questions about how being justified in favouring your loved ones over strangers relates to the more specific claim that you are justified in prioritizing honouring your lost loved ones over saving the lives of strangers.

I will here bypass these questions and assume that it is justifiable for you to honour your lost loved one (at least in some way, on some occasion), even if this means you will fail to save the lives of five strangers. This assumption is not enough to establish the conclusion that you are justified in giving to Cancer Charity *as a way of honouring your lost loved one.* There are at least two obstacles between the assumption and the conclusion.

First, it is not clear that giving to Cancer Charity is the best way of honouring your lost loved one, on any plausible account of what honouring consists in. There are many things you can do to honour them: host a celebration of life, talk to their friends, write a memoir, create a slideshow, plant a memorial tree, retrace their footsteps (and put yourself in their shoes), complete their projects, and so on. Arguably many of these activities would honour your loved one to a greater degree than giving to Cancer Charity, given the richer role you would play in them than simply filling in your credit card details on Cancer Charity's website. If you took one-fifth of the money you would have given to Cancer Charity, and spent it on a celebration of life, slideshow, and memorial tree, you could take the remaining four-fifths and give it to Malaria

Charity. Arguably then you would both honour your loved one to a greater degree *and* save more strangers than if you spent all the money on Cancer Charity.

Second, unless fighting cancer was one of your lost loved one's projects, it is unclear that fighting cancer (by giving to Cancer Charity) honours them in a way that could justify you in failing to save lives. What makes their *cause of death* stand out as particularly honour-relevant, as opposed to their beliefs, aims, talents, hobbies, culture, and so on? Even if we could provide a plausible answer to this question, it is unclear how 'fighting cancer' relates to their cause of death. For example, you would not, in fighting cancer, be fighting *the particular cancer cells* that caused your loved one's death. Even if these particular cancer cells had miraculously survived your loved one's death, it is dubious you would be justified in going out of your way to destroy them if this meant failing to save the lives of several strangers. So why think you would be justified in going out of your way to fight cancer – at most the *type* of cause of your loved one's death – if this meant failing to save the lives of several strangers? Moreover, why is the relevant type of cause of death not broader, e.g. 'terminal diseases'?

On reflection, it seems implausible that fighting cancer would, in and of itself, honour your lost loved one in a way that would justify you in giving to Cancer Charity over Malaria Charity.

CONCLUSION

I have argued that, given the assumption that partiality to people is justified, we can go *some* distance toward justifying partiality to charities by appealing to psychological pain and ground projects. These defences of partiality to charities are limited, and do not cover the full range of cases in which many people claim that partiality to charities is justified. I have considered an attempt at filling in this gap that appeals to giving as a way of honouring your lost loved one. I have argued that this attempt does not succeed. I suspect that there is a general tendency to move quickly and uncritically from partiality to people to partiality to charities, and from the belief that the former is justified to the belief that the latter is, too. I recommend that we proceed more cautiously, and view partiality to charities with far greater scepticism.

NOTES

1 For very helpful comments, I am grateful to Roger Crisp, David Edmonds, Benjamin Lange, and Hannah Pummer.
2 Jeremy Bentham's dictum, 'everybody to count for one, nobody for more than one' is an early statement of the conception of impartiality described here. See John Stuart Mill's Utilitarianism, ed. Roger Crisp, Oxford: Oxford University Press (1861/1998). For an impartial defence of routinely favouring one's near and dear in deciding how to act, see: Peter Railton, 'Alienation, Consequentialism, and the Demands of Morality', Philosophy and Public Affairs 13: 134–171 (1984); and Julia Driver, 'Consequentialism and Feminist Ethics', Hypatia 20: 183–199 (2005).
3 For some relevant literature, see: Susan Wolf, 'Morality and Partiality', Philosophical Perspectives 6: 243–259 (1992); Partiality and Impartiality: Morality, Special Relationships, and the Wider World, eds. Brian Feltham and John Cottingham, Oxford: Oxford University Press, 2010; Simon Keller, Partiality, Princeton: Princeton University Press, 2013; and Roger Crisp, 'Against Partial Benevolence', The Lindley Lecture, Lawrence: University of Kansas (2018).
4 In the final sentence of his wonderful article defending the claim that, other things being equal, it is wrong to save one stranger over five others, Derek Parfit offers the following variant of Bentham's dictum, 'Each counts for one. That is why more count for more'. See: 'Innumerate Ethics', Philosophy and Public Affairs 7: 285–301 (1978), at p. 301.
5 René Bekkers and Pamala Wiepking, 'A Literature Review of Empirical Studies of Philanthropy: Eight Mechanisms That Drive Charitable Giving', Nonprofit and Voluntary Sector Quarterly 40: 924–973 (2011).

6 For a justice-based argument for giving, see Elizabeth Ashford's 'Severe Poverty as an Unjust Emergency', Chapter 4 of *The Ethics of Giving: Philosophers' Perspectives on Philanthropy*, ed. Paul Woodruff, New York: Oxford University Press (2018).

7 William MacAskill, *Doing Good Better: Effective Altruism and a Radical New Way to Make a Difference*, London: Faber & Faber (2015) and 'The Definition of Effective Altruism', in *Effective Altruism: Philosophical Issues*, eds. Hilary Greaves and Theron Pummer, Oxford: Oxford University Press (forthcoming).

8 www.givewell.org/

9 This is not to suggest that the rankings can be precise. For some comparisons of charities, especially those that have very different aims (e.g. saving lives versus preserving the environment), there might be no fact about whether a gift to one would do more good than the same gift to another.

10 What effective altruists call 'cause-neutrality' consists in open-mindedly and even-handedly considering every cause area (be it global poverty, animal suffering, existential risks, or political reform) in our attempts to identify how to help others as much as possible. One needn't be a perfect, effective altruist to be perfectly committed to cause-neutrality, so defined.

11 Hayden Wilkinson, Juliet Bowater, and Per-Erik Milam, 'Full Report: Cancer (Part 1 of 2)'. For further details, see: www.givingwhatwecan.org/cause/cancer/

12 For a sympathy-based view of ethics, see Michael Slote, *The Ethics of Care and Empathy*, Routledge (2007). For criticism of some implications of Slote's view, along the lines sketched previously, see Richard Chappell, 'Overriding Virtue', in *Effective Altruism: Philosophical Issues*, eds. Hilary Greaves and Theron Pummer, Oxford: Oxford University Press (forthcoming).

13 For discussion of projects and partiality, see: Samuel Scheffler, 'Projects, Relationships, and Reasons', in *Reason and Value: Themes From the Philosophy of Joseph Raz*, eds. R.J. Wallace, P. Pettit, S. Scheffler, and M. Smith, Oxford: Clarendon Press (2004), 246–269; and Sarah Stroud, 'Permissible Projects, Partiality, and Plural Agency', in *Partiality and Impartiality*.

14 J. Jeremy Wisnewski, 'What We Owe the Dead', *Journal of Applied Philosophy* 26: 54–70 (2009).

Ethics and social media

Part Five

Eleven

Rebecca Roache

Social media gets a bad press. Boomers shake their heads at millennials who rely on their smartphones as if they were vital organs. Parents wring their hands when their 9-year-olds start asking about Facebook and Instagram, opening the door to a murky, silent world of cyber bullying, 'thinspiration', pornography, and career paedophiles. We read online articles like '7 ways Facebook is bad for your mental health' (Kenrick 2014) and 'Is social media bad for you?' (Brown 2018). Chamath Palihapitiya, a former Facebook executive, claimed that the site is 'ripping apart the social fabric of how society works' (Sini 2017). We regard a 'digital detox' – a period of time spent abstaining from the devices we use to access social media – as a healthy thing to do (Hayes 2018). So ubiquitous are concerns about the negative effect of social media use on our lives that Facebook itself has responded in a blog post (Ginsberg and Burke 2017).

Are we right to worry about social media? I want to explore this issue here. We'll begin by looking at the science. Then we'll consider some conceptual issues relating to what friendship is and the extent to which our interactions with people via social media can give us what we usually get offline. We'll also consider an important way in which those of us for whom social media wasn't available until adulthood are likely to overestimate the disadvantages of social media and under-estimate its advantages. To keep things simple (and because I am not hugely adventurous with social media), we'll focus mainly on Facebook.

THE SCIENCE ON SOCIAL MEDIA AND HAPPINESS

Social media can make us feel bad. A 2015 study found that social media was linked to stress, particularly in women – although the level of stress can be mitigated by having more education, being married or living with a partner, being younger, and being employed (Hampton et al. 2015). Facebook use has been shown to increase negative mood, especially by making users feel that they have wasted their time, and we routinely overestimate the extent to which using Facebook will make us feel better (Sagioglou and Greitemeyer 2014). Symptoms of depression and anxiety have been shown to increase with the number of social media platforms used (Primack et al. 2017).

On the other hand, however, there is evidence that Facebook users are more trusting, have closer relationships, get more social support, and are more politically engaged than non-Facebook users (Hampton et al. 2011); that social media users are more aware than others of major events in the lives of people close to them (Hampton et al. 2015); and that Facebook users are more likely to be made happier by their friends' happy posts than they are to be made less happy by their friends' unhappy posts (Coviello et al. 2014). It turns out, too, that the way we interact on social media matters: while negative social interactions on social media are correlated with depression, positive interactions are not (Davila et al. 2012).

A survey of the empirical data on the effect on us of social media use is, of course, relevant when trying to decide whether it makes our lives better or worse. But focusing on the data also encourages us to take a consequentialist view of things. That is, it encourages us to believe that using social media is a good thing if it brings good consequences (makes us less depressed, more cheerful, and so on) and a bad thing if it makes us feel bad. This way of looking at things ignores much that is important and relevant in considering whether we should be concerned about Facebook. Living a good and fulfilling life does not depend solely on doing things that make us feel good and avoiding things that make us feel bad. Abandoning a desperate friend in her hour of need in favour of going out partying might make us feel cheerful, but behaving in that way is not part of what being a good friend is, and friendship is something that we value. Good friends support each other through the hard times, and often make personal sacrifices to do so. How do we work out whether social media supports and enriches our friendships, rather than undermines them, given that having our friendships supported and enriched is not necessarily going to result in the more positive outcomes identified in the studies mentioned previously – less stress, less depression, less anxiety?

FACEBOOK AND THE ARISTOTELIAN VIRTUES

One attempt to address this issue has been made by Shannon Vallor (2012). Focusing on an Aristotelian virtue-ethics conception of friendship, she tests whether the sort of interactions that people have via Facebook can exemplify and support true friendship. Virtue ethics is sometimes said to be one of the three major ethical approaches, along with deontology and consequentialism. Deontology evaluates and explains why certain behaviour is ethical primarily with reference to duties and rules; consequentialism does so primarily with reference to the consequences of the behaviour. Virtue ethics focuses on virtues or character traits. On a virtue ethics account, certain actions are right primarily because they express and/or cultivate certain virtues, such as courage, temperance, or practical wisdom. Actions are wrong primarily because they express and/or cultivate vices.

Aristotle's virtues were intended to be applicable in a wide range of situations. As a result, despite the fact that he died over 2,000 years before the appearance of the internet, his virtue-based conception of friendship is flexible enough to apply even to today's electronically mediated interactions. Vallor tells us that one way of using Aristotle's account of friendship to evaluate the impact of social media on our friendship involves reflecting on 'how various uses of new social media could impact the development of specific virtues or vices. We might, for example, consider whether specific new media practices are likely to hinder or promote the development of ethical traits' (Vallor 2012: 187). Vallor notes that Aristotle used the term 'friendship' in several ways, not all of which resemble today's use. She identifies four Aristotelian virtues as relevant to our friendships today: reciprocity, empathy, self-knowledge, and the shared life.

Vallor argues that all of these virtues are to some extent supported by our Facebook interactions. Reciprocity – social 'give and take' – is at the heart of most of Facebook's features: sending and accepting friend requests, 'liking' and commenting on posts, tagging friends, and so on. These interactions also support empathy – the capacity to feel the joy and suffering of others – as we see when people post about their hangovers, illnesses, weddings, promotions, etc., and others respond by celebrating or commiserating with them. Self-knowledge (of the sort of people we are and how we fit into the world) can be advanced by Facebook interactions; as can the shared life, which involves a community of people living together with shared values and actions.

Vallor notes, however, that these four friendship-constituting virtues are not all expressed and supported to equal extents in our Facebook interactions. For example, while Facebook expressions of empathy are better than no empathy, there is something especially valuable about empathy expressed in person, as when we comfort a grieving friend with a hug. And since our Facebook interactions need not involve living and striving together with a community of people with whom we interact in a sustained, intimate way, the opportunities afforded by Facebook for development of self-knowledge and a shared life are inferior to those that arise in offline settings.

LOSS AVERSION, STATUS QUO BIAS, AND THE VALUE OF FACEBOOK

One problem with the analysis conducted by Vallor – which is, I think, an example of a much more general bias when we consider the impact of Facebook on our friendships – is that it proceeds by evaluating our Facebook-mediated friendships against the gold standard of traditional friendships. We think of traditional friendships as confined to meatspace; that is, to the world outside the internet. This latter model of friendship is natural to anyone born earlier than the mid-1980s, since they (okay, *we*) first formed adult friendships without the aid of social media. Facebook and other social media are, for this group of people, later optional add-ons to the institution of friendship, rather like Candy Crush and Tropicats are later optional add-on games to the institution of Facebook. Taking meatspace-only friendships to be the norm against which alternatives are evaluated affects the way we see differences between the two models. People in general care more about avoiding losing valuable things that we already have than about gaining new valuable things – even when the value lost or gained in each case is equal. This phenomenon was first described by psychologists Daniel Kahneman and Amos Tversky in 1979, and is called *loss aversion*. It means, roughly, that in order for us to welcome a change in the status quo, the benefits of the change may need to be significantly larger than the drawbacks.

As a result, it should not surprise us when people who were born earlier than the mid-1980s – a group that includes most (perhaps all) of the researchers cited in this chapter – express the view that Facebook is bad for friendship. People in this group are likely to weigh what Facebook might be *costing* our friendships far more heavily than what our friendships *gain* from Facebook.

By contrast, we can expect younger people whose first adult friendships have been formed in the age of social media to attach more weight to the good that Facebook adds to friendship. This is what they would lose were they to lose Facebook. For these people, the suggestion that Facebook has impoverished friendships must feel rather like the suggestion that telephones or cars have impoverished friendships. There is a sense in which these suggestions are impossible to conceive: younger people no more have memories of (adult) friendships pre-Facebook than they do memories of (adult) friendships pre-telephones and pre-cars. It does not matter that not everyone uses Facebook, just as it does not matter that not everyone has a telephone or a car; what matters is living in a world in which these technologies are available and normal.

Another related thought is this: we tend to prefer the status quo. Psychologists call this *status quo bias*. People who grew up and formed friendships before the appearance of Facebook are more likely to favour the sort of friendships that were cultivated pre-Facebook, and younger people whose friendships have been formed in the age of social media are more likely to favour the sort of friendships that they have cultivated and enjoy against the backdrop of social media.

Given status quo bias, how can we work out whether a given alteration to friendships – such as the explosion in popularity of Facebook over the last decade or so – really is a bad thing, or whether some people are simply led to believe it is a bad thing as a result of their biases? One approach is to weigh the arguments from both sides: from the pre-mid-1980s brigade who grew up without Facebook, and from the younger people whose friendships developed alongside it. Younger people currently publish very little in this area, but are increasingly likely to argue their case in academia and elsewhere.

Another way is to conduct a 'reversal test'. This is a heuristic developed by Nick Bostrom and Toby Ord to examine value judgments about the desirability of human enhancement. They set it out as follows:

> *Reversal Test:* When a proposal to change a certain parameter is thought to have bad overall consequences, consider a change to the same parameter in the opposite direction. If this is also thought to have bad overall consequences, then the onus is on those who reach these conclusions to explain why our position cannot be improved through changes to this parameter. If they are unable to do so,

then we have reason to suspect that they suffer from status quo bias.

(Bostrom and Ord 2006: 664–665)

Bostrom and Ord use the reversal test to assess judgments about alterations that occur in a linear way; in particular, improvements in intelligence brought about by genetic engineering. The effect that Facebook has had on friendship is much messier, and not at all linear. Facebook has resulted in us being more available to contact from friends, better able to interact with people from anywhere in the world, better able to keep in contact with childhood friends and people who live very far away, it has increased the ease with which we can discuss news stories and other events with a wide group of people, and so on. It might be possible to apply the reversal test to some of these individual changes; but it is not possible to apply it to all these changes together. The reversal test is much more useful for assessing judgments about the desirability of intelligence enhancement than it is for assessing judgments about the desirability of Facebook.

TESTING FACEBOOK'S VALUE: A THOUGHT EXPERIMENT

We can, though, devise a way to assess judgments about the desirability of Facebook that is inspired by the reversal test. Specifically, we can entertain a scenario that reverses the status quo, and consider how certain changes to that status quo might be received by people who experience them. With this in mind, imagine that Facebook has always been around, and that it was always as ubiquitous as it is now. There was never friendship without Facebook. Even while Aristotle was writing about friendship in the *Ethics*, he was pausing to share cat memes on his Facebook page and challenging Alexander the Great to Words With Friends. Your parents were Facebook friends with each other, as were your grandparents, your great-grandparents, and your great-great-grandparents. Let's call this world *Eternal Facebook World*, or EFW. To imagine what EFW would be like at our current point in history requires more thought and mental gymnastics than I plan to devote to it here; however, we can be sure of one thing. That is, if – in a mirror of what has happened in the actual world over the last decade or so – people in EFW were faced with the gradual decline and eventual elimination of Facebook over the course of about a decade, we could expect them to be concerned about what they would lose out on as a result. They would, of course, lose exactly what we have gained as a result of the increasing popularity of Facebook, but since we tend to care more about avoiding losses than we do about making corresponding gains, we can expect people in EFW to place more weight on these features than we do.

What sort of anxieties might such people have, faced with the prospect of losing Facebook? Taking a broad view, losing Facebook would restrict the nature and extent of one's interactions with friends, family, colleagues, and acquaintances. Losing Facebook would, after all, entail losing one of the most convenient methods of interacting with people. Facebook makes it easy for us to keep up to date with the lives of a large group of people, regardless of their distance from us. In a few seconds, we can announce a major life event – a birth, a marriage, a promotion, a video of a cat running into a glass door – to hundreds of people, and those responding can interact not only with us but also with each other. Other forms of social media aside, we lack any alternative way of quickly and easily communicating in this way.

That Facebook enables us to keep in touch with people regardless of where they (or we) are in the world has far-reaching consequences for our friendships. Before social media, and especially before earlier technologies like email, telephones, and motorised transport, friendships were heavily restricted by geography. The closer you lived to a person, the easier it was to maintain a friendship with them. It was less easy, in those days, to select friends based primarily on common interests: if you were the only liberal-minded person in a city inhabited by conservatives, or the only fan of satanic death metal in a village full of devout Christians, you had to work at finding areas of common interest with local people if you wanted to have friends. By largely freeing our friendships from the constraints of geography, Facebook makes it easy for us to seek out people who share our interests and values, wherever they might live: we can use Facebook to connect with fellow yoga enthusiasts, fellow victims of domestic violence, fellow Marxists, and so on.

It is not an unmitigated good thing for people to cluster into groups of common interest. It is often complained that this results in an 'echo chamber' in which people are less likely to be exposed to views divergent from their own, and that as a result people have an impoverished understanding of different people and are perhaps less tolerant of them. On the other hand, the ability to seek out people like oneself can be a great source of support to people who might otherwise feel quite isolated. We can expect that people in a world where Facebook has always existed, faced with the prospect of losing Facebook, would resent losing the ability easily and conveniently to sustain relationships with people around the world. Were they to learn that being restricted to friendships with more local people would likely lead them to be more understanding of others – especially those with views and values different to their own – it is unlikely that they would regard this as sufficient compensation for the loss of Facebook, especially since losing Facebook is not a necessary condition for realising that benefit (they could, for example, implement social measures to encourage a diverse range of people to associate with each other without giving up Facebook).

Another reason for people in EFW to lament the impending loss of Facebook is that this loss is likely to hit some people harder than others: people who live in isolated areas, people who don't have (or can't afford) transport to enable them easily to meet up with friends, elderly people and people with incapacitating disabilities or illnesses, and people who can't afford (or who simply don't enjoy) the activities that go hand-in-hand with seeing friends in person, like dining out or drinks in the pub. It's likely that many would demand that some public measure be introduced to offset the difficulties that such people would face in a Facebookless world. After all, it is common for comparable demands to be made whenever a group in society is adversely affected by some measure – such as the closure of facilities like post offices, bus routes, and medical centres in rural areas.

FACEBOOK AND THE ARISTOTELIAN VIRTUES, AGAIN

Let's revisit the Aristotelian virtues discussed by Vallor in the context of this thought experiment. How might an Aristotelian EFW inhabitant view the impact of the loss of Facebook on the virtues relevant to friendship? We noted earlier that while Facebook supports the virtue of reciprocity, Vallor found that it is less supportive of the other three friendship-related virtues she considered: empathy, self-knowledge, and the shared life. There is something valuable about meatspace interactions that is lost when we interact via Facebook, meaning that while Facebook expressions of empathy, advances in self-knowledge, and participation in the shared life are better than nothing, more valuable still are the face-to-face interactions that help develop and advance these virtues in us. There is, Vallor argues, a physical dimension to empathy: she tells us that 'the best comfort to a grieving friend is often a quiet physical embrace' (2012: 193). Development of self-knowledge requires living in a one-to-one relationship with friends who 'mirror [our] virtues and noble achievements' (2012: 194) – a kind of relationship that is common offline, but less common (thinks Vallor) on Facebook. The shared life involves investing with others in 'shared projects and commitments' (2012: 197); yet while Facebook facilitates the sorts of exchanges of information that support shared living, Vallor worries that the way Facebook is actually used (especially by young people) is not conducive to the shared life.

One notable aspect of Vallor's analysis is that she frequently (though not always) sets up Facebook friendships in opposition to meatspace friendships. Facebook fares worse than meatspace at supporting empathy, for example, because it does not provide the opportunity to interact in certain important physical ways with people. Yet, while many of us have Facebook friends whom we are yet to meet, most people use Facebook for maintaining existing relationships rather than for creating new ones – as Vallor notes, citing a study by Subrahmanyam et al. (2008). Our most valued Facebook friendships, then, involve interactions with people we met through means other than Facebook. In most cases, these are people we have met in meatspace, making them friends with whom we interact on Facebook *as well as* offline. Some of these – such as childhood friends who live far away from us – are people with whom we would likely have lost touch, were it not for Facebook. In other cases, our Facebook interactions supplement our offline interactions. Even conceding that the virtues of empathy, self-knowledge, and the shared life are best supported when we interact offline with our friends, Facebook need not detract from offline benefits. There are, of course, ways of using Facebook that undermine valuable aspects of offline activity – but the same can be said for other technologies, too. By driving a car too much we miss out on exercise, by using a calculator we risk losing our mathematical skills, by using a word processor we risk our handwriting deteriorating, and so on. Given the positive value that all these technologies add to our lives, the fact that there are also drawbacks to using them does not entail that they are on balance bad. Rather, it should lead us to use them thoughtfully, so as to maximise their benefits whilst minimising their drawbacks.

CONCLUSION

Are we right to worry about Facebook? This is the question from which we began. I think that the answer, in short, is: we are indeed right to worry about what Facebook might be costing us, but if we want a balanced appraisal of Facebook, we would do well to keep in mind what we gain from Facebook, too. And, given that we tend to weigh losses more heavily than gains, we should be wary of underestimating the benefits of Facebook – especially those of us who grew up without it.

REFERENCES

Bostrom, N. and Ord, T. 2006: 'The reversal test: eliminating status quo bias in applied ethics', *Ethics* 116 (July): 656–679.

Brown, J. 2018: 'Is social media bad for you? The evidence and the unknowns', *BBC Future*, 5th January. Available at www.bbc.com/future/story/20180104-is-social-media-bad-for-you-the-evidence-and-the-unknowns

Coviello, L., Sohn, Y., Kramer, A.D.I., Marlow, C., Franceschetti, M., Christakis, N.A., and Fowler, J.H. 2014: 'Detecting emotional contagion in massive social networks', *PLOS One* 9/3: e90315.

Davila, J., Herschenberg, R., Feinstein, B.A., Gorman, K., Bhatia, V., and Starr, L.R. 2012: 'Frequency and quality of social networking among young adults: associations with depressive symptoms, rumination, and corumination', *Psychology of Popular Media Culture* 1/2: 72–86.

Ginsberg, D. and Burke, M. 2017: 'Hard questions: is spending time on social media bad for us?', *Facebook Newsroom*, 15th December. Available at https://newsroom.fb.com/news/2017/12/hard-questions-is-spending-time-on-social-media-bad-for-us/

Hampton, K., Rainie, L., Lu, W., Shin, I., and Purcell, K. 2015: 'Psychological stress and social media use', *Pew Research Center*, 15th January.

Hampton, K., Sessions Goulet, L., Rainie, L., and Purcell, K. 2011: 'Social networking sites and our lives', *Pew Research Center*, 16th June.

Hayes, M. 2018: 'How to quit your tech: a beginner's guide to divorcing your phone', *The Guardian*, 13th January. Available at www.theguardian.com/technology/2018/jan/13/how-to-quit-your-tech-phone-digital-detox

Kahneman, D. and Tversky, A. 1979: 'Prospect theory: an analysis of decision under risk', *Econometrica* 47: 263–291.

Kenrick, D.T. 2014: '7 ways Facebook is bad for your mental health', *Psychology Today*, 11th April. Available at www.psychologytoday.com/us/blog/sex-murder-and-the-meaning-life/201404/7-ways-facebook-is-bad-your-mental-health

Primack, B.A., Shensa, A., Escobar-Viera, C.G., Barrett, E.L., Sidani, J.E., Colditz, J.B., and Everette James, A. 2017: 'Use of multiple social media platforms and symptoms of depression and anxiety: a nationally-representative study among U.S. young adults', *Computers in Human Behavior* 69: 1–9.

Sagioglou, S. and Greitemeyer, T. 2014: 'Facebook's emotional consequences: why Facebook causes a decrease in mood and why people still use it', *Computers in Human Behavior* 35: 359–363.

Sini, R. 2017: '"You are being programmed", former Facebook executive warns', *BBC Trending*, 12th December. Available at www.bbc.co.uk/news/blogs-trending-42322746.

Subrahmanyam, K., Reich, S.M., Waechter, N., and Espinoza, G. 2008: 'Online and offline social networks: use of social networking sites by emerging adults', *Journal of Applied Development Psychology* 29: 420–433.

Vallor, S. 2012: 'Flourishing on Facebook: virtue friendship & new social media', *Ethics and Information Technology* 14: 185–199.

Twelve

Carissa Véliz

In 2013, American YouTube music and comedy sensation Chrissy Chambers witnessed her reputation crumble when her ex-boyfriend uploaded seven videos of them having sex to dozens of porn sites. Chambers didn't even know he had filmed her. As the videos spread through the internet, she was harassed by misogynistic trolls. For months after discovering the videos online, Chambers suffered from night terrors, and body shame so intense that she could not stand to be touched or to look at herself in the mirror. She started drinking, and was diagnosed with post-traumatic stress disorder. In 2017, after four years of legal battles, she reached a settlement with her ex. She received compensation for damages, copyright of the videos, and an apology. It is more than most victims of revenge porn get, but compensation cannot undo psychological damage. And in the Chambers case, her ex's name was not disclosed; as part of the settlement, he kept his privacy.[1]

WHAT IS PRIVACY?

Privacy is the quality of having one's personal information and one's personal 'sensorial space' unaccessed. In other words, you have privacy with respect to another person to the extent that the other person does not have access to your personal information and your personal space – that is, to the degree that they do not know anything personal about you and that they cannot see, touch, or hear you in contexts in which people typically do not want others' attention.

Personal information is the kind of information about ourselves that is common for people in a certain society not to want anyone, other than themselves (and perhaps a very limited number of other people chosen by them) to know about. For example, people typically do not want just anyone to know details about their sex life. Personal information also includes information that the subject is particularly sensitive about and has taken measures to conceal from others. Imagine a person who is shy about her achievements and wishes to keep them secret so as not to become the centre of attention. Similarly, the limits of our sensorial space are set by what people are typically comfortable exposing to others. There are two ways this space can be violated. First, when someone sees, hears, or touches us in a zone in which there are cultural expectations to be free from the eyes, ears, touch, and presence of others (e.g. in the toilet). Access can be obtained through direct or indirect perception (such as cameras and microphones). Second, when we are witnessed engaging in some activity or being the subject of some event that typically evokes the desire to have no witnesses or very few chosen witnesses (e.g. being naked).[2]

Chambers' ex-boyfriend violated her privacy because he published content online without her consent that contained sensitive information – that she had had sexual intercourse with a man. This information was particularly problematic because in online communities she described herself as a lesbian. The violation of her privacy was compounded by the use of images – except for exhibitionists, most people do not want to be seen naked nor witnessed when having an intimate experience with another person.

But why should we value privacy?

Well, because having our personal information accessed and our sensorial space invaded makes us vulnerable. Privacy protects us from both individual and collective harms.

INDIVIDUAL HARMS

One set of harms that privacy protects us from is illustrated by revenge porn – the non-consensual sharing of nude or sexual images – and related harms such as blackmail. Others' attention and judgment can cause people to feel self-conscious at best, and humiliated or shunned at worst.

Revenge porn is not uncommon. According to a survey of nearly 4,300 people, one in five Australians has been a victim of image-based abuse. In some cases, sensitive images get shared and exposed; in other cases, the threat of exposure is used to coerce, extort, or harass the victim.[3] In England and Wales, 1,160 cases were reported to the police in the first nine months after the legislation on revenge porn was passed in 2015. Some victims were as young as 11 years old.[4]

Other individual harms include identity theft and fraud. A woman who got hold of Ramona María Timaru's personal details used them to impersonate her and take out loans that were never paid back in banks across Spain. It is surprisingly difficult to prove you did not commit a crime when someone is committing them in your name. Timaru has been detained multiple times, and she has spent years and a substantial amount of money defending herself in many trials in different parts of Spain. When the newspaper El País interviewed her, she said that her life 'was being ruined,' and that she was taking tranquillisers to fight anxiety.[5]

Some other individual harms are more difficult to notice, but can be just as damaging. One is discrimination. Data brokers are companies that strive to collect all the data they can on internet users. Information can include census and address records, driving records, web-browsing history, social media data, criminal records, academic records, credit records, medical records, and more. They then sell these files to banks, would-be employers, insurance companies, and governments, among others.

Imagine two candidates are equally qualified for a particular job, but the data broker's file on one of them shows that he suffers from health issues. The company decides to hire the healthy candidate and tells the other one that there was someone more qualified for the job. In theory, discrimination is illegal. In practice, it is very hard to prove; companies can always come up with untruthful explanations for their decisions, and victims may not even realise they have been discriminated against. Discrimination may take several forms: if your genetic information is not private, an insurance company that suspects you to have bad genes can charge more expensive premiums for something over which you have no control and for which you cannot be blamed.

COLLECTIVE HARMS

Privacy damages can also be collective. In the 2018 Cambridge Analytica scandal, it was revealed that personal data from 87 million Facebook accounts had helped build psychological profiles of internet users who were then sent personalised political propaganda. Cambridge Analytica worked on both the 2016 US election and the EU referendum campaign in Britain that same year. During the referendum, the firm was on the 'leave' side; voters who were leaning towards voting 'leave' got information that reinforced their views, including false news regarding immigration, while voters who were thinking of voting 'remain' might have been sent information that discouraged them from going to the ballot box. Propaganda is not new, but in the past it was something public – everybody could see what each party was advertising. What is particularly unhealthy about personalised propaganda is that it contributes to polarisation through showing each person different and potentially contradictory information, and it takes advantage of people's personality traits to be more effective in influencing them. In the past, propaganda may have been just as misleading, but at least we all had access to it. Personalised propaganda causes individuals to be blind to what others are seeing. It fractures the public sphere into atomic individual spheres.

One lesson of the Cambridge Analytica case is the collective nature of privacy. Privacy is not only collective because of the consequences of its loss – even if 'only' 87 million Facebook users lost their privacy, all of the citizens of the manipulated democracies were indirectly harmed. Privacy is also collective in another way: when you expose information about yourself, you inevitably expose others as well.

Only 270,000 Facebook users actually consented to Cambridge Analytica collecting their data. The other 87 million people were friends of the consenting users whose data was harvested without their knowledge or consent. We are responsible for each other's privacy because we are connected in ways that make us vulnerable to each other. Think of all the contacts you have on your mobile phone. If you give a company access to that phone, you give it access to your contacts too. If you divulge genetic information, you expose your parents, siblings, and children. If you reveal your location data, you inform on people with whom you live and work. If you disclose your habits and psychological make-up, you expose people who resemble you.

Collective harms facilitated by privacy losses can be dramatic. The Nazis were more effective in finding Jews where there were better civil registers. It is no coincidence that the Nazis were great innovators in techniques of registration and identification of individuals. It is worth noting – given the new power of technology companies – that it was a technology company, IBM, who assisted them in these objectives through the development of punch cards.[6]

These examples may come from what might seem the distant past. But as I write this chapter, the Chinese government is implementing a system of 'social credit' through which people are given a grade that represents their reputation. It is calculated on the basis of all the data that is held on them. A poor grade may limit their access to opportunities. In February 2017, the Supreme People's Court announced that 6.15 million people had been banned from taking flights in the last four years for having committed 'social misdeeds.' Another 1.65 million people on the blacklist are banned from taking trains.[7] The Chinese government is creating a system of control over its citizens in which as many individual actions are recorded as possible; those who deviate from established norms are punished with social exclusion or worse. The government knows so much about its citizens that dissidence can be squashed before it can express itself in an organised fashion. And if it does appear, those who engage in it can be easily targeted for punishment.

For those of us lucky enough to live in reasonably democratic societies, the mere existence of data on us is still a risk. Democratic countries have not always been democracies, and may cease to be so in the future. Data is like water – it rarely stays still and isolated. It tends to combine and flow. There is no telling in whose hands it may end up.

DATA HYGIENE

Hoarding personal data is a risky practice. This information is coveted by many agents – from personal enemies, jealous exes, and bad neighbours, to insurance companies, business competitors, data brokers, banks, and governments. Information is hard to keep safe in the digital age. Attackers will always have an advantage over defenders. An attacker can choose the time and method of attack, while defenders have to protect themselves from any type of attack at all times. A sufficiently skilled, motivated, and well-funded cyber-attacker has a high probability of success. And that is if the defender is doing everything it can to protect data. But netizens cannot trust that governments and companies will be careful enough with their data. Even if they do not sell data – which, in this data economy, should not be taken for granted – governments and businesses can be sloppy about keeping data safe. In 2015, the American government was hacked and sensitive information on 21.5 million people who had undergone background checks for security clearances was stolen.[8]

Since data is vulnerable, data subjects and anyone who stores data are also vulnerable. This is why security expert Bruce Shneier calls personal data a 'toxic asset.'[9] It is like keeping a bomb in the shed that could explode at any moment.

Given the destructive potential of personal data, one strategy is to lose as little privacy as possible. This advice, however, is not very practical in the current digital environment. To be fully functional members of society, most of us feel compelled to use services like Facebook and Twitter that force us to give up a substantial amount of privacy. These platforms have become the new public square; suggesting we stay away from them may be too much to ask. As democracies, we also do not want to discourage citizens from participating in new forms of public engagement. In any case, companies like Facebook track netizens online even if they do not have a Facebook account; opting out is not always an option.

Fortunately, 'abstinence' is not the only or even the safest way to protect privacy online. Useful advice includes being conservative in all privacy settings, covering your cameras with tape or a sticker, staying away from online quizzes that ask personal questions, using ad blockers, turning off your phone's Wi-Fi and Bluetooth when you leave home, choosing services that are better at protecting privacy (e.g. DuckDuckGo instead of Google, ProtonMail instead of Gmail, etc.), and using obfuscation. Obfuscation means confusing online trackers, losing them with noise.[10] In some cases, like government webpages, the law requires you to reveal your identity. But online companies do not have a claim on your personal data. If they force you to give up personal data in exchange for services, you are entitled to give them misleading information about your birth date (as long as you are not a minor trying to access a service for adults, or an adult pretending to be a minor), gender, location, or preferences. There are a few tools that have been designed to facilitate obfuscation. TrackMeNot, for example, issues randomised search-queries to popular search engines to hide your actual searches and interests.

Most important of all is to periodically delete old data that is no longer necessary. Privacy expert Max Schrems deletes his tweets after they have been published for two months. You might find that deleting personal data is hard. The temptation is to hold on to it as a way of holding on to your history, your identity. But keeping personal data online is dangerous. Getting rid of it is a way of making sure you will not get stuck in the past or in a mistake – a drunken night, a bad relationship, an unreflective comment, or an opinion you no longer hold or in any case don't want a record of it to exist in the public domain.

That is the motivation behind the European right to be forgotten. In May 2014, the European Court of Justice ruled against Google in *Costeja*, a case brought by a Spanish man, Mario Costeja González, who requested the removal of a link to a digitised 1998 article in a newspaper about an auction for his foreclosed home, for a debt that he had subsequently paid.[11] If he had already paid his debts, he successfully argued, it was unfair for his reputation to continue to be tarnished. If our mistakes become the only thing we are known for (as people usually read only what comes up first on a search engine), we will never be allowed to move past them.

Under the European General Data Protection Regulation (GDPR), data subjects now have the right to ask institutions and businesses to erase their data, stop sharing their data, and have third parties halt processing of the data. Although the law only applies to European citizens, many companies, including Facebook, have vowed to extend the same rights to all its users. The success of the legislation will partly depend on users demanding our rights. No good will come from the right to be forgotten unless netizens ask for their data to be deleted.

CONCLUSION

In 2010, Facebook founder Mark Zuckerberg suggested that privacy was no longer 'a social norm,' that we had 'evolved' beyond it. His buying of the four houses surrounding his for privacy reasons casts doubt on the sincerity of his statement. What is clear, in any case, is that he was wrong. Privacy is as important and relevant as ever – in fact, in the digital age, it is more relevant than ever. When we fail to protect privacy, individuals and societies get harmed.

These harms suggest that privacy is not only a right on account of the interests we have in protecting our personal information and sensory space; it is also an obligation. We do not only put ourselves at risk when we are careless with our privacy. We also jeopardise our family, friends, flatmates, colleagues, fellow citizens, and people with whom we share habits and personality traits. A culture of exposure creates a hostile environment for anyone identified as an outlier. Protecting our privacy is thus not only an act of self-care, but it is also necessary to protect others' privacy.

The need for privacy is as important as the need for companionship and community. In fact, these goods are complementary. Privacy is necessary for individuals and communities to flourish. We are not creatures who thrive in fishbowls.

NOTES

1 Kleeman (2018).
2 Véliz (2017).
3 Henry, Powell, and Flynn (2017).
4 Sherlock (2016).
5 Hernández (2016).
6 Black (2012).
7 Botsman (2017).
8 Zengerle and Cassella (2015).

9 Schneier (2016).
10 Powles (2015).
11 Bygrave (2015).

REFERENCES

Black, Edwin. IBM and the Holocaust. Washington, DC: Dialog Press, 2012.

Botsman, Rachel. 'Big Data Meets Big Brother as China Moves to Rate Its Citizens.' Wired, 2017.

Bygrave, Lee Andrew. 'A Right to Be Forgotten?,' Communications of the ACM, 58:1, 35–37, 2015.

Henry, Nicola, Anastasia Powell, and Asher Flynn. Not Just 'Revenge Pornography': Australians' Experiences of Image-Based Abuse. Melbourne: RMIT University, 2017.

Hernández, José Antonio. 'Me Han Robado La Identidad Y Estoy a Base De Lexatín; Yo No Soy Una Delincuente.' El País, 24 August 2016.

Kleeman, Jenny. 'The Youtube Star Who Fought Back Against Revenge Porn – And Won.' The Guardian, 18 January 2018.

Powles, Julia. 'Obfuscation: How Leaving a Trail of Confusion Can Beat Online Surveillance.' The Guardian, 24 October 2015.

Schneier, Bruce. 'Data Is a Toxic Asset, So Why Not Throw It Out?' CNN, 2016.

Sherlock, Peter. 'Revenge Pornography Victims as Young as 11, Investigation Finds.' BBC, 27 April 2016.

Véliz, Carissa. On Privacy. Oxford: University of Oxford, 2017.

Zengerle, Patricia, and Megan Cassella. 'Millions More Americans Hit by Government Personnel Data Hack.' Reuters, 9 July 2015.

Fake news and free speech

Thirteen

Neil Levy

As the world changes, the problems that confront us change,
too, in unexpected and unpredictable ways. The problem of
fake news is a perfect illustration of this phenomenon.

But what exactly is the problem, and how should we
respond to it?

By "fake news," I mean false information, especially about
political figures and events, that masquerades as or is mistaken
for genuine news. That definition is rough and leaves many
questions unanswered (are satirical magazines or satirical
online sites like *The Onion* fake news?). However, it is sufficient
for our purposes.

Fake news apparently has real world effects. It has been
blamed (or credited) for changing the outcome of important votes (such as the 2016 US presidential election and the
Brexit referendum in the UK). Consider this example, from
the 2016 presidential campaign. In March 2016, John Podesta,
the chairman of Hillary Clinton's election campaign, had his
email hacked. Several months later, a number of these emails
were published by Wikileaks. Apparently as a joke, some people posting on social media and discussion boards began to
speculate that the emails contained code words referring to
paedophilia, and to allege that senior figures in the Democratic Party were involved in the trafficking of children for

sex. Allegedly, food-related words in the emails referred to sex with children (for instance, "cheese pizza" meant "child pornography," since they share initial letters).

As the conspiracy theory transmuted, it came to be associated with the Comet Ping Pong restaurant, a Washington D.C. pizzeria owned by a Clinton supporter, which had hosted fundraising events for Barack Obama. Comet Ping Pong was alleged to host parties involving paedophilia and sexual abuse of children. At least some of the people who fabricated ever wilder versions of these stories or spread them were trolls or pranksters. Some, in fact, probably thought that they were harmless jokes because they were so implausible. But others took them seriously. An opinion poll in December 2016 asked Americans whether they believed the rumours that the emails contained code words for paedophilia and satanic ritual abuse. More than a third of respondents, and nearly half of Republicans, reported that they believed the rumours were "probably" or "definitely" true.[1] At least some people believed the rumours strongly enough to be motivated to take action. On 4 December 2016, Edgar Maddison Welch drove to Comet Ping Pong with an assault rifle. He was there, he said, to investigate the claims and free any child slaves he found. He fired multiple shots before he was arrested.

No one died at Comet Ping Pong. The incident illustrates, however, how consequential fake news can be. It may have swung elections. It may have motivated terrorist bombings. Think of how rumours concerning George Soros, a prominent liberal Jew, seem to have motivated one American terrorist who sent pipe bombs to him to and other liberal figures, and another terrorist who shot and killed 11 people at a Pittsburgh synagogue in 2018; perhaps fake news has also played a role in motivating Islamic terrorists. It may be playing a role in our (insufficient) response to climate change and the growing problem of vaccine scepticism. Arguably, it is the ethical problem of our times.

It is a problem that can usefully be understood as involving three different kinds of agents; each raises a different set of questions and requires a different kind of response. First, there is the question of the ethical assessment of the *producers* of fake news, who may be individuals with a variety of motivations, or who may instead be organisations. Second, there is a question concerning the ethical assessment of *consumers* and perhaps *sharers* of fake news. Finally, there is a more social and political dimension to the problem, concerning how institutions and the law should respond to fake news. I will address these questions in reverse order.

In liberal societies such as the UK, there is a strong presumption in favour of free speech. Most of us believe that governments should restrict speech (here understood broadly, to include writing and even posting memes or GIFs on social media) only rarely, when there are strong reasons to fear that significant harms are likely to arise from the speech. While we may want to punish individuals who shout "fire!" in a crowded place purely to cause panic, we are reluctant to extend prohibition further (some countries, including the UK but not the US, have laws forbidding hate speech – the vilification of individuals and groups on the basis of race, religion, or sexuality; these laws are often highly controversial). Most of us believe that lies and propaganda are best countered with more and better speech, not by bans or restrictions.

The best-known and most influential set of arguments for why speech should be unrestricted unless it is clearly and directly harmful to others is owed to the great nineteenth-century philosopher, John Stuart Mill. In *On Liberty* (1985/1859),

Mill argued that each of us has a right to act as we like so long as we don't harm others without their consent. With regard to speech specifically, Mill advanced several arguments. First, he argued, we can rarely be entirely sure that we are already in possession of the truth, so banning opposing views robs us of an opportunity to learn better. Second, even when we are right, hearing opposing arguments provides us with an opportunity to come to a clearer understanding of our own view by testing it. Third, granting to government the power to restrict speech risks tyranny.

Mill recognised, of course, that there were risks with allowing unrestricted speech: it may mislead the gullible, for instance. But he believed that the risks were small. Underlying this belief was a confidence in our reason: truth tends to defeat untruth when they confront one another. Extending Mill's ideas to the contemporary world, we might say that the best response to fake news is to combat it with truth. Perhaps we need more and better fact-checking sites (like Snopes.com).

But is Mill right to be optimistic that truth will tend to defeat lies, given the opportunity?

There is in fact a great deal of evidence that people are *motivated believers*. That is, we tend to believe claims if we would like them to be true and disbelieve them if they are uncomfortable. It is no accident that twice as many Republicans as Democrats believed that Pizzagate was definitely or probably true. It is also no accident that Republicans are far more likely to be climate change sceptics than Democrats (effective action on climate change may require control of the free market, and support for a free market is a very strong predictor of climate change scepticism).[2]

There is also a lot of evidence that correcting misinformation often fails to lead people to reject it.[3] In fact, sometimes an authoritative correction actually *increases* people's belief. One study found that people who believed that Saddam Hussein had weapons of mass destruction (the putative reason for the 2003 US invasion of Iraq) were even more convinced after receiving an authoritative correction from the US congressional report that found he had no such weapons.[4] Education is no cure (in fact, better educated Republicans were more likely to believe that former US President Barack Obama is a secret Muslim, not less). This body of psychological research[5] provides us with strong reason to think that Mill was overly optimistic to think that truth will always, or even typically, crowd out falsehood.

That does not – necessarily – imply that we must ban fake news. Perhaps there are responses available that are less restrictive than prohibition but more restrictive than supporters of Mill envisage. Perhaps, for instance, there are steps we can take to limit exposure to fake news. Part of the solution to the social and institutional problem of fake news might lie at the level of producers and consumers. I turn to these aspects of the problem before returning to the social and institutional dimension.

If we acknowledge that fake news has costs to individuals and to society, then perhaps we might best tackle the problem by addressing production. Fake news is produced by a variety of different people with different motivations. Some do it as a joke, not intending that others will take it seriously (if *The Onion* is fake news, it is clearly designed for entertainment purposes only – though as literallyunbelievable.org demonstrates, that fact doesn't prevent some people from being taken in by it). Others who produce fake news with the aim of entertaining themselves and third parties in mind don't care whether consumers are taken in, or even hope they will be. Some produce fake news in order to make money, either by providing "click-bait" for websites or because they are paid to produce it (like the Macedonian teenagers who were allegedly responsible for up to one-third of the fake news spread during the 2016 US presidential election). Finally, some people produce fake news in order to change people's behavior, usually to promote political agendas. Allegedly, much of the pro-Trump fake news was produced or funded by Russian agencies with an interest in swaying the election.

This variety of motivations is relevant to the moral assessment of those who produce fake news. Some of these motivations are legitimate, considered in themselves. The urge to entertain is usually permissible. There is nothing illegitimate *per se* about wanting to be paid. However, while it is sometimes permissible, and sometimes even praiseworthy, to want to entertain or to be remunerated in many contexts, these motivations are obviously not always permissible, let alone praiseworthy. It is, *prima facie*, immoral to spread false information – to lie – and the producers of fake news knowingly engage in this activity. Those producers who take reasonable steps to ensure that their productions will not be believed (by tagging it clearly as satire, for example), may be exempt from moral condemnation, but those who either do not care whether it is believed or actively seek to have it believed act immorally. Plausibly, the latter act more immorally than the former (just as the intentional infliction of harm is held to be worse by the law than the reckless infliction of harm). All the major moral theories converge on this assessment. *Consequentialists* will condemn the spread of fake news as likely to lead to false beliefs which in turn will impede the effective pursuit of our interests (most obviously, in this context, it may lead me to vote for a candidate whose policies will negatively affect me). *Kantians* will condemn these actions as disrespectful toward rational beings. *Virtue ethicists* will condemn them as manifesting vices, like contempt toward others.

Let's turn, now, to the consumers of fake news: you and me. Under the heading of consumption, I include not only the reading of fake news but also spreading it (say by sharing it on social media). Like producers, those who consume fake news have a variety of motivations. We may knowingly consume fake news for entertainment purposes. Or we may unknowingly consume it, mistaking it for genuine news. Similarly, we may spread it in order to entertain or to (mis)inform. Our motivations and our mental states make an important difference to how we should be morally assessed.

If we spread fake news in order to deceive others, or are indifferent to whether they are taken in, we obviously deserve some degree of moral criticism. But do we deserve moral condemnation if we consume it for entertainment? Or if we are taken in by it? There is room for disagreement here. There are two grounds for criticising those who consume fake news for entertainment. First, they may be criticised for helping to sustain the market for fake news (our clicks are counted and contribute toward the revenue of the websites that host fake news). Of course, the contribution of each individual is very small, so perhaps the criticism should be correspondingly mild (though non-consequentialists may think that complicity with an industry that is immoral deserves serious censure).

Second, we may criticise people in the light of the psychological research mentioned previously. While we may think that we can safely consume fake news without having our attitudes changed, there is evidence suggesting that even alert readers have their attitudes altered.[6] Even if we don't believe the allegations about Hillary Clinton and Pizzagate, we may find ourselves nevertheless with more negative attitudes toward her. This may work indirectly. Perhaps as a consequence of reading fake news, we will tend to dwell more than we otherwise would on those – genuine – aspects of her character that paint her in a bad light, and that may cause us to have a less favourable overall view than, arguably, we should have. Since the research that suggests that we cannot insulate ourselves from the effects of consuming fake news is not widely known, it is difficult to blame people for reading it for entertainment value. It might nevertheless be *bad* without being *blameworthy*.

We might also criticise those who consume fake news mistaking it for the real thing. According to some philosophers, traits like gullibility or a lack of intellectual curiosity are so-called epistemic vices – criticisable character traits related to how we behave in the domain of knowledge – just as cruelty or lack of empathy are moral vices; these philosophers often claim that we can appropriately criticise those who manifest these vices.[7]

Having discussed the production and the consumption of fake news, let's return to social and institutional issues. We have seen that production and consumption is often criticisable. But there are good reasons to think that at least some producers and some consumers are not well-placed to understand the ways in which their actions are wrong. They may not realise it has harmful effects. It is also very difficult to avoid fake news, some of which is easily mistaken for genuine news and is often to be found alongside it (e.g. in your Facebook news feed). Because it is better to prevent fake news from proliferating than to attempt to correct it (indeed, corrections seem often to fail), and because it is (currently) unreasonable to expect people to avoid fake news, it may be more effective to focus on institutional responses that limit the degree to which it is produced or that minimise exposure to it.

The dangers John Stuart Mill highlighted are surely genuine: though we have good reason to minimise exposure to fake news, we should be reluctant to ban speech. There are a variety of policy responses we can utilise to steer between these twin dangers. Some of these responses are best implemented by private companies (although they may only do so under pressure from government and the public). For example, Facebook and Twitter can take steps to vet content, to try to make fake news less prominent than it currently is – and thereby reduce exposure. Doing so could be expected to reduce the amount of fake news that is produced, since reduced exposure translates into a reduction in incentives for producing it.

Government arguably has a more direct role to play in combatting fake news. Government can promote certain kinds of speech and discourage others, through the use of taxation policy or through direct subsidy. One reason that fake news does so well is that the traditional media is increasingly unable to play its role when so much content is available for free. Government subsidies to national broadcasters and perhaps even to private companies upholding high standards of journalistic integrity might help to level the playing field. Fake news is an international problem – much of it is produced outside the national borders in which it is consumed – so there are limits on what any single nation may do on its own. A comprehensive response will require international agreement. This will be extremely hard to pull off, given that different countries have different interests. But if fake news comes to be a problem everywhere (because every country is targeted by malicious agents outside the country), it might be achievable. Again, an international agreement should promote certain kinds of speech: bans should be used very sparingly or not at all.

Fake news may not be an entirely new problem.[8] But it confronts us in ways that are unprecedented, in a world in which information can spread from person to person and across national borders almost instantaneously, and in which we no longer have agreed sources of trustworthy information. We also now possess new psychological knowledge about the effects of disinformation, even on knowing consumers. In this environment, we may need to address falsehoods in ways that Mill did not envisage. To the extent to which it is a genuinely new problem, we need to find genuinely new solutions.

NOTES

1 Blake (2016).
2 Lewandowsky et al. (2013).
3 Lewandowsky et al. (2012).
4 Nyhan and Reifler (2010).
5 Much of which is summarised in Levy (2017).
6 See Levy (2017) for review.
7 See, e.g., Battaly (2014).
8 Darnton (2017).

REFERENCES

Battaly, H. 2014. Varieties of Epistemic Vice. In Jon Matheson and Rico Vitz (eds). *The Ethics of Belief: Individual and Social*, Oxford: Oxford University Press, 2014.

Blake, A. 2016. Nearly Half of Republicans See Truth in "Pizzagate" Theory: Poll. *Washington Times*, December 28. www.washingtontimes.com/news/2016/dec/28/pizzagate-theory-believed-by-nearly-half-of-republ/

Darnton, R. 2017. The True History of Fake News. *NYR Daily*, February 13. www.nybooks.com/daily/2017/02/13/the-true-history-of-fake-news/

Levy, N. 2017. The Bad News About Fake News. *Social Epistemology Review and Reply Collective* 6: 20–36. https://social-epistemology.com/2017/07/24/the-bad-news-about-fake-news-neil-levy/

Lewandowsky, S., Ecker, U. K. H., Seifert, C. M., Schwarz, N., and Cook, J. 2012. Misinformation and Its Correction: Continued Influence and Successful Debiasing. *Psychological Science in the Public Interest* 13: 106–131.

Lewandowsky, S., Oberauer, K., and Gignac, G. E. 2013. NASA Faked the Moon Landing – Therefore, (Climate) Science Is a Hoax: An Anatomy of the Motivated Rejection of Science. *Psychological Science* 24: 622–633.

Mill, J. S. 1985 [1859]. *On Liberty*. London: Penguin Books.

Nyhan, B. and Reifler, J. 2010. When Corrections Fail: The Persistence of Political Misperceptions. *Political Behavior* 32: 303–330.

Democracy

Part Six

Fourteen

Operation Rescue, the Army
of God, and the Nashville
Declaration of Conscience

Steve Clarke[1]

> Let every soul be subject to the governing authorities. For there
> is no authority except from God, and the authorities that exist
> are appointed by God. Therefore whoever resists the authority
> resists the ordinance of God, and those who resist will bring
> judgment on themselves. For rulers are not a terror to good
> works, but to evil. Do you want to be unafraid of the authority?
> Do what is good, and you will have praise from the same. For he
> is God's minister to you for good. But if you do evil, be afraid;
> for he does not bear the sword in vain; for he is God's minister,
> an avenger to *execute* wrath on him who practises evil.
>
> (Romans 13:1–4)

'Extremist' is a pejorative term, which is often used by people
who hold mainstream views, to describe people who do not
hold mainstream views and of whom they disapprove. Attempts
to pin down the meaning of the term 'extremist' usually end
up by defining it in relation to the non-extreme. According to
one definition an extremist is someone 'whose views are outside the mainstream on some issue or dimension'.[2] A second
definition locates the meaning of 'extremist' by contrasting
extremist views with 'balanced views'.[3] Another account has it
that we Westerners use the term extremist to label those who

Extremism

175

reject our core values – the values of 'Western democracy'.[4] When someone describes a third party as an extremist, they suggest not only that the third party's views are outside the mainstream, but also that those views are misguided or otherwise objectionable. However, branding views as extremist does nothing to explain why they are mistaken or flawed.

In many countries, there is an ongoing policy debate about the appropriate level of expenditure that the national government should commit to maintain the country's armed forces. Almost all participants in such debates hold that their national government ought to commit some funds for this purpose, though they disagree about how much. An uncompromising pacifist who held that the armed forces should be abolished would be taking an extreme position, relative to more usual, mainstream positions. So, it would be appropriate to refer to that uncompromising pacifist as an extremist. This would not be appropriate in a country in which the proposal to abolish the armed forces was a mainstream policy position, held by many participants in policy debates.

The political economist Ronald Wintrobe notes that people who are willing to use violent means to promote their favoured political position are especially liable to be labelled as extremists.[5] He is right about this. I take it that we are disposed to label those who are willing to resort to violence to promote their favoured position as extremists because we regard the use of violent means as extreme relative to the means which are usually employed to promote political positions in well-ordered Western societies.

*

The focus of this chapter is the use of the term 'extremist' to describe political activity. I have two goals – first, to illustrate the point that extremism is a relative term and that as society changes, what counts as extremist behaviour can also change; and second, to argue that the charge of being an extremist lacks normative content. That is to say, the fact that something is 'extreme' tells us nothing about whether it is good or bad. There may well be significant moral objections to many extremist positions, but the way to demonstrate this is to focus on the details of those positions and not on their relationship to mainstream positions.

An example from history is useful here. Abolitionism – the view that slavery ought to be abolished – had been an extreme view in the United States during the eighteenth century, but by the 1850s, in the lead up to the US Civil War of 1861–1865, it had become a mainstream view. By that time, slavery had been abolished in several US states, including Vermont and New York. Other states, including Maine and California, had entered the Union as 'free states' in which slavery was not permitted. John Brown, a leading abolitionist of the mid-nineteenth century, was widely regarded as an extremist, not because he held an extreme view, relative to the mainstream, but because he was willing to employ extreme measures to promote that view. The best known of these was his armed raid on a US Government armoury at Harper's Ferry, Virginia (now West Virginia), in October 1859. Brown and his followers intended to capture weapons and use these to help incite a slave uprising, first in Virginia, and then across all of the US states in which slavery was still practiced. The plan failed and Brown was captured and then convicted of treason, murder, and insurrection. He was hanged in December 1859. This sequence of events was instrumental in polarizing US public opinion about the morality of slavery and contributed to the outbreak of the US Civil War.

In recent decades, public opinion in the United States has become polarized over another issue: the morality of abortion. Abortion has been a subject of dispute in the United States for a long time, but while abortion was illegal in most parts of the United States, the public conversation over its morality was not particularly prominent and not especially polarized. This all changed with the 1973 US Supreme Court decision *Roe v. Wade*, which disallowed a number of state and federal restrictions on abortion, effectively legalizing abortion in all states. The US public debate over abortion soon became very prominent and highly polarized.[6] I will go on to discuss the use of extreme means by people who are sometimes labelled as 'anti-abortion extremists'. A point I will bring out is that if circumstances change in particular ways, today's moderate, who feels that it is not justifiable to use extreme means to promote their favoured cause, can become tomorrow's extremist.

It has become conventional to think of participants in the US debate about abortion as being divided into two camps. Those who are in favour of abortion remaining legal are referred to as 'Pro-Choice', while those who wish to make (at least ordinary instances of) abortion illegal are referred to as 'Pro-Life'. The view that abortion is immoral and, therefore, ought to be illegal is not an extreme view, in the context of the current US debate. However, there are members of the Pro-Life camp who are said to be extremists, because they are willing to use extreme methods to oppose abortion. Most people who are Pro-Life are happy to restrict their methods of opposition to abortion to ones that are legally sanctioned. They vote for Pro-Life candidates in elections, attend peaceful anti-abortion protests, donate money to mainstream Pro-Life organizations, and so on. But a few opponents of abortion think that abortion is such an important issue that they are willing to break the law in order to promote the Pro-Life cause. They are appropriately referred to as extremists.

A group often referred to as extremist is Operation Rescue. They describe themselves as a 'Pro-Life Christian activist organization'.[7] Operation Rescue opposes abortion in a variety of ways, including harassing physicians who perform abortions, employees of abortion clinics, and women seeking abortions. In the late 1980s and early 1990s, Operation Rescue organized large-scale acts of civil disobedience, coordinating the activities of their followers who blocked entrances to abortion clinics.[8] In 1989, this campaign led to the arrest of over 12,000 Pro-Life activists. In 1994, Congress passed a new law recognizing the specific crime of impeding access to abortion clinics and introducing severe penalties for harms to others committed during demonstrations outside abortion clinics. After the new law was passed, the number of organized blockades of abortion clinics dropped off drastically.[9]

Operation Rescue explicitly denounces the use of violence on behalf of the Pro-Life cause,[10] but at times members have behaved in ways that might be construed as inciting violence. One of their early slogans was 'if you believe abortion is murder, act like it's murder'.[11] Given that it is commonly accepted that one is entitled to act violently to prevent oneself or a third party from being murdered, this slogan is easy to interpret as an incitement to violence. In 2009, Scott Roeder, a supporter of Operation Rescue, shot and killed a physician who provided abortions, in Wichita, Kansas.[12] Operation Rescue had moved their headquarters to Wichita in 2002. Because the slain physician, George Tiller, was one of the few physicians based in Wichita who performed abortions, and because he provided controversial late-term abortions, his clinic was a frequent target of Operation Rescue's protests. Operation

Rescue was quick to distance itself from Roeder after Tiller was killed. Its president described Roeder's actions as both immoral and stupid.[13]

One Pro-Life organization which supported Roeder's killing of George Tiller was the Army of God. On its website, Roeder is described as an 'American Hero'.[14] An associate of the Army of God, Shelley Shannon, had been convicted of attempted murder for shooting and wounding Tiller in 1993.[15] The Army of God describes its members as serving under the command of their general: God.[16] They also have a 'Chaplain', Pastor Michael Bray.[17] The fact that the Army of God have a general and a chaplain might suggest that it is a well-structured organization. In fact, it is a loose network of activists who rarely communicate with one another. It has no official leaders and no central office.[18] It is a name that is invoked by extremist Pro-Life Christians who conduct, and threaten to conduct, violent acts on behalf of the Pro-Life cause.[19]

The Army of God's Chaplain, Michael Bray, is the author of the book *A Time to Kill*, in which he outlines a justification for the killing of abortionists. Bray's main line of justification for killing abortionists is the 'justifiable homicide' defence.[20] The right to self-defence against unjust attack is a well-established legal and moral right; it is often argued that it is justifiable to use lethal force in self-defence if this is necessary to prevent unjust attack. It is usually also accepted that third parties are entitled to assist people who are defending themselves against unjust attack, and that these third parties are also entitled to use lethal force, if necessary.[21] Bray argues that foetuses are unborn people who can be placed under threat of unjust attack by abortion-providing physicians. He further argues that he and other anti-abortion activists are entitled to use lethal force if it is necessary to protect those foetuses from threats to their lives.[22] When they do use such lethal force, they are committing acts of 'justifiable homicide', he asserts.[23] As should be obvious, the justifiable homicide defence of violence against abortion providers will be unacceptable to those who reject the view that unborn humans have the same moral status, and possess the same right to life, as born humans.

Scott Roeder was tried for murdering George Tiller and pled 'not guilty', employing the justifiable homicide defence in an attempt to establish his innocence. This was judged to be unsuccessful, both because abortion is legal in Kansas and because Tiller did not pose an imminent threat to either the born or the unborn at the time that Roeder shot him. Tiller was not conducting an abortion when he was killed. He was standing inside a church.[24] It seems clear that Roeder was relying on a very expansive notion of 'justifiable homicide'. On this expansive notion, one is justified in using lethal force to prevent a threat to the life of an unspecified person that, it is anticipated, will happen at an unspecified time in the future.

This, however, seems implausible. If I find out that someone is a professional contract killer, then I have good reason to think that they pose a threat to the life of an unspecified person at an unspecified time in the future. Surely my knowledge of their profession does not give me the right to defend this unspecified person against the threat to their life at an unspecified time by killing the contract killer wherever and whenever I want. It only entitles me to use lethal force if it is necessary to prevent an imminent violent attack against a specific person by the contract killer. At most, the (appropriately restricted) justifiable homicide defence of violence against abortion providers entitles an anti-abortion activist to act violently to prevent an abortion when that abortion is about to take place, and it only entitles the activist to use lethal force if there is no other way to prevent that abortion.

Given that most people who are Pro-Life regard abortion as murder and given that it is widely accepted that one is entitled to use lethal force if it is necessary to prevent an imminent act of murder, it might be assumed that most people who are Pro-Life accept the (appropriately restricted) justifiable homicide defence of violence against abortion providers. But this is not the case. Most people who are Pro-Life regard violence against abortion providers as unjustified. According to the Army of God website, this shows that many of the Pro-Lifers are hypocrites.[25]

In 1994, a defence against the charge of hypocrisy was provided in the 'Nashville Declaration of Conscience', a document which has been very influential in the American Pro-Life community. The Nashville Declaration is headed 'The Struggle Against Abortion: Why the Use of Lethal Force is Not Morally Justifiable'. It is a consensus statement issued by a number of leading Southern Baptist theologians and academics. The signatories to the Nashville Declaration are all firmly committed to the Pro-Life cause. They agree with Operation Rescue and the Army of God that the 1973 legalization of abortion in the United States, and the estimated 30 million abortions that have followed it, are a 'moral outrage'.[26]

Many Christians are pacifists, but the signatories to the Nashville Declaration do not wish to be counted amongst them. They draw on Scripture to argue that there is a small set of circumstances in which the taking of human life is morally justifiable. They also draw on Scripture to argue that divine authorization for the use of lethal force is granted to legitimate governing authorities and not to ordinary citizens.[27]

So, they view violent anti-abortion activists as vigilantes who illegitimately take the law into their own hands.[28] The signatories do not, however, think that ordinary citizens should always follow laws that they regard as unjust. They hold that Christians should lobby to have abortion laws changed, and they argue that acts of non-violent civil disobedience, by anti-abortion activists (such as Operation Rescue), are morally permissible if such acts are aimed at having unjust laws changed and if the overall benefits of civil disobedience outweigh the harms.[29] Their objection is specifically to violent forms of civil disobedience.

The response to violent anti-abortion activism in the United States by the signatories to the Nashville Declaration hinges on the legitimacy of the US Federal Government, and given that the US Federal Government now permits abortion, anti-abortion activists may be tempted to argue that it is no longer a legitimate government; and that, therefore, it is permissible for anti-abortion vigilantes to take the law into their own hands. The signatories to the Nashville Declaration anticipate this line of reasoning and attempt to rebut it by identifying two conditions which must both be fulfilled before a government can lose its legitimacy: when it 'sets itself against divine law' and when it 'loses the popular support of its people'.[30] They argue that only one of these conditions has been fulfilled in the United States. The signatories to the Nashville Declaration draw an analogy to the situation that many Christians of the 1850s, who were convinced that slavery was immoral and against the will of God, found themselves in. The signatories argue that, back then, it was morally permissible to violate the fugitive slave laws and assist slaves to escape to freedom. However, they see the violent acts of John Brown and his supporters as morally impermissible.[31]

As we have seen, according to the signatories to the Nashville Declaration, the case against anti-abortion vigilantism in a particular country depends on the legitimacy of the government of that country, which in turn depends on its popular support. So, by the lights of their own reasoning, the signatories to the Nashville Declaration would lack grounds to disapprove of violent anti-abortion activism in unpopular dictatorships. We can imagine America developing in ways which would render the line of argument irrelevant in the United States, too. Suppose that the population of the United States was to become overwhelmingly Pro-Life in the not-too-distant future and elected a government on a promise to make abortion illegal. Suppose also that this government failed to act on its promise and became very unpopular as a result. In such circumstances, that government could fairly be said to have lost the popular support of its people, so the case against anti-abortion violence, as laid out in the Nashville Declaration, would no longer hold.

Operation Rescue and the Army of God are extremist organizations relative to other Pro-Life organizations. They advocate taking extreme measures on behalf of a mainstream cause. If a sufficiently significant proportion of Pro-Life activists became willing to act violently or became willing to commit acts of civil disobedience, to try to prevent abortions, then acts of violence and civil disobedience, undertaken on behalf of the Pro-Life cause, would no longer count as extremist actions. They would have become mainstream actions. There would still be people who would count as anti-abortion extremists, but these would be people who were willing to perform acts that are more extreme than those currently performed by members of Operation Rescue and the Army of

God. Examples of such activities might include attempting to kill people merely because they are Pro-Choice.

When we examine the case against violent anti-abortion activism in the United States, set out in the Nashville Declaration of Conscience, it becomes apparent that the line between extremism and moderation can be thin. On the case for moderation presented in the Nashville Declaration, a moderate, committed opponent of abortion, who became convinced that the US government lacked the legitimacy provided by popular support, would be entitled to conclude that violent opposition to abortion was justified in the United States. Today's moderate would have become tomorrow's extremist.

Because moderates can become extremists and extremists can become moderates, without changing their positions, there cannot be any normative significance that attaches to the pejorative term 'extremist'. If an action is labelled 'extremist', that alone tells us nothing about its morality. If serious ethical criticisms are to be levelled at extremists, these must be made on grounds other than that they are extremists.

NOTES

1 Thanks to Piero Moraro, Jacques Rousseau, Anne Schwenkenbecher, and Leighann Spencer for helpful comments on an earlier draft of this chapter. Research leading to the development of this chapter was supported by Australian Research Council Discovery Grant DP150102068.
2 See Wintrobe (2006, p. 6).
3 See Winter and Hasan (2016, p. 669).
4 See Resnick (2008, p. 108).
5 See Wintrobe (2006, p. 6).
6 Debate about the morality of abortion gained prominence in advance of *Roe v. Wade* in a handful US states in which abortion had been legalized before the US Supreme Court's landmark 1973 decision. For discussion, see Williams (2016).

7 See: www.operationrescue.org/about-us/who-we-are/ (Accessed 13 April 2018).

8 The meaning of the term 'civil disobedience' is somewhat ambiguous and on some accounts 'uncivil' acts, such as blocking the entrances to clinics and harassing people, would not count as acts of civil disobedience. Here I rely on a broad conception of civil disobedience, equating it with non-violent protest that involves breaking the law.

9 See Stern (2003, p. 154) and www.operationrescue.org/about-us/history/ (Accessed 29 March 2018).

10 See: www.operationrescue.org/about-us/who-we-are/ (Accessed 29 March 2018).

11 See Clarke (2014, p. 180, n. 31).

12 For further discussion of the killing of George Tiller, see Clarke (2014, pp. 164–167).

13 See Newman (2009).

14 See www.armyofgod.com/POCScottRoederIndexPage.html (Accessed 29 March 2018).

15 See Juergensmeyer (2003, p. 21).

16 See Jefferis (2011, p. 53).

17 See Clarke (2014, p. 165).

18 See Stern (2003, p. 150).

19 See Doan (2007, p. 108).

20 See Jefferis (2011, pp. 54–58).

21 For further discussion of the right to self-defence, see Clarke (2014, pp. 91–93).

22 See Bray (1994).

23 The appeal to 'justifiable homicide' is the major line of justification that anti-abortion activists offer for violence against abortion providers, but it is not the only line of justification they offer (Clarke 2014, pp. 166–167).

24 See Clarke (2014, p. 165).

25 See Jefferis (2011, p. 104).

26 See the Ethics and Religious Liberty Commission of the Southern Baptist Convention (1994, section 3.10).

27 See the Ethics and Religious Liberty Commission of the Southern Baptist Convention (1994, section 2.5 and Section 5.5).

28 See the Ethics and Religious Liberty Commission of the Southern Baptist Convention (1994, section 2.8).

29 See the Ethics and Religious Liberty Commission of the Southern Baptist Convention (1994, sections 4.10–4.15).

30 See the Ethics and Religious Liberty Commission of the Southern Baptist Convention (1994, section 5.12).

31 See the Ethics and Religious Liberty Commission of the Southern Baptist Convention (1994, section 5.14).

REFERENCES

Bray, Michael. (1994). *A Time to Kill: A Study Concerning the Use of Force and Abortion*. Portland: Advocates for Life.

Clarke, Steve. (2014). *The Justification of Religious Violence*. Malden: Wiley-Blackwell.

Doan, Alisha E. (2007). *Opposition & Intimidation*. Ann Arbor: The University of Michigan Press.

Ethics and Religious Liberty Commission of the Southern Baptist Convention. (1994). *The Nashville Declaration of Conscience*. Accessed 1st April 2018: http://mail.erlc.com/article/nashville-declaration-of-conscience

Jefferis, Jennifer. (2011). *Armed for Life: The Army of God and Anti-Abortion Terror in the United States*. Santa Barbara: Praeger.

Juergensmeyer, Mark. (2003). *Terror in the Mind of God: The Global Rise of Religious Violence*, 3rd ed. Berkeley: University of California Press.

Newman, Troy. (2009). 'Shooting Abortionists Isn't Just Immoral – It's Stupid'. *Troy's Blog: Thoughts From Troy Newman – President of Operation Rescue*, 29 July 2009. Accessed 30th March 2018: www.operationrescue.org/troys-blog/

Resnik, David. (2008). 'Can Autonomy Counteract Extremism in Traditional Education?'. *Journal of Philosophy of Education* 42, 1, pp. 107–118.

Stern, Jessica. (2003). *Terror in the Name of God*. New York: HarperCollins.

Williams, Daniel K. (2016). *Defenders of the Unborn: The Pro-Life Movement Before Roe v. Wade*. New York: Oxford University Press.

Winter, Charlie and Hasan, Usama. (2016). 'The Balanced Nation: Islam and the Challenges of Extremism, Fundamentalism, Islamism and Jihadism'. *Philosophia* 44, pp. 667–688.

Wintrobe, Ronald. (2006). *Rational Extremism: The Political Economy of Radicalism*. Cambridge: Cambridge University Press.

Fifteen

Regina Rini

Jacqueline is at her first party since coming to university. Like in her classes, she is one of the few non-white people here. She is standing alone when a young white man approaches.

"Hey", he says. "Where are you from"?

"From Essex", Jacqueline replies.

"Cool", says the young man. "But, uh, where are you *really* from"?

"I told you, I'm from Essex. I was born there and I grew up there".

The young man looks a bit confused, but then he shrugs and asks what kind of music she likes.

Jacqueline knows what this was all about. The man doesn't want to know where she was born. He wants to know where her parents came from. He's really asking: what *are* you? Jacqueline could tell him the whole story: that her dad was born in Singapore, that her mum was born in London but her parents were born in Ghana. That's what the man really wants to know. But Jacqueline isn't going to satisfy his curiosity. She's been through this so many times before and she is tired of it. If "from Essex" would be a good enough answer for a white person, why isn't it a good enough answer for her? Why can't people who look like her be from Essex, like any other British person?

What's happened to Jacqueline is an example of micro-aggression. A microaggression is a relatively small insult or indignity aimed at a member of a socially disadvantaged group. One microaggression by itself might not be that big a deal. If this were the first time a white person ever asked Jacqueline where she is *really* from, maybe she wouldn't be so bothered. But this wasn't the first time, and it won't be the last. Microaggressions form pieces of a *pattern*. Often, people who are targeted by microaggressions can easily see the pattern, even if the person doing the microaggressing cannot.

Microaggressions pose several challenges for ethical analysis. In this chapter we will examine the harms of microaggressions and the moral questions they provoke. The section on "What microaggressions are" will give an overview of the background of the microaggression concept and its relation to oppression. The section "The harms of microaggression" will explore the various ways microaggression are harmful. The section "Moral responsibility for microaggression" will consider whether we can blame people who commit microaggressions, even when they might not have meant to cause harm. Finally, the section on "Social responses to microaggression" will look at the ethics of responding to microaggression as a society. Can we reduce the harms of microaggression without intruding on free speech or reducing people's ability to manage challenging social dynamics?

WHAT MICROAGGRESSIONS ARE

The word "microaggression" was coined in 1970 by Harvard Psychiatry professor Chester Pierce. Pierce was an expert on stress and extreme environments. Earlier in his career, he visited a military base in Antarctica to study the effects of six months without daylight. Now, in the late 1960s, he was studying the effects of racism on black Americans' psychology. Pierce was black himself and drew upon his own experiences to illustrate the situations he wanted to analyze. For example, he noticed that, even though he was an established senior faculty member at Harvard, white students would still come up after class with unsolicited feedback on his teaching.[1]

Pierce knew that these students might not have meant to be disrespectful. But he theorized that the students were acting out a kind of racist dominance without fully realizing it. According to Pierce's theory, white people raised in a racist society, like mid-twentieth-century America, were trained from childhood to expect deference from non-whites. Small acts of insult or indignity – like telling a professor how to teach – were subtle ways of reminding black people of their inferior status.

Pierce did not assume that all white people were intentionally doing these things. Instead, he made an analogy to another concept from psychiatry: the *defense mechanism*. A person who doesn't want to confront challenging information will create psychological barriers, such as blaming other people. Pierce asked: couldn't there also be *offensive* mechanisms? Maybe a person's unconscious mind could cause them to do subtly cruel things to others, as a way of putting them in their place. This, Pierce argued, is what the white students were doing when telling him how to teach. Though they didn't necessarily realize it, white supremacy was acting through their routine, automatic ways of treating other people.

Hence the idea of "microaggression". A microaggression, according to Pierce, is an act of asserting someone else's lesser social status. But, unlike obvious acts of hatred, it is an act subtle enough that even the perpetrator sometimes doesn't realize it is happening. Pierce was a practicing clinical psychiatrist, in addition to being a researcher. His focus was not on blaming people for the harms of racism, but instead on finding solutions. He thought that diagnosing the subtle mechanisms behind microaggression would be a step toward ending racial injustice.

Though Pierce first wrote about microaggression nearly 50 years ago, we are unfortunately still far from full racial equality. Pierce died, at age 89, in 2016. Building on his ideas, other theorists have extended the concept of microaggression to include social categories other than race. Microaggressions, as psychologists now understand them, can also be targeted at sex, gender, sexual orientation, religion, disability status, nationality, socio-economic class, and other things.[2]

The key idea is that microaggressions are related to oppression. Oppression occurs when members of certain social groups find that their choices are systematically limited by how others treat them. Philosopher Marilyn Frye compared the operation of oppression to the bars of a bird cage: one single bar of metal can't keep a bird from flying away, but many bars arranged together certainly can. If you look at just one bar, you miss the point of the cage. Similarly, to see oppression, you need to look at how many social restrictions hang together around certain people.[3]

Frye pointed out that oppressed people are in trouble no matter what they do. If you cooperate with oppressive requirements, then your freedom is limited, but if you don't cooperate, then you'll be punished. She called this the "double bind" of oppression.

Microaggressions are related to oppression in two ways. First, some microaggressions are the bars of the oppressive cage. When the young man at the party asks Jacqueline where she's really from, she has only two choices. She can play along and tell him what he really wants to know, or she can give him the answer any white person would be allowed to give – and then get rebuffed by the man's awkward lack of engagement. She is caught in oppression's double bind.

There's a second way in which microaggressions are related to oppression. Microaggressions are the smaller parts of a much bigger oppressive system, which includes overt acts of discrimination and prejudice, like refusing service at a restaurant to a person of color, or shouting misogynistic slurs at a woman on the street. Part of what makes microaggressions harmful is their victims' awareness of the connection to these other forms of injustice. Jacqueline knows what the man at the party really wants to hear because she's had a lifetime of experiences of white people being clueless and sometimes even hostile. She realizes that this young man's question is the narrow end of a bigger wedge whose heavier side includes the Home Office unfairly deporting elderly non-white immigrants.

The systematic relationship between microaggression and oppression is very important to keep in mind. It's what distinguishes microaggression from ordinary rudeness. Everyone has to deal with rude people sometimes; if you ignore patterns of discrimination, then some microaggressions look like ordinary rudeness, not something that deserves special ethical concern. But the pattern of oppression that lies behind microaggression makes it crucially different from ordinary rudeness, as we'll now see by looking at the distinctive harms of microaggression.

THE HARMS OF MICROAGGRESSION

When ethicists say that a person has been harmed by an event, they usually mean that the person's life would have gone better if that event hadn't happened to them. Philosophers call that the "counterfactual" concept of harm. There is more than one type of harm. Some are obvious, such as physical or psychological pain. Other types of harm might be less apparent to their victims. Imagine you have a winning lottery ticket, though you haven't realized it yet. When you aren't looking, I switch your ticket with a loser, and then go cash yours and keep the money for myself. You never notice the switch, so you never *feel* any pain. But I've still harmed you by stealing your ticket – I've made your life go worse than it otherwise would have.

This point helps us to appreciate that microaggression can be harmful in a variety of ways. To start, there's the obvious psychological pain. A person who knows they are being microaggressed is aware that they are being treated differently than anyone else because of who they are – and that *hurts*. But there may be other effects.

Psychologist Derald Wing Sue has studied microaggression extensively. He classifies the harms of microaggression into several types: biological stress (higher blood pressure and weakened immune activity), emotional effects (anxiety, depression), cognitive effects (losing confidence in one's own abilities), and behavioral effects (hypervigilance about further microaggressions).

Philosophers have noticed an additional sort of harm caused by microaggression. This is *epistemic harm*. Epistemology is the study of knowledge – how we know about the world and how we share this knowledge with others. Philosopher Miranda Fricker has pointed out that women and people of color are often treated as less competent when they try to share knowledge with others. Fricker says this is a form of epistemic injustice, the victim of which has been "wronged in her capacity as a knower".[4] Many cases of epistemic injustice are the result of microaggressions. Philosopher Kristie Dotson points out that people who are used to being disbelieved or ignored may eventually give up on trying to share their knowledge at all, an effect she calls "testimonial smothering".[5]

Perhaps worst of all, victims of microaggression are often disbelieved about microaggressions themselves. Philosopher Saba Fatima wrote, regarding her experience as a woman of color in America, that white people's constant suggestion she had misinterpreted remarks pushed her to "the epistemic border of thinking of oneself as paranoid and of being secure in one's perception of reality".[6]

Most of us depend on other people to confirm and validate our perceptions of reality. People who are systematically disbelieved when they report being treated unfairly may slowly come to doubt themselves, causing harm to self-esteem and the ability to function comfortably in society. Microaggressions cause this sort of harm precisely because they are so subtle and hard to prove.

MORAL RESPONSIBILITY FOR MICROAGGRESSION

As we've seen, microaggressions play a role in oppression and harm their victims in a number of ways. Should we therefore blame people who commit microaggressions against others? Should we blame the young man at the party for reminding Jacqueline that she won't be treated like other people?

Ethicists use the term moral responsibility to talk about questions like these. Just because someone does something harmful, that doesn't necessarily mean they are morally responsible. Sometimes it's a genuine accident, perhaps because the person didn't realize what they'd done. Suppose I take your umbrella on a rainy day, leaving you to get soaked. It turns out that my umbrella looks identical to yours, and I forgot that I didn't bring mine. I should apologize, but it would be strange for you to put much blame on me. That's because I didn't really mean to do it.

Other times, we say that a person isn't morally responsible because they weren't in control of themselves. For example, suppose I've just come from the doctor and have taken some strong painkillers. I might be confused and clumsy. If I drop a heavy book on your foot, hopefully you'll understand that I didn't have control and you won't blame me.

Both of these aspects of moral responsibility – knowing what you are doing and having control over it – are complicated in many cases of microaggression. Let's take them in turn.

The first complication has to do with knowledge, and relates to something we've already talked about. Much of the harm of microaggression involves its *cumulative* impact. Again, the young man's question about Jacqueline's origins wouldn't be that big a deal if it had never happened before. And the man, presumably, doesn't know about Jacqueline's personal history with that question, or the fact that it fits into a bigger pattern of racist oppression. He probably wasn't thinking about it at all. Is it fair to blame him for contributing to a build-up of harm when he doesn't know the whole background?[7]

Ethicists often distinguish between *culpable* ignorance and *non-culpable* ignorance. Suppose I am about to turn off the light switch at the bottom of a long flight of stairs. I don't know that someone is about to start down from the top, and they will trip and fall if things suddenly go dark. Can I be blamed when that happens? Well, it depends. *Should* I have known there might be someone there? I could have called up to the top of the stairs and checked. On the other hand, what if I reasonably thought that I was the only one home? Maybe then my ignorance is a good excuse.

What about ignorance of the oppressive social patterns that microaggression fits into? Is that sort of ignorance culpable? Philosopher Charles Mills has argued that, in many modern societies, white people's ignorance of racist history is not easily excused. Often, white people *have an interest* in being unaware of the continuing effects of enslavement, colonization, and discrimination on non-white people. Fully acknowledging history might make people feel guilty, or admit that they benefit from inequalities that they did nothing to earn.[8] Understood that way, the ignorance behind some microaggressions looks much less innocent.

We can see this happening in other contexts, not just race. Some people still say "that's so gay", when they mean to call something worthless. This is a homophobic microaggression. Sometimes, if someone challenges them, they will insist that they "didn't know" what they were saying was such a big deal. They didn't "really mean" to insult gay people – it's just a phrase people use. If you explain that the phrase is part of a bigger oppressive system making queer people's lives go worse, they might even agree that they shouldn't use this phrase again. But does that mean it's not fair to blame them for having done so before? Is this the sort of ignorance that excuses?

The second complication with moral responsibility for microaggression has to do with control over actions. Remember Chester Pierce's theory: many microaggressions are the result of unconscious "offensive mechanisms" that are so subtle even the microaggression perpetrator doesn't entirely know what they are doing. Is it fair to blame people for causing harm through unconscious habits trained into them by a prejudiced society?

The big problem here is that it might be very hard to fix unconscious prejudice without blaming people. If you are going around doing harmful things because of your unconscious psychology, maybe you need to be shaken up. Maybe the discomfort of being called out for microaggression will motivate you to try to learn new habits, so you become less likely to do harmful things unthinkingly.

Philosopher Cheshire Calhoun has made this point about systemic sexism. It might be true that some sexist behavior is habitual, so that we can't *expect* people to easily change. Some sexists may not fully understand the harm of what they are doing, or be fully in control of their behavior. But saying nothing about sexist behavior allows it to continue. As Calhoun puts it: "If the excuse for wrongdoing is the normalcy and social legitimacy of one's actions, this same excuse can be repeated for ongoing resistance to seeing that there is anything wrong with what one is doing".[9] Calling someone out on sexist behavior might be the only way to get them to notice the problem and work on establishing control in the future.

The idea, then, is that *even* if microaggressions typically aren't under our control, we should treat people as responsible for them anyway. That doesn't necessarily mean punishing people, or exiling them from our community. But it might mean using words that people don't like to hear, such as "you shouldn't have done that", or "that was wrong". It might even mean being angry with people who commit microaggressions repeatedly and make no effort to change.

Notice, though, that this last point assumes that we *can* change microaggressive behavior. This is contentious territory in psychology.

Setting aside the issue of holding individual microaggressors responsible, what can we do to *reduce* the harms of microaggression? One promising answer is *institutional*: we can change community rules and symbols to communicate support for anti-oppression. For example: in recent years, students at several universities have called upon their administrations to rename institutions named for prominent historical oppressors. Georgetown University changed the names of two buildings from slave-dealing former presidents to those of some of the enslaved people they sold. Yale changed the name of a college named after a politician who defended slavery as a "positive good".

The theory behind these changes is that they make communal spaces more welcoming to all. Having to attend classes in a building named after someone who enslaved your great-grandparents is not very welcoming. The change is meant to create a different atmosphere – less conducive to microaggression. Other initiatives involve microaggression education and training.

Critics have presented two main objections to efforts like these. First, they worry about intruding upon freedom of speech. Second, they say that these efforts "coddle" students and do not prepare them for the harshness of the real world.

The first objection seems a bit off-base. Very few responses to microaggression actually threaten free speech. If renaming buildings named after slaveholders intrudes on free speech, then wouldn't renaming a building after a wealthy donor *also* intrude on free speech? We usually accept that institutions have the right to name their components however they please.

More problematic might be university and corporate "speech codes", which restrict what community members may say. But normally these only cover the most extreme cases, such as explicit and deliberate use of racial slurs. There is very rarely any punishment for more typical microaggressions, such as the "where are you really from?" question, that Jacqueline received.

The other objection is more interesting. Psychologist Jonathan Haidt and campus activist Greg Lukianoff have claimed that attention to microaggression "coddles" young people.[10] They worry that students who are protected from microaggression will not learn how to cope with a world full of mistreatment. In 2016, the University of Chicago issued a similar statement to its incoming freshman class, claiming that its commitment to "freedom of expression" made it impossible to take efforts to reduce microaggression.

One problem with this critique is that it often fails to distinguish between ordinary rudeness and oppressive microaggression. Lukianoff and Haidt talk about microaggression as if it were just the routine sort of unpleasantness that everyone experiences. This causes them to miss a crucial point: when they worry that students protected from microaggression will not develop coping skills, they forget that oppressed people learn those skills long before university. Similarly, the University of Chicago statement appears to mistakenly assume that students cannot distinguish between ordinary interpersonal difficulty and the special challenges of microaggression. As Cameron Okeke, a black Chicago graduate, wrote:

> During my time on campus, I met more than couple people who believed in the genetic inferiority of black

people. I was never afraid of their thinly veiled bigotry, just bored and disappointed. I needed a space where I, a biology major, was not expected to give free race theory classes.[11]

Perhaps the most compelling response to the "coddling" objection is the following: "coddling" is only a problem if we assume that people will always face microaggressive harm. But why assume this? Why not work to change it? And how will we change it unless we begin confronting microaggression throughout education?

There are still complicated ethical questions about how to balance concerns like these against the need to challenge microaggression. Where is the line between hate speech and less extreme microaggression? Which sorts of acts require administrative enforcement, and which are best handled through education and non-coercive encouragement? Should we *ever* hold back from discussing literature or history related to oppression? Are there people who should not be officially invited to speak at universities because of their past actions?

None of these questions are settled, and working through them is part of how we decide together what to do about microaggression.

NOTES

1 See Pierce (1970).
2 See Sue (2010).
3 See Frye (1983).
4 Fricker (2007, p. 44).
5 See Dotson (2011, p. 244).
6 Fatima (2017, p. 148).
7 See Friedlaender (2018).
8 See Mills (1997).

9 Calhoun (1989, p. 393).
10 See Lukianoff and Haidt (2015).
11 Okeke (2016).

REFERENCES

Calhoun, Cheshire (1989). 'Responsibility and Reproach'. *Ethics* 99(2): 389–406.

Dotson, Kristie (2011). 'Tracking Epistemic Violence, Tracking Practices of Silencing'. *Hypatia* 26(2): 236–257.

Fatima, Saba (2017). 'On the Edge of Knowing: Microaggression and Epistemic Uncertainty as a Woman of Color'. In *Surviving Sexism in Academia: Feminist Strategies for Leadership*, ed. Kirsti Cole and Holly Hassel. Abingdon: Routledge: 147–157.

Fricker, Miranda (2007). *Epistemic Injustice: Power and the Ethics of Knowing*. Oxford: Oxford University Press.

Friedlaender, Christina (2018). 'On Microaggressions: Cumulative Harm and Individual Responsibility'. *Hypatia*. Early Access Online: http://onlinelibrary. wiley.com/doi/10.1111/hypa.12390/full

Frye, Marilyn (1983). 'Oppression'. In her *The Politics of Reality*. Trumansburg: Crossing Press: 1–16.

Lukianoff, Greg and Jonathan Haidt (2015). 'The Coddling of the American Mind'. *The Atlantic*.

Mills, Charles W. (1997). *The Racial Contract*. Ithaca: Cornell University Press.

Okeke, Cameron (2016). 'I'm a Black Uchicago Graduate. Safe Spaces Got Me Through College'. *Vox*. www.vox.com/2016/8/29/12692376/ university-chicago-safe-spaces-defense

Pierce, Chester (1970). 'Offensive Mechanisms'. In *The Black Seventies*, ed. Floyd B. Barbour. Boston: Porter Sargeant: 265–282.

Sue, Derald Wing (2010). *Microaggressions in Everyday Life: Race, Gender, and Sexual Orientation*. Hoboken: Wiley.

Sixteen

Roger Crisp

Look at any newspaper or news website on any day and you will find issues involving freedom of speech. One especially problematic area in recent years, for example, has been that of hate speech. In the United Kingdom, expressions of hatred towards another based on, for example, their race, disability status, nationality, religion, gender identity, or sexual orientation, are forbidden by law, while in the United States, discussion of hate speech has primarily revolved around the First Amendment to the Constitution, which protects freedom of speech.

In 2004, the English radical feminist Julie Bindel published an article in *The Guardian* called 'Gender Benders, Beware'.[1] The article argued that transgender women – people born male who now identify as women – should not be treated as women, and ended: 'I don't have a problem with men disposing of their genitals, but it does not make them women, in the same way that shoving a bit of vacuum hose down your 501s does not make you a man'. Bindel was seen as 'transphobic' and the National Union of Students UK officially adopted a 'no platform' policy, banning Bindel from speaking at any of their events. She has been prevented from speaking at various universities and colleges, while many feminists and others have defended her on grounds of freedom of speech. Who is right? To answer that question, we must first decide exactly what counts as 'freedom of speech'.

WHAT IS FREEDOM OF SPEECH?

Freedom of speech is a value as old as democracy, which began two-and-a-half millennia ago in ancient Athens, where the citizens believed that their freedom to say what they thought was part of what distinguished them from slaves. That freedom was central to their culture. Playwrights mercilessly mocked the celebrities of their day, including politicians.

Since the Enlightenment of the eighteenth century, and the development of so-called 'liberal' democracies in the West, the idea of freedom of speech has been extended to cover not just speaking, but expressive acts in general, such as the burning of a flag. These acts needn't be seen as 'making a statement'. In the 1970s, the debate about pornography moved from issues of obscenity and decency to whether pornography itself was protected by a right to freedom of speech, broadly construed. Pornography, or pornographers, may be making a statement, perhaps about how women should be treated; but even if they are not – even if pornography is merely for sexual gratification – whether pornography should be restricted has become a question of free speech. Free speech covers any kind of communicative act, including the communication of images as well as opinions and ideas.

Almost no one believes that free speech in the public domain should be unlimited. Context is all important. You shouldn't shout 'Fire!' in a crowded theatre – unless of course you've discovered a blaze behind the curtain. Or, to use a famous example of the nineteenth-century British philosopher John Stuart Mill, it is one thing to publish an article in the newspaper arguing that corn-dealers are starvers of the poor, quite another to say it to a mob gathering outside the house of a corn-dealer.

It is important to remember that morally criticizing some form of expression will often not be a violation of any right to freedom of speech. We may claim that some piece of modern art is disgusting or corrupting, perhaps in the presence of its creator, and quite consistently go on to argue strongly in favour of the artist's right to create it. In a phrase usually attributed to the eighteenth-century writer Voltaire, I may disapprove of what you say, but defend to the death your right to say it. Sometimes, however, moral criticism is used – often by groups – in an attempt to silence someone, and then it becomes a possible violation of the right to free speech. Consider, for example, the orchestrated internet trolling of someone who has expressed some view online not to the liking of the trolls. Julie Bindel has had her fair share of aggressive abuse online (and although it hasn't silenced her, it may have prevented others speaking out).

However, most debates about freedom of speech involve the use of legal or quasi-legal coercion. One extreme example is the censorship of the media and even private communication by the Nazis from 1933 until the end of World War Two. Another milder form of legal censorship is the Obscene Publications Act (1959), which is still in force in the United Kingdom, forbidding publications which can be shown to have a tendency to 'deprave and corrupt'.

Freedom of speech is primarily freedom from coercion. This is what the twentieth-century philosopher Isaiah Berlin called 'negative' freedom – freedom from interference by others.[2] But freedom of speech may also be 'positive' – freedom *to*. It may be claimed, for example, that the state has a duty to make it possible for its citizens to communicate their views to others, or to educate its citizens to become appropriate participants in democratic debate, either for their own benefit or the benefit of others and the community as a whole.

WHY DOES IT MATTER? (1) UTILITARIANISM

The most important and influential defence of freedom of speech in modern times is that of Mill, in his book *On Liberty*, first published in 1859.[3] Mill was concerned with liberty or freedom in general. He says that the point of his essay is to put forward a single simple principle: 'the only purpose for which power can be rightfully exercised over any member of a civilized community, against his will, is to prevent harm to others' (p. 14). This is now usually called the *harm principle*, and it is fairly easy to see how it might be taken to permit the banning of a speaker such as Bindel, whom some allege to be 'anti-trans'. The claim might be that she risks harming those who are trans, transitioning, or questioning, by offending them or even inciting violence against them.

Mill would not have approved of attempts to ban Bindel from speaking, and we'll come to his specific arguments in a moment. But first note another claim he makes, just after stating the harm principle:

> I forego any advantage which could be derived to my argument from the idea of abstract right, as a thing independent of utility. I regard utility as the ultimate appeal on all ethical questions; but it must be utility in the largest sense, grounded on the permanent interests of man as a progressive being.

(p. 15)

Mill is a *utilitarian*, who denies the existence of independent moral rights. That is to say, he doesn't believe we have a *right* to free speech. Before proceeding further, we need to understand the debate between utilitarians and rights-theorists.

Mill is using 'utility' as a technical term for 'happiness'. His ethical position can be captured in another simple principle: that what makes an action right is that it maximizes overall happiness, that is, the balance of pleasure over pain. Whether the action of banning anti-trans speakers is justified, then, depends entirely on whether that action produces the most happiness. But then what is the relation between the harm principle and the principle of utility? Imagine a no-platform policy which bans certain speakers, who are neither advocating harm to others nor posing any risk of harm to others, just because those imposing the ban are prejudiced against such speakers and so take immense satisfaction from banning them. And imagine that this satisfaction vastly outweighs the harm done by any ban (such as the hurt and offence to potential speakers) and any good that such speakers might bring about. Here the harm principle and the utility principle come into direct conflict.

At this point, it is very important to understand that utilitarianism is a theory about *what makes actions right*. It is not a theory about how to *decide* how to act. Mill would criticize anyone who sought to impose a ban on another's speech on the basis of their own prejudice because *in general* making decisions on the basis of prejudice will produce less overall happiness than using the harm principle. In other words, Mill is recommending that we adopt the harm principle not because it is a truly fundamental ethical principle, but because adopting it will produce the greatest happiness overall. We'll soon explain how this view emerges into his defence of free speech in particular.

WHY DOES IT MATTER? (2) RIGHTS

Utilitarianism remains a popular view, but many think there is more to morality than producing the greatest happiness overall. In particular, what about rights, and the right to free speech? The rights theorist claims that there are *other* things, in addition to happiness, that make actions right or wrong. In the earlier example, a rights theorist might object to the ban on certain speakers based only on the satisfaction prejudiced people get from banning them. The rights theorist might insist that these speakers have a *right* to speak.

In today's culture, many believe in a basic right, or human right, to freedom of speech. Article 19 of the 1948 UN Declaration of Human Rights, for example, guarantees freedom of speech, and that article has been written into the legislation of many countries. Utilitarians tend to agree with such laws, because they do so much good overall. So when you have to come to a philosophical view on whether some restriction of freedom of speech is right or wrong, you would be wise to work out first whether you believe in utilitarianism, a theory of basic rights, or some other position. The truth about what makes actions right and wrong may not be something you should use to guide your actions; but you should use it – or your view of it – when you are thinking philosophically about what is right and wrong, independently of some practical decision you have to make.

MILL'S ARGUMENTS

What we have learned, then, is that utilitarians like Mill believe that actions are right in so far as they produce the greatest overall happiness, but when it comes to making real-life decisions, we might well be justified in appealing to a principle advocating a right of free speech. Behind Mill's defence of free speech, as we have seen, lies the harm principle; and behind the harm principle lies the utility principle. Since his arguments on free speech have been by far the most important and influential in recent times, we should now examine them more carefully.

At the end of Chapter 2 of *On Liberty*, which covers liberty both of thought and of expression, you'll find a helpful summary by Mill of his four main arguments. First, he says, 'if any opinion is compelled to silence, that opinion may, for aught we can certainly know, be true. To deny this is to assume our own infallibility' (p. 59). We might call this the *infallibility argument*: Mill is reminding us of the possibility that a view, however unpopular, may nonetheless be correct, and that if we deny this we are (quite mistakenly) assuming that we must be in the right.

But what if the silenced opinion is incorrect? Well, it may still contain *part* of the truth, and 'it is only by the collision of adverse opinions, that the remainder of the truth has any chance of being supplied' (p. 59). In this *partial truth* argument, then, Mill is pointing out that there may be some truth even in a view which is largely mistaken, and this truth will only emerge in open discussion.

What if there isn't *any* truth in the silenced opinion, and the usual view contains the whole truth? Suppressing the false view, Mill suggests, will mean that the correct view will 'be held in the manner of a prejudice, with little comprehension or feeling of its rational grounds' (p. 59). In the *argument from prejudice*, Mill is suggesting that we won't properly understand the reasons for a view, even if it is true, if we just take it as read and never hear any opposition to it.

Even worse, we might lose touch with what the true doctrine really means, and hence any advantages it might have for our 'character and conduct'. According to this *argument from dogma*, then, true beliefs that are held without reflection will be unable to produce the good in the world which might arise in a context of free discussion.

Now we have to remember that Mill does not place any ultimate value on truth itself, or on knowing the truth. What matters is happiness, and so the question we must be asking of each of these arguments is whether we accept the connections Mill is implying between the promotion of knowledge of truth, on the one hand, and happiness, on the other.

If we return to the ban on Bindel, those imposing the ban can side-step the infallibility argument. They might admit that they could be mistaken, claiming that they are banning her not because her views are incorrect but because of the harm that she may do in expressing them. Their argument, then, is analogous to that of those who would ban the expression of anti-corn-dealer views outside a corn-dealer's house. Mill sometimes seems to assume that *complete* liberty of expression is required for us to be warranted in holding our own view. But this forgets the importance of context. Those banning Bindel from universities may concede that there are other contexts, such as a newspaper or journal, in which anti-trans views should be allowed.

Nevertheless, Mill is surely right that there is a relation between discovering the truth and happiness. For one thing, if we discover the truth about happiness, then we are more likely to be able to achieve it for ourselves and others. So the partial truth argument has some force. The third and fourth arguments are a little overstated (there's nothing wrong with my belief that Paris is the capital of France, even though I've never heard anyone question it), but their general implication seems right that in most cases the truth will produce more good in a context of free and open discussion. Complacency can be detrimental to overall happiness, for example by enabling harmful practices to continue longer than they should. (Mill, whose book *The Subjection of Women* was a major contribution to the development of feminism, might have mentioned, for example, the restriction of the franchise to men.)

The question, then, is how we weigh up the value in the anti-trans speech of the possible contribution to knowledge and hence to happiness against the possible harm caused by the speech itself, or the mere knowledge that it is being made.

At this point, someone may try to distinguish harm from mere offence. Those offended by a speech from Bindel are not really harmed, it could be argued: that would require something much more serious, like a physical assault. Mill cannot easily accept this distinction, however. He is concerned with happiness, and happiness can be decreased as much by the pain of offence as physical pain.

So . . .

SHOULD BINDEL BE BANNED?

On *Liberty* is a more rhetorical work than most of those by Mill. He was clearly extremely concerned about the dangers he saw in a growing 'tyranny of the majority' (p. 8), in which those who refuse to believe what everyone else believes are ignored or even persecuted. This, he believed, would make it impossible for human beings to make progress on understanding which ways of life will most advance 'the permanent interests of man as a progressive being' (p. 15). And he also recognized the value many human beings can and do place on free intellectual inquiry and discussion, the acquisition of understanding, and the living of informed and autonomous lives whether as valuable in themselves or as objects of deep enjoyment. Those values require at least some significant degree of freedom of speech. I am certain that Mill would think the no-platform policy against Bindel was a mistake. If she is invited to speak at a university or college, he would say, she should be allowed to do so, and those who disagree with her may, if they wish, protest or disagree with her, but they may not prevent her expressing her opinion.

Mill's argument, however, is that there should be a presumption of free speech unless a clear and persuasive harm-based argument can be provided against it. In modern times, as Neil Levy shows (see Chapter 13), given what we now know about human irrationality – and the damage that people can do when exposed to strong opinions and (sometimes false) information – harm-based arguments in favour of censorship are beginning to gain serious traction. That is, it does seem that there are times when free speech may genuinely cause more harm than good. If there is a basic right to free speech, those harm-based objections to free speech are going to be somewhat harder to make. But any plausible theory of rights cannot allow the right to free speech to be absolute. At some point, it must be trumped or cancelled by the greater good of happiness. The same would go for a ban on anti-trans speakers in a world in which prejudice against trans people had escalated and anti-trans speeches were really equivalent to inciting the mob outside the corn-dealer's house.

FREE SPEECH AND DEMOCRACY

In closing, let me return to the roots of freedom of speech in democracy. The word 'democracy' means, in effect, 'rule by the people'. Just as autonomy, or self-government, requires the capacity to engage in open discussion with others about aspects of the world relevant to the living of one's own life, so true democracy must involve freedom of speech. Democracy, ancient and modern, also involves a particular conception of citizens: they are equal, deserving to be treated with equal respect and concern, and with an equal right to vote or to make their voice heard. It is for this reason that people sometimes describe the current control of the media by a small number of rich people and corporations as 'undemocratic'.

Representative democracy will function best when there are free channels of communication to which all citizens have access; this enables politicians to understand the views and interests of their electorate, which of course if they wish to be re-elected they have a reason to respect. Further, it is almost certain that electorates will make better decisions in elections in a context of freedom of discussion, despite the problems arising from fake news and other kinds of misinformation.

Fundamental freedoms of speech and thought remain under threat, and one of the central problems of the twenty-first century will be understanding which forms of expression are, in effect, equivalent to shouting fire in a crowded theatre or inciting the mob, and which are not. Restricting expression should be a last resort, but should be seen not as a violation of freedom of speech, but as an attempt to enable it, by creating a civic culture of trust in which the equal freedoms of all can be exercised to the benefit of all. We have to hope that there will never be a time when it is right to silence ethical and political statements about the nature of women, such as those made by Bindel; but if there ever is such a time, the justification for silencing will be at least partly that it may help us return to a world in which freedom of speech is properly respected.

NOTES

1 www.theguardian.com/world/2004/jan/31/gender.weekend7
2 Berlin, I., 1969, 'Two Concepts of Liberty', in I. Berlin, *Four Essays on Liberty*, London: Oxford University Press. Reprinted in Berlin 2002.
3 J.S. Mill, 'On Liberty', in J. Gray (ed.), *On Liberty and Other Essays*, Oxford: Oxford University Press, 1991.

Part Seven

Rights and their claim

Part Seven

Seventeen

Brian D. Earp

PRÉCIS

In this chapter, an infringement of bodily integrity (BI) is defined as any penetration into a bodily orifice, breaking of the skin, or alteration of a person's physical form. A violation of a person's right to BI is any infringement of their BI that wrongs them. An autonomous person is wronged by an infringement of their BI if they did not consent to it. If a person is incapable of consenting because they are temporarily non-autonomous – as in the case of an intoxicated adult or a pre-autonomous child – the infringement should be delayed until the individual becomes autonomous and can make their own decision. It is only when the infringement cannot be delayed without putting the person into a situation they would be *even less likely* to consent to (if they were autonomous) that the infringement does not wrong them. Given the seriousness of violating anyone's right to BI, and especially that of the most vulnerable persons, the appropriate likelihood-of-consent for proceeding with a BI infringement on a child is argued to be at or near the 'medically necessary' threshold.

INTRODUCTION

Suppose you are a healthy adult, minding your own business, and a stranger comes along and cuts you with a knife. Not badly – just a little slice out of your arm, let's say – but enough to draw blood. If you did not consent to this, it seems obvious that this stranger has seriously wronged you. In fact, you might say you have a right against other people intentionally cutting you (or otherwise crossing your physical boundaries) without your consent, no matter how mildly. This is sometimes expressed as a right to 'bodily integrity.'[1]

Let's say that *bodily integrity* (BI) refers to the physical state of being all in one piece, unbroken, undivided, intact. So, skin puncturing of any kind would negate this. What about borderline cases, like if I jam my finger in your ear? I'd have entered your bodily sphere, in some sense, and if you don't want my finger there, I am most likely wronging you in some way. But it isn't clear whether I am actually infringing on your 'bodily integrity' as we have defined it. So let's just stipulate that any intentional (or negligently accidental) penetration into a bodily orifice, breaking of the skin, or alteration of your physical form, counts as a BI infringement.

Now we have to draw a distinction: 'merely' infringing on someone's BI is not necessarily the same thing as *violating their right* to BI. This is because not all infringements of a person's BI wrong them, and if you have not wronged someone (we'll suppose) you also have not violated their rights. So let's go ahead and define a violation of a person's *right* to BI as an infringement of their BI that *wrongs* them.

Why should we think that not all infringements of a person's BI wrong them? Well, suppose you have a sudden heart problem. You need emergency surgery or you will probably die. You are rushed to the hospital and, in this case, you give your consent to have your chest cut open so the surgeon can fix the problem: let's assume that 'consent' means *valid, informed* consent here and for the rest of this chapter. As it happens, the surgeon in this scenario will have to cut you in a much more serious and invasive way than the stranger who sliced your arm. But since you gave your consent, she clearly does not wrong you by opening up your chest cavity. In other words, although she certainly *infringes* on your BI when she cuts you open, and while she also causes significant local harm in damaging certain bodily tissues, she does not *violate your right* to BI as we have defined it.

Now, the two cases of cutting obviously differ in various ways apart from whether you gave your consent. In the heart problem case, for example, you *need* to be cut to have a decent chance of survival, and that is plausibly at least part of what makes the cutting permissible: that is, the local harm to specific bodily tissues is instrumental to, even necessary for, and above all, clearly outweighed by, the expected benefit of the surgery to your body as a whole. In fact, even if you *couldn't* consent – because you passed out on the way to the hospital, let's say – it would still be permissible under ordinary circumstances for the surgeon to operate to save your life. We'll explore why that is in the following sections. But in most cases, if you *are* capable of consenting to a potential infringement of your BI and you *don't* consent – and especially if you actively *withhold* your consent – then it is seriously wrong to cut you (or otherwise intrude into your bodily sphere).

UNDERLYING INSIGHT AND TWO CONDITIONS

What is the basic idea behind this principle? It's rather simple. Our bodies are very precious to us (even if we don't always take good care of them). In an important sense, they are part of who we are.[2] They house our minds and our personalities and are the means by which we navigate the world and interact with others. They are deeply connected to how we understand ourselves, including our sexuality and gender identity.[3] And for better or worse, they are with us to the end. You can lose virtually everything else – friends, family, house, job; even the clothes off your back – and still soldier on. But if your body gives out, that's it. Unless you believe in souls and the like, without our bodies, we would not exist.

Moreover, the particular *state* of our bodies often matters to us a great deal. We care whether we are healthy or sick, fat or thin, hairy or hairless, light-skinned or dark-skinned. We care whether we have scars, and where they are, and how they got there. In fact, meaningful concern about the state of our bodies can come down to the tiniest detail, sometimes in ways that are not obvious to others: the specific location of a favorite freckle that is deeply cherished by someone we love (for instance). Or the fullness of our beard as a sign of devotion to our religion. Or a small tattoo we got in remembrance of our sister who died in the war. In other words, profound layers of meaning can become associated, quite intimately, with various aspects of our bodies, most often in ways that we alone are best positioned to appreciate.

Given their role in anchoring such personal meanings in our lives, as well as enabling our agency, shaping our identity, and facilitating – or frustrating – our general well-being, it makes sense that *we* should get to decide what happens to our own bodies. How they are treated, whether or in what ways they are altered, what goes into them, who even gets to see or touch them. And this means that except in very odd circumstances (for example, we are attacking someone and they are defending themselves within reason), no one has a right to infringe on our bodily integrity, not even to remove a freckle. Unless, that is, one of two conditions holds:

1 we *consent* to the infringement (often because we judge it to be in our overall best interests); or

2 we *can't* consent, because we are temporarily unconscious or otherwise impaired in some way, but we *would* consent if we were able – like in a medical emergency.

We will come back to these two conditions throughout this chapter, and attempt to clarify why they matter and how to apply them. For example, what is so important about your consent in the first condition, and how exactly does it relate to your best interests? And for the second condition: How do you know what BI infringements a person 'would' consent to, if they are not in a position to tell you, and how certain do you have to be of your judgment?

For now, it is enough to say that this general framework is pretty uncontroversial, at least when it comes to autonomous individuals (roughly speaking, adults). Here, 'autonomous' means having the mental capacity to make adequately informed and reasoned decisions about important self-affecting matters, taking into consideration the potential long-term consequences.[4]

BODILY INTEGRITY FOR CHILDREN

What about non-autonomous individuals, though? Or more specifically, *pre*-autonomous individuals, like children? Here things get more complicated. This is because both of the conditions we listed in the previous section (for when an infringement of someone's BI does not wrong them) are rooted in the notion of consent. But children, depending on their level of maturity, are not yet *able* to consent to a wide range of important actions that affect them, including potential BI infringements.[5]

So how do they fit into this framework? Specifically, how can we tell if a child is *wronged* by a BI infringement, and therefore that their *right* to BI has been violated?

Typically, when it comes to things that go beyond their ability to understand what is at stake and make their own informed decisions, children depend on their adult caretakers – most often their parents – to decide for them. The thinking is that parents usually love their children and sincerely want what's best for them; and they also *know* more about their children and their particular needs than just about anybody else. So it makes sense that they should be the ones to decide. Of course, there are exceptions to this. Some parents are indifferent to their children or actively abuse them. Other parents have good intentions but still make bad decisions that undermine their children's welfare. Either way, resulting traumas can last a lifetime. So it's very important to get clear about what the moral limits should be for what parents can do – or have done – to their children's bodies.

Setting exceptions aside, though, most parents *do* love their children, and really do want to see them flourish. And not just in childhood, but for the rest of their lives. So the aim should be to help them grow up physically and mentally secure, so they can develop the tools necessary to think for themselves and eventually act on their own behalf. Accordingly, there are – or should be – increasing *degrees* of autonomy as children approach adult status, ranging from a helpless baby (almost no autonomy) to an older teenager (almost full autonomy, as defined by what is characteristic for adults).

This has implications for how we should think about children's BI. Based on what we said in the previous section (about the importance of getting to decide for ourselves what happens to our own bodies), it means that there should be shifting priorities for how we treat children's bodies, depending on where on the spectrum of autonomy they are. Specifically, the more helpless a child is, the more it needs protection from BI infringements that are not clearly in its best interests, whereas the more autonomous a child is, the more it needs authority over what happens to its own body – both in a positive sense (what to do with its body) and a negative sense (what to keep from happening to its body). In both cases, the goal is to avoid BI infringements during childhood that would limit the child's ability, in the future, to make important decisions about their own BI as informed by their ever-maturing preferences and values.[6]

AUTONOMY AND CONSENT

This is where consent comes in, and why it is so important. Just think of your own case. Consent is what lets you decide about something that will primarily affect your own embodied self, typically based on what you take to be in your best interests. But you might also decide to do something that is plausibly not in your best interests, such as donating one of your kidneys to a sibling. Either way, though, the choice should be yours. We would not want to live in a world where others had a right to interfere with our bodies based on what they thought was in our best interests, without first asking our permission. This is why consent, rather than best interests, is built into the two conditions from before for when someone can infringe on your BI without wronging you, and so avoid violating your right to BI: (1) you *consent* to the infringement, or (2) you *can't* consent, because you are temporarily non-autonomous (TNA), but you *would* consent if you were able.

We have already seen that children, especially very young children (like toddlers and babies), are not *capable* of consenting to all sorts of things, including potential BI infringements. So for them, the first condition doesn't seem to do much good. What about the second condition? This one seems more promising. In particular, it invites us to think of children, depending on where they are on the autonomy spectrum, as being more or less TNA. According to this picture, older children and teenagers are TNA for a shorter stretch of time, whereas younger children and babies are TNA for a longer stretch of time. But in both cases, the relative lack of autonomy is temporary, barring some tragedy or abnormality.

Now, there is an important caveat here. And that is that no child is non-autonomous with respect to decisions that match – or fall within – their level of autonomy. Remember that we defined autonomy as simply 'having the mental capacity to make adequately informed and reasoned decisions about important self-affecting matters, taking into consideration the potential long-term consequences.' In other words, having the capacity to *consent*. Depending on what the proposed BI infringement is, then, children will sometimes be able to consent – or withhold their consent – to a proposed alteration of their bodies in a way that is appropriate for their developmental stage. Presumably most 15-year-olds, for instance, will be entirely capable of making an informed decision about whether or not they want to get their ears pierced or have cosmetic orthodontia wired onto their teeth; and if they do *not* want either of those things done, to simply force it on them against their will would wrong them, and therefore violate their right to BI.

What, then, about proposed infringements that go *beyond* a child's capacity to give their own consent? Here we can turn to the second half of condition (2), which refers to what a person 'would' consent to if they were able. But how do you *know* what someone would consent to, if they are not in a position to tell you? Someone who is unconscious, for example, like when you passed out on the way to the hospital in our thought experiment? Or more to the point for this chapter, someone who is pre-autonomous like a child?

You can make an educated guess, of course; but you can't really *know* unless the person tells you. So in most situations, the surest way to avoid violating someone's right to BI is simply to wait. Wait, that is, until they are no longer unconscious, or pre-autonomous, or otherwise TNA, so they can assess the situation and any relevant trade-offs in light of their own considered values, and then consent to the infringement, or withhold their consent, on their own terms and on their own behalf.

This point should not be taken lightly. Sometimes, you think you know what a person would want for their body, but you turn out to be very wrong. For example, you might think that someone would want to be touched sexually, though they are temporarily impaired (perhaps from too much drinking). And you might even be *right* that, if they could consent, that is what they would want. But what if you are wrong? Because the potential harms, emotional and otherwise, that are often associated with unwanted sexual contact are so profound, if there is *any doubt at all* about the other person's consent – much less their capacity to consent – it is very wrong to touch them. Now just extend this lesson to the whole range of possible infringements of a person's BI that have the potential to cause harm or resentment.[7]

As we saw with the cherished freckle in an earlier section, even seemingly 'trivial' aspects of a person's body may have great value or meaning for them, in ways that only they can understand. In such cases, it could seriously harm the person if those aspects were changed without their permission. So, if you are thinking about infringing on someone's BI who is not currently capable of consenting to the infringement, and you can wait for them to become autonomous without putting them in a situation they would be even less likely to consent to, you should.

JUDGING FOR OTHERS

How can you know if failing to infringe on someone's BI while they are TNA would put them in a situation they would be even less likely to consent to, if they were autonomous, than the proposed BI infringement itself?

There are easier and harder cases. On the easiest end of the spectrum are things like feeding and washing a child who cannot yet manage those tasks on their own, as well as giving them required vaccinations, all of which preserve their future bodily autonomy with minimal interference. There are also 'medically necessary' interventions for any TNA person, like the open heart surgery we imagined at the beginning. For a quick definition, these are interventions that are needed to alter a bodily state, where the bodily state in and of itself poses a serious and immediate threat to the person's well-being, and the intervention is the least harmful way of changing the bodily state to one that substantially alleviates the threat. These cases are easy because nearly everyone would consent to having their BI infringed if it was necessary to save their life, preserve their future bodily autonomy, or otherwise reliably promote their well-being to a similarly high degree.

When a BI infringement is almost universally regarded as something that promotes well-being in this way, and when judgments to that effect are likely to remain stable over the course of a person's lifetime despite plausible changes in circumstance or perspective, the chance it will wrong the person, and therefore violate their right to BI, is very small. The less universally a BI infringement is regarded as something that promotes well-being, or when judgments to that effect are not as robust against changes in circumstance or perspective, the greater the chance it will violate the person's right.[8]

There are various ways a BI infringement could come to be widely – and robustly – regarded as an overall well-being promoter. But a major way is to have its expected benefits rooted in norms or values that are relatively fixed across cultures and times: values like preserving core bodily functions or avoiding premature death, for example, when there is no other feasible way to achieve those ends in a less harmful way. Where things get more difficult is in cases where the very status of a BI infringement as an overall well-being promoter (versus diminisher) depends on relatively unstable, contested, or parochial norms or values, or when its intended benefits could be feasibly achieved in a less harmful way: for example, a way that didn't involve a BI infringement.

The main examples in this category are what are sometimes called 'cultural' surgeries, or other socially driven body modifications that are not strictly medically necessary. Things like breast implantation,[9] traditional body scarification or tattooing,[10] partial finger amputation,[11] ritual tooth extraction,[12] non-therapeutic male circumcision,[13] and female genital cutting of various kinds.[14] In these cases, there is no life-threatening illness to treat or physical function to restore. Almost no one would claim that the current bodily state of the person – often a child who cannot consent – poses a serious or immediate threat to their well-being. So why are these BI infringements carried out?

Usually, there is a background cultural norm in the person's group that stigmatizes the healthy body part in question, or that attaches perceived or intended social, aesthetic, symbolic, prophylactic, or spiritual benefits to its being altered or removed. Among the Dinka and Nuer people who live along the banks of the Nile River, for example, if a child does not have its front teeth pulled out, it may be teased or seen as unattractive.[15] Among the Dani people of central New Guinea, if a girl does not have one of her fingers partially amputated after a relative dies, this may be seen as disrespectful.[16] Among practicing Jews and Muslims, if a boy does not have the foreskin of his penis cut off, he may be seen as physically or symbolically impure or as excluded from a certain relation to the divine.[17]

A problem with these cases is that many people, both within and outside of the relevant communities, either do not agree that the intended benefits are actually benefits (for example, if they do not share the cultural or religious beliefs of the majority), or they disagree that the benefits outweigh the disadvantages, or they see the benefits as being based in norms that are themselves morally objectionable.[18] In cases like this, where there is disagreement among reasonable people about the very status of the BI infringement as an overall well-being promoter versus diminisher, it is harder to predict what any given child would consent to if it were autonomous. And guessing incorrectly could lead to serious resentment.

To illustrate: having a prominent scar or tattoo on your body, or missing your front teeth, the top half of your finger, or sensitive tissue from your penis, might be something you grow up to appreciate – if you strongly identify with the religion or culture of your parents, for example, or if you end up endorsing the relevant background norms and values. But if you grow up to dissociate from your parents' culture or religion, or to reject those norms or values, you might feel harmed or even mutilated by the very same bodily changes.[19]

What this suggests is that parents should think twice about subjecting their children to any BI infringement whose status as a well-being promoter is vulnerable to such shifts in perspective. This is especially the case when (1) opinion among informed and reasonable people is polarized: between those who see the infringement as an overall benefit and those who see it as an overall harm,[20] and (2) the infringement is irreversible. Anyone who wishes they had been subjected to a polarizing, irreversible BI infringement when they were TNA may have the option to undergo the infringement now that they are autonomous. By contrast, someone who resents that they were subjected to such an infringement when they were TNA has no comparable recourse: they cannot 'undo' what has already happened.

CONCLUSION

We live in an interconnected world. People from different cultures now constantly interact, and move from place to place, and get exposed to new ideas, and as a consequence often revise their beliefs and attitudes.[21] This means that the risk of wronging a child by permanently altering its body on behalf of norms or values that are neither universal nor stable is much greater than it may have been in the past – when people lived in more isolated settings and their future preferences could be more easily controlled and predicted.

In other words, unlike the values associated with avoiding premature death or preserving core bodily functions (which are constant over time and shared by almost everybody), the values associated with particular cultural or religious practices are much less robust against possible changes in perspective over a lifetime. Indeed, it is increasingly common for people to adopt new cultural identities upon reaching adulthood, or to lose the religious beliefs they may have had as children.[22] For BI infringements that are based in such identities or beliefs, then, there is often a subset of affected children who grow up to feel, not just apathetic or mildly irritated about what was done to their bodies without their consent, but significantly harmed by what was done.[23]

This suggests that, for any BI infringement carried out on a pre-autonomous child, especially if it is irreversible, the degree of certainty one should have about what the child would consent to if it were autonomous should be very high indeed before proceeding – at or near the 'medically necessary' threshold. If the BI infringement can be delayed until the child is sufficiently autonomous to make their own decision (without placing the child into a situation they would be even less likely to consent to), it should be delayed.[24]

NOTES

1 In this chapter, we'll be talking about a *moral* right to bodily integrity, as opposed to a *legal* right, although these rights often overlap. A *moral* right is something that places ethical limits (or requirements) on others for how they can (or should) treat you, whatever the law may say. So, even if there were some country where cutting an adult without their consent didn't happen to be illegal, it would still be *wrong* to do this because, among other reasons, it would violate that person's *moral* right to not be assaulted. For more on the right to bodily integrity as discussed in this chapter, see Earp (2017a); Fox and Thomson (2017);

Hill (2015); Koll (2010); Ludbrook (1995); and Mazor (2018, 2019). Thanks to Laurie Paul, Clare Chambers, Joseph Mazor, Joe Fischel, Robert Darby, Steve Latham, and David Edmonds for feedback on these ideas..

2 See Bermúdez (2018); Jensen and Moran (2013).

3 See Earp and Steinfeld (2018). See also Munzer (2018).

4 For discussion, see Owen et al. (2009).

5 For discussion, see Carmack et al. (2016).

6 See Darby (2013); Maslen et al. (2014); Möller (2017).

7 For a very good discussion of why non-consensual sexual contact is wrong, see Archard (2007). For further discussion, see Earp (2015c). These discussions clarify that sex without consent is wrong not simply because of the harms, such as psychological trauma, that it may cause, as in some cases it does not appear to cause such harms. Nor is it wrong simply because it *tends* to cause such harms. Rather, it is wrong, first and foremost, because it infringes on a person's 'sexual integrity' – to use Archard's (2007) term – without their consent. In this, it denies that the person is worthy of respect with regard to something that is central to their personhood, namely, their ability to decide who may engage with their embodied sexuality under what conditions. In other words, regardless of the harms that may or may not follow from non-consensual sex, the sex is wrong *because* it is non-consensual. Similarly, non-consensual infringements of a person's BI are wrong, whether or not the person is harmed or goes on to feel harmed by the infringement.

8 See Earp and Shaw (2017).

9 See Chambers (2004).

10 See Ojo (2008).

11 See Bosmia et al. (2014).

12 See Willis et al. (2005). For an argument that prophylactic extraction of third molars (wisdom teeth) in so-called developed nations is essentially a medicalized ritual with little evidence of benefits outweighing risks, see Friedman (2007).

13 See Earp and Darby (2017).

14 See Shahvisi and Earp (2019).

15 See Pinchi et al. (2015).

16 See Kirkup (2007).

17 See Glick (2005).

18 See Chambers (2018); Earp (2014); Earp and Darby (2019); Juth and Lynøe (2014); McMath (2015); Sarajlic (2014); Ungar-Sargon (2015).

19 See Earp (2017b).

20 See Earp (2015a, 2016).

21 See Johnsdotter and Essén (2016).

22 See Haaretz Staff (2012); Pew Research (2015).

23 See Earp and Steinfeld (2017); Hammond and Carmack (2017); Johns-
    dotter (2018); Lightfoot-Klein et al. (2000); Sahiyo (2018), Taher
    (2017), Willis et al. (2005).
24 For extended discussions, see Earp (2015b, 2016).

REFERENCES

Archard, D. (2007). The wrong of rape. *The Philosophical Quarterly*, 57(228),
    374–393. https://doi.org/10.1111/j.1467-9213.2007.492.x

Bermúdez, J. L. (2018). Bodily ownership, psychological ownership, and
    psychopathology. *Review of Philosophy and Psychology*, in press. https://doi.
    org/10.1007/s13164-018-0406-3

Bosmia, A. N., Griessenauer, C. J., and Tubbs, R. S. (2014). Yubitsume: Ritualistic
    self-amputation of proximal digits among the Yakuza. *Journal of Injury
    and Violence Research*, 6(2), 54–56. https://doi.org/10.5249/jivr.v6i2.489

Carmack, A., Notini, L., and Earp, B. D. (2016). Should surgery for hypospa-
    dias be performed before an age of consent? *The Journal of Sex Research*, 53(8),
    1047–1058. https://doi.org/10.1080/00224499.2015.1066745

Chambers, C. (2004). Are breast implants better than female genital muti-
    lation? Autonomy, gender equality and Nussbaum's political liberalism.
    Critical Review of International Social and Political Philosophy, 7(3), 1–33. https://
    doi.org/10.1080/1369823042000269366

Chambers, C. (2018). Reasonable disagreement and the neutralist dilemma:
    Abortion and circumcision in Matthew Kramer's 'Liberalism with Excellence.'
    The American Journal of Jurisprudence, 63(1), 9–32. https://doi.org/10.1093/ajj/
    auy006

Darby, R. (2013). The child's right to an open future: Is the principle appli-
    cable to non-therapeutic circumcision? *Journal of Medical Ethics*, 39(7),
    463–468. https://doi.org/10.1136/medethics-2012-101182

Earp, B. D. (2014). Hymen 'restoration' in cultures of oppression: How can
    physicians promote individual patient welfare without becoming com-
    plicit in the perpetuation of unjust social norms? *Journal of Medical Ethics*,
    40(6), 431–431. https://doi.org/10.1136/medethics-2013-101662

Earp, B. D. (2015a). Addressing polarisation in science. *Journal of Medical Ethics*,
    41(9), 782–784. https://doi.org/10.1136/medethics-2015-102891

Earp, B. D. (2015b). Female genital mutilation and male circumcision:
    Toward an autonomy-based ethical framework. *Medicolegal and Bioethics*,
    5(1), 89–104. https://doi.org/10.2147/MB.S63709

Earp, B. D. (2015c). 'Legitimate rape,' moral coherence, and degrees of sexual
    harm. *Think*, 14(41), 9–20. https://doi.org/10.1017/S1477175615000172

Earp, B. D. (2016). Between moral relativism and moral hypocrisy: Reframing the debate on 'FGM.' *Kennedy Institute of Ethics Journal*, 26(2), 105–144. https://doi.org/10.1353/ken.2016.0009

Earp, B. D. (2017a). Gender, genital alteration, and beliefs about bodily harm. *The Journal of Sexual Medicine*, 14(5, Supplement 4), e225. https://doi.org/10.1016/j.jsxm.2017.04.182

Earp, B. D. (2017b). The right to bodily integrity and the concept of sexual harm. *The Journal of Sexual Medicine*, 14(5, Supplement 4), e239. https://doi.org/10.1016/j.jsxm.2017.04.153

Earp, B. D., and Darby, R. (2017). Circumcision, sexual experience, and harm. *University of Pennsylvania Journal of International Law*, 37(2-online), 1–57. https://www.researchgate.net/publication/315763686_Circumcision_sexual_experience_and_harm

Earp, B. D., and Darby, R. (2019). Circumcision, autonomy and public health. *Public Health Ethics*, 12(1), 64–81. https://doi.org/10.1093/phe/phx024

Earp, B. D., and Shaw, D. M. (2017). Cultural bias in American medicine: The case of infant male circumcision. *Journal of Pediatric Ethics*, 1(1), 8–26. https://www.researchgate.net/publication/316527603_Cultural_bias_in_American_medicine_the_case_of_infant_male_circumcision

Earp, B. D., and Steinfeld, R. (2017). Gender and genital cutting: A new paradigm. In T. G. Barbat (Ed.), *Gifted Women, Fragile Men*. Brussels: ALDE Group-EU Parliament. Retrieved from http://euromind.global/brian-d-earp-and-rebecca-steinfeld/?lang=en

Earp, B. D., and Steinfeld, R. (2018). Genital autonomy and sexual well-being. *Current Sexual Health Reports*, 10, 7–17. https://doi.org/10.1007/s11930-018-0141-x

Fox, M., and Thomson, M. (2017). Bodily integrity, embodiment, and the regulation of parental choice. *Journal of Law and Society*, 44(4), 501–531. https://doi.org/10.1111/jols.12056

Friedman, J. W. (2007). The prophylactic extraction of third molars: A public health hazard. *American Journal of Public Health*, 97(9), 1554–1559. https://doi.org/10.2105/AJPH.2006.100271

Glick, L. B. (2005). *Marked in Your Flesh: Circumcision From Ancient Judea to Modern America*. Oxford: Oxford University Press.

Haaretz Staff. (2012, August 20). New poll shows atheism on rise, with Jews found to be least religious. *Haaretz*. Retrieved from www.haaretz.com/jewish/news/new-poll-shows-atheism-on-rise-with-jews-found-to-be-least-religious-1.459477

Hammond, T., and Carmack, A. (2017). Long-term adverse outcomes from neonatal circumcision reported in a survey of 1,008 men: An overview of health and human rights implications. *The International Journal of Human Rights*, 21(2), 189–218. https://doi.org/10.1080/13642987.2016.126 0007

Hill, B. J. (2015). Constituting children's bodily integrity. *Duke Law Journal*, 64(1), 1295–1362.

Jensen, R. T., and Moran, D. (Eds.). (2013). *The Phenomenology of Embodied Subjectivity* (Vol. 71). New York: Springer.

Johnsdotter, S. (2018). The impact of migration on attitudes to female genital cutting and experiences of sexual dysfunction among migrant women with FGC. *Current Sexual Health Reports*, 2(1), 1–7. https://doi.org/10.1007/s11930-018-0139-4

Johnsdotter, S., and Essén, B. (2016). Cultural change after migration: Circumcision of girls in Western migrant communities. *Best Practice & Research Clinical Obstetrics & Gynaecology*, 32, 15–25. https://doi.org/10.1016/j.bpobgyn.2015.10.012

Juth, N., and Lynøe, N. (2014). Are there morally relevant differences between hymen restoration and bloodless treatment for Jehovah's Witnesses? *BMC Medical Ethics*, 15(89), 1–7. https://doi.org/10.1186/1472-6939-15-89

Kirkup, J. R. (2007). Ritual, punitive, legal and iatrogenic causes. In *A History of Limb Amputation* (pp. 35–44). London: Springer. https://doi.org/10.1007/978-1-84628-509-7_4

Koll, M. (2010). Growth, interrupted: Nontherapeutic growth attenuation, parental medical decision making, and the profoundly developmentally disabled child's right to bodily integrity. *University of Illinois Law Review*, 2010, 225–264.

Lightfoot-Klein, H., Chase, C., Hammond, T., and Goldman, R. (2000). Genital surgeries on children below an age of consent. In L. T. Szuchman and F. Muscarella (Eds.), *Psychological Perspectives on Human Sexuality* (pp. 440–479). New York: John Wiley & Sons.

Ludbrook, R. (1995). The child's right to bodily integrity. *Current Issues in Criminal Justice*, 7(2), 123–132.

Maslen, H., Earp, B. D., Cohen Kadosh, R., and Savulescu, J. (2014). Brain stimulation for treatment and enhancement in children: An ethical analysis. *Frontiers in Human Neuroscience*, 8(953), 1–5. https://doi.org/10.3389/fnhum.2014.00953

Mazor, J. (2018). On the child's right to bodily integrity: When is the right infringed? *Journal of Medicine & Philosophy*, in press. http://eprints.lse.ac.uk/id/eprint/84662

Mazor, J. (2019). On the strength of children's right to bodily integrity: The case of circumcision. *Journal of Applied Philosophy*, 36(1), 1–16.

McMath, A. (2015). Infant male circumcision and the autonomy of the child: Two ethical questions. *Journal of Medical Ethics*, 41(8), 687–690. https://doi.org/10.1136/medethics-2014-102319

Möller, K. (2017). Ritual male circumcision and parental authority. *Jurisprudence*, 8(3), 461–479. https://doi.org/10.1080/20403313.2017.1339535

Munzer, S. R. (2018). Examining nontherapeutic circumcision. *Health Matrix*, 28(1), 1–77.

Ojo, O. (2008). Beyond diversity: Women, scarification, and Yoruba identity. *History in Africa*, 35, 347–374. https://doi.org/10.1353/hia.0.0015

Owen, G. S., Freyenhagen, F., Richardson, G., and Hotopf, M. (2009). Mental capacity and decisional autonomy: An interdisciplinary challenge. *Inquiry*, 52(1), 79–107. https://doi.org/10.1080/00201740802661502

Pew Research. (2015, November 3). *U.S. public becoming less religious*. Retrieved November 26, 2017 from www.pewforum.org/2015/11/03/u-s-public-becoming-less-religious/

Pinchi, V., Barbieri, P., Pradella, F., Focardi, M., Bartolini, V., & Norelli, G.-A. (2015). Dental ritual mutilations and forensic odontologist practice: A review of the literature. *Acta Stomatologica Croatica*, 49(1), 3–13. https://doi.org/10.15644/asc49/1/1

Sahiyo. (2018). Thaal Pe Charcha highlights: 'I was cut with a fingernail.' *Sahiyo Newsletter*, 3(7), July 18.

Sarajlic, E. (2014). Can culture justify infant circumcision? *Res Publica*, 20(4), 327–343. https://doi.org/10.1007/s11158-014-9254-x

Shahvisi, A., and Earp, B. D. (2019). The law and ethics of female genital cutting. In S. Creighton and L.-M. Liao (Eds.), *Female Genital Cosmetic Surgery: Solution to What Problem* (pp. 58–71)? Cambridge: Cambridge University Press.

Taher, M. (2017). *Understanding Female Genital Cutting in the Dawoodi Bohra Community: An Exploratory Survey* (pp. 1–82). Sahiyo: United Against Female Genital Cutting. Retrieved from https://sahiyo.files.wordpress.com/2017/02/sahiyo_report_final-updatedbymt2.pdf

Ungar-Sargon, E. (2015). On the impermissibility of infant male circumcision: A response to Mazor (2013). *Journal of Medical Ethics*, 41(2), 186–190. https://doi.org/10.1136/medethics-2013-101598

Willis, M. S., Schacht, R. N., and Toothaker, R. (2005). Anterior dental extractions among Dinka and Nuer refugees in the United States: A case series. *Special Care in Dentistry*, 25(4), 193–198. https://doi.org/10.1111/j.1754-4505.2005.tb01649.x

Eighteen

Guy Kahane

In 2002, news outlets around the world reported the birth of a baby named Gavine. Gavine was conceived via artificial insemination to a lesbian couple in the US. But that's not why Gavine made the headlines. You see, his parents, Sharon Duchesneau and Candy McCullough, are a deaf lesbian couple and they wanted their child to be deaf like them. They had asked a series of sperm banks to provide them with sperm from a congenitally deaf donor but all these sperm banks refused their request. So they approached a deaf friend who had several generations of deafness in his family. The deaf friend donated his sperm and this was how Gavine was created.

Deliberately choosing to create a deaf child is rather unusual. It's much more common for couples to use reproductive technology to *prevent* or *avoid* disability. Many couples, for example, use pre-natal screening to find out if their foetus has Down's syndrome, and many of these couples abort the foetus if this is the case. They *don't* want to have a disabled child. But is it morally wrong to actively seek to create a disabled child? Is it wrong to actively seek to avoid having a disabled child – and even to abort foetuses that will grow to be disabled?

These are contentious questions. Many people were outraged to hear that a couple would deliberately create a deaf child. A growing number of people, especially in the disabled community, are upset that the general public regards disability as something that should be cured rather than celebrated – let alone a reason to abort a foetus. These responses reflect radically different views about what it even means to be disabled. The *Medical Model* of disability sees disability as something we need to cure. The opposing *Social Model* of disability sees disability as primarily a social problem. I will introduce these two influential views of disability and highlight some of their problems. I'll then suggest an alternative approach that builds on the insights contained in both views.

THE MEDICAL AND SOCIAL MODELS OF DISABILITY

The Medical Model of disability is basically the common-sense view. As its name indicates, it is the view that has dominated medical practice, at least until recently. On this view, disability is a deviation from normal human species functioning and an inherently harmful condition. On the Medical Model, we should think of disability as something similar to a disease. It is a physical condition that is inherently undesirable or, at best, a serious burden. It is something that should be prevented, corrected, and removed whenever possible. We should therefore screen foetuses for disability just as we screen them for serious diseases. And we should devote our resources to finding medical cures to disabilities or otherwise ways to bring disabled people closer to normal functioning. For example, cochlear implants – surgically implanted electronic devices – can provide a sense of sound in people who are deaf or severely hard of hearing.

The opposing view of disability is known as the Social Model and was developed primarily by people with disability. Proponents of the Social Model agree that disabled people are impaired in the sense of deviating from the normal species functioning of humans. The majority of humans can hear, and in that sense, being deaf is an abnormality. But according to the Social Model, this abnormality is a mere difference – roughly akin to differences in gender, sexual orientation, or skin colour. On this view, while disabled people do live lives that are in some respects different from those of abled people, such lives are not inherently worse, and disability does not automatically entail a lower quality of life.

For many 'able-bodied' people, this is hard to believe. In fact, if you ask people to predict how they will feel if they became disabled, they tend to predict a catastrophic effect. They say that they will feel utterly miserable. But, in most cases, that's not what actually happens. Many studies have found that individuals with various kinds of disabilities report high levels of satisfaction with their quality of life – in some cases, higher than that of many abled-bodied people. Even people who become disabled later in life, due to accident or illness, usually eventually feel as satisfied with their lives as they were before the accident. And shouldn't we base our view of disability on what disabled people actually tell us rather than just assert, from our 'able-bodied' perspective, that disability is a serious burden?

Still, able-bodied people might persist, isn't it obvious that it is better to have two healthy, functioning legs than to need a wheelchair to move around? Well, why, exactly? Someone in a wheelchair can often move faster than someone who walks, and if you're waiting in a long queue, it is better to sit in a chair than to stand. And if we turn from wheelchairs to prosthetic legs, it is even harder to pin down the disadvantage. Oscar Pistorius, the South African athlete, lost his legs as a baby. But, using prosthetic legs, he can run faster than most people on Earth.

The Social Model doesn't deny that disability is associated with a significant degree of disadvantage. There may be difficulties finding a job or a romantic partner. There are many places that are inaccessible to someone in a wheelchair. So there are certainly obstacles. But according to the Social Model, these obstacles are imposed by society. They are not inherent to the physical condition itself. If people overcame their prejudiced attitude to disability, if we arranged things to accommodate the distinctive needs of people with impairment, this advantage would disappear. The *disability* would disappear – even if the impairment remained. According to the Medical Model, we should change disabled people to fit the existing world and to be more like the 'normal' majority. According to the Social Model, the problem is not medical but social. We don't think that women or black people should adjust to fit a sexist or racist society. What needs to change is society. And in the same way that we change society to eradicate sexism and racism, we should change it to eradicate *ableism* in its many forms. Even to describe a paraplegic or amputee as *confined* to a wheelchair is itself a subtle expression of ableism.

The critic of the Social Model may remain unconvinced. After all, even if society were radically adjusted to accommodate disabilities, the blind would still not be able to see those they love, to fully appreciate movies or the Mona Lisa. But this objection is less powerful than it might seem. For example, perhaps it is an advantage not to be affected by how people look. In any case, none of us can access all the goods that are out there. You need to lead a certain life, and invest a great deal of time and effort and sometimes money, to be able to engage in, and enjoy, extreme athletic achievement or Anglo-Saxon literature or fine wine. Many of us cannot engage in these goods, but this hardly means that we cannot live good lives. Men cannot experience pregnancy and childbirth, but this is no reason to think that the lives of men are fundamentally inferior to those of women. So it does not follow from the fact that the deaf cannot enjoy music that their lives are worse in any interesting way. Indeed, they can instead benefit from the unique culture of the deaf community, a culture to which few hearing people have entry. When a new deaf child is created, it is a welcome addition to that community. And, to actively select against disability, or to try to 'cure' it, is to erase a valuable difference, to make the world more monotonous and less diverse. To seek to 'cure' impairments such as blindness or deafness – for example, by giving cochlear implants to deaf children – is, according to the Social Model, the same as trying to 'cure' homosexuality.

Some people think that it is inherently bad to be disabled because disability necessarily involves a dysfunction of some kind in normal human functioning. It is natural for human beings to be able to walk or see or hear, and to have certain cognitive capacities. This is why disability is a bad thing. Now disability does involve an abnormality. The deaf are a small minority. And our ears and eyes did evolve to hear and see. But so what? What's so good about being natural or normal? Our modern lives are dramatically different from the lives of our ancient hunter-gatherer ancestors. For example, childbirth is naturally extremely painful, but this is not a good reason to withhold painkillers from women during labour. Human aggression is natural, but that's not a reason to cherish it. It matters whether one has mobility because it's extremely useful to be able to move around, not because it's 'normal'. And it doesn't terribly matter whether one moves using 'natural' limbs or prosthetic ones or, for that matter, a wheelchair.

Perhaps the most powerful objection to the Social Model is that it seems to have implications that few would be willing to accept. According to the Social Model, it is wrong for couples to try to use pre-natal screening to prevent the birth of disabled children. And it is just fine for disabled (or indeed, 'able-bodied') couples to want to have disabled children. The view also seems to imply that it would be fine to make a perfectly healthy person disabled. If disability is just a difference, and not any kind of inherent harm, how could that be wrong? But the idea that it's okay to make people blind or amputate their legs is surely absurd if not deeply repugnant.

This argument is a bit too quick.[1] If I cut your long hair while you slept, I did something wrong, even if having short hair is just different than having long hair. In fact, it would be wrong even if you would look better with short hair. The wrong is in interfering with people's lives without their consent. In the same way, it would obviously be wrong to blind someone who can see, even if there is nothing inherently disadvantageous about being blind.

So it's wrong to just cause disability in someone even if disability is just a difference. But what if someone *wants* to become disabled and is happy to undergo the difficult transition process? This idea may sound bizarre, but there are people who have that wish. Some people have a condition known as 'bodily integrity identity disorder'. These people feel that some of their healthy limbs aren't really theirs. Some of them deeply desire, for example, to have their legs amputated and much prefer to be in a wheelchair than to walk. According to the Medical Model, these people are irrationally seeking to harm themselves. But on the Social Model, it's not clear what difference there is between a person who wants to lose her limbs and a blind person who wants to undergo an operation to restore her vision. In both cases, the move is not from better to worse – it's just a change in one's form of life.

This seems hugely implausible – perhaps because this bizarre disorder is hard to get one's head around. But another argument against the Social Model of disability can be developed in a more straightforward way. The defender of the Social Model can concede that it is wrong to cause an able-bodied adult to be disabled because this would wrongly interfere with their lives and because the transition to a disabled life can be difficult. Neither of these points, however, would apply in the case of an infant. We cannot ask for an infant's consent, and parents are generally given broad license to shape the lives of their children in ways they see fit. We don't see such parental choices as wrongful interference. And infants who were just born have not yet adjusted to a seeing or hearing life. A simple operation could remove their ability to see or hear and they would grow up fully adjusted to that condition. Surely very few would agree that such a procedure is justified. Indeed, many would regard it as monstrous.

What can defenders of the Social Model say in response? They can 'bite the bullet', pointing out that our deepest intuitions often reflect unfounded prejudices: not so long ago, nearly everyone would have found the idea of equality of women preposterous. They could point out that we would also be disturbed by the idea of a procedure that would change an infant from male to female. We can be disturbed by the idea of changing someone's nature in this way while still thinking that gender is a mere difference.

There is a problem with this reply. We are as disturbed by the idea of changing an infant from male to female as we are of changing an infant from female to male. But we don't find the idea of giving vision to a blind infant remotely as disturbing as blinding a seeing infant. This asymmetry is hard to explain in terms of the Social Model. Or imagine that a condition affected a seeing infant which, if not counteracted, would soon turn it blind. Here it seems not just right but urgent to intervene to stop the process. Few of us would think that we should intervene in a similar way in a parallel case where a blind infant is acquiring the capacity to see.

THE WELFARIST MODEL OF DISABILITY

What, then, are we to conclude? The Medical Model remains the dominant view of disability. But it faces serious challenges. It treats impairments such as deafness and paraplegia as inherently disadvantageous while ignoring the massive role of the social environment in producing this disadvantage. It treats abnormality as such as a bad thing. And it ignores what disabled people themselves say about their condition. At the same time, it is not easy to accept the Social Model's claim that the overall disadvantage associated with disability is *entirely* due to a prejudiced and oppressive society; the idea that disability is a mere difference has disturbing implications. Is there a middle path that will incorporate insights from both views?

I will now sketch one such approach. It is called the *Welfarist Model*. According to this view, we should think of disability as a stable physical or psychological condition of a person that tends to reduce the person's potential for well-being in a given expected environment, even in circumstances that do not involve prejudice and injustice. According to the Welfarist Model, disabilities are not inherently negative conditions – they are only harmful through their effects in specific environments. In order to address this harmful effect, we can change either the disabled person or the environment. But unlike the Medical Model and the Social Model, there is no special priority to be given to one over the other. Both medical and environmental interventions should be explored. More-over, since mere deviation from what is normal for humans is not negative or harmful in itself, to assess whether a given condition is a disability, and to what extent, is a matter for empirical investigation. We need to assess the expected effect of the condition on the person's well-being in the environment they are expected to inhabit. Such an investigation may reveal some disabilities to be far less harmful than commonly assumed, and others may turn out not to be real disabilities at all, or even advantages. It may still be the case, however, that many familiar disabilities are significant disadvantages in the world we currently inhabit. We need to consider the evidence on a case-by-case basis, rather than merely appeal to our own intuitions or assume that what holds in the case of one disability must also hold in the case of another.

One important feature of the Welfarist Model is that it sees disability as highly context dependent. A deaf child raised by loving deaf parents and surrounded by a thriving community of other deaf people may suffer from only the mildest of disadvantages. And in an environment where there is constant loud noise in the background, being deaf can be a significant advantage. Or take colour blindness. For most of us, becoming colour blind would be a trivial disability at best. But for a painter at the height of her career, becoming colour blind might be a devastating disability. Disability is not inherently disadvantageous – it reduces a person's well-being in some contexts, but not in others.

Another feature of the Welfarist Model is that disability becomes a matter of degree – and so common. For example, asthma is a disability because it makes breathing more difficult in certain environments commonly encountered in the developed world – places with dust or smoke or pets. It hinders physical activity. Myopia and dyslexia are other examples of common but mild disabilities. In this way, all of us can be said to suffer from disabilities – conditions inherent to our nature that reduce our well-being and make it more difficult to realize a good life in the context we inhabit.

People sometimes associate disability with visible and overt features of people's bodies, or with very severe mental limitations. But genetics, biology, and psychology will identify many other internal impediments to well-being. It may turn out, for example, that having poor impulse control is, in many contexts, a more acute obstacle to a good life than being deaf or missing an arm. That is, having poor impulse control may adversely affect well-being, and thus be a greater disability than losing an arm. The fact that certain characteristics of people are more salient than others may distort our understanding of the weight they have in shaping people's lives and the proper prioritization of medical research and treatment. The Welfarist Model tries to correct this distortion by defining disability in a broader and more inclusive way.

To see the difference between these three models of disability, let us think about a controversial real-life case. Ashley is a girl from Seattle who was born with static encephalopathy, a severe brain impairment that left her unable to walk, talk, eat, sit up, or roll over. Ashley would never go beyond the developmental level of a 3-month-old baby. In 2004, when Ashley was 9 years old, she was given high-dose oestrogen therapy to stunt her growth, and her uterus and breast buds were removed to prevent menstrual discomfort and to limit the growth of her breasts. Ashley's parents argued that this treatment was intended 'to improve our daughter's quality of life and not to convenience her caregivers'.[2]

This so-called Ashley treatment is very controversial. Some people have claimed, in line with the Social Model, that

Ashley's condition is detrimental only because of adverse social circumstances and that it is only these circumstances that need to be changed – for example by providing further support for the parents to lift or transfer Ashley, and so forth. These people think that the Ashley treatment is profoundly unethical. By contrast, on both the Welfarist Model and on the Medical Model, Ashley was born with a severe disability. Nonetheless, their verdicts on this case radically diverge. On the Medical Model, the Ashley treatment would greatly increase her disability – driving her even further from what is normal for humans. But according to the Welfarist Model, in the context of Ashley's brain impairment, and assuming that the claims made for the effects of the treatment on Ashley's well-being were correct, the treatment would be not disabling but enhancing.

The bitter debate between proponents of the Medical and Social models of disability has been going on for decades. But I have argued that we don't need to choose sides. There is nothing inherently negative about deviating from what is biologically normal, but to hold that the disadvantage associated with disability is wholly due to social factors also goes too far. The Welfarist Model offers a better alternative. It places disability on a continuum with many other ways in which our biology places potential limits on our well-being. These limits can only be understood in a given context. And to remove, or ease them, we need to pursue both social and medical interventions.

NOTES

1 My discussion of this objection draws on Barnes, Elizabeth (2015) *The Minority Body: A Theory of Disability* (Oxford: OUP), chapter 5.
2 'The "Ashley Treatment": Toward a Better Quality of Life for "Pillow Angels",' http://ashleytreatment.spaces.live.com/.

REFERENCES AND FURTHER READING

Shakespeare, Tom (2013) 'The Social Model of Disability'. In Lennard Davis, ed. *The Disability Studies Reader* (London: Routledge), 214–221.

Barnes, Elizabeth (2015) *The Minority Body: A Theory of Disability* (Oxford: OUP).

Kahane, Guy and Julian Savulescu (2009) 'The Welfarist Account of Disability'. In Kimberley Brownlee and Adam Cureton, eds. *Disability and Disadvantage* (Oxford: OUP), pp. 14–53.

Nineteen

Katrien Devolder

In 2002, I attended a conference on embryo research. It was about the extraction of stem cells from early embryos, and the use of these embryonic stem cells in research. Not long before the conference, it had been discovered that embryonic stem cells are promising tools for the development of treatments for devastating diseases such as Parkinson's and Huntington's diseases. Most talks at the conference addressed the scientific and legal aspects of embryonic stem cell research, but one talk addressed its ethical acceptability. The speaker gave a passionate presentation about how immoral it is to use embryos for biomedical research. His view was clear: we should never do this. It fails to respect the moral status of the embryo. To my surprise, his talk was met with loud applause. But the people near where I was sitting were not applauding. They were in wheelchairs and suffered from diseases that embryonic stem cell research could potentially help to cure, perhaps within their lifetime. To them, it was as though the speaker was encouraging a death sentence, and with the audience cheering him on.

This experience made a great impression on me, and I spent much of the next 15 years researching the ethics of embryonic stem cell research. Do the lives of embryos really matter more than the lives of the people suffering from devastating diseases?

INTRODUCTION

Before delving into the ethics of embryo research, we need to know what sorts of embryos we are talking about and what sort of research.

In this chapter, we have in mind only *human* embryos that have been created and grown in the laboratory and have not been implanted in a woman's womb. We will also focus only on early human embryos – embryos that are less than 14 days old. These embryos are hollow balls of cells of about 0.2 mm diameter in size. In at least 12 countries, including the US and the UK, it is unlawful for researchers to conduct research on embryos beyond 14 days. The great majority of embryos used for research are embryos created in the course of an *in vitro* fertilisation (IVF) treatment, but no longer wanted for reproductive purposes; sometimes embryos are also especially created for the purpose of research.

As for what sort of research we have in mind, one type is *embryonic stem cell* research. Embryonic stem cells are cells that can be extracted from five-day-old embryos. Embryonic stem cells can give rise to any cell type of the body, such as liver or heart cells, and can indefinitely replicate themselves. It is thus possible to produce a large number of embryonic stem cells and to coax them into developing into any cell type. This makes them promising tools for stem cell therapies. For example, embryonic stem cells could potentially be induced to develop into heart muscle cells to repair or replace damaged heart tissue, into insulin-producing cells to treat diabetes, or into neurons and their supporting tissues to repair spinal cord injuries.

Embryonic stem cells are also powerful tools for biomedical research. For example, we can use them to study how our cells differentiate into different body parts as an embryo develops into a foetus and then a child. This could provide insight into how tissues are maintained throughout life, and into why things sometimes go wrong; for example, in birth defects. Other major uses of embryonic stem cells in biomedical research include the creation of *in vitro* models (*in vitro* means 'in the glass') for the study of diseases and for drug discovery and toxicity testing. Diseases could be studied, or drugs could be tested on stem cells and their derivatives in a petri dish, rather than in humans or animals. This could make studies safer and more efficient.

Not all embryo research focuses on embryonic stem cells. Some embryo research studies whole embryos. Examples include research done to improve techniques for storing, freezing, testing, and implanting embryos in the context of fertility treatments, such as IVF, which involves the fertilisation of an egg with sperm in a petri dish.

Thus, embryo research may lead to knowledge and the development of therapies that will lengthen lives, alleviate suffering, and allow people to better achieve their reproductive goals. These all seem like worthwhile and important goals. So what's the catch? Why is embryo research so controversial?

The difficulty is that embryo research typically involves destroying the embryos being studied, either in the course of the research, or after the research, when scientists may be legally required to discard the embryo. It is this embryo destruction that, according to some, makes embryo research unacceptable, or at least problematic.

EMBRYO RESEARCH IS MURDER

Consider this hypothetical case:

> *Lethal Experiment*: Tim, a scientist, hopes to find a treatment for a devastating disease that affects hundreds of

thousands of patients. The most efficient way to do this is by doing invasive experiments on one adult patient, which will foreseeably result in her death. Tim anaesthetises the patient and conducts the experiments, without her consent, and she indeed dies.

Most would agree that Tim's action is wrong. Even if our aims are laudable, we can't just do to a person whatever we want. A person has rights or interests that limit what we can permissibly do to her. In philosophy, this is captured by the concept of 'moral status'. Moral status refers to the value something or someone has in and of itself regardless of how valuable that someone or something is to others. A toaster, for example, does not have moral status. It is only valuable to the extent that it is useful to us, presumably by helping us to make toast. We don't have to treat it in a certain way for its own sake. But you and I do have moral status. We have value regardless of how useful we are to others. Scientists can't just take our organs to conduct research, even to benefit others. They are morally required to take into consideration our interest in remaining alive, or our 'right to life'. Only in exceptional circumstances may this interest or right be overridden. Perhaps it could be overridden if killing one person were necessary to rescue a million others.

Some believe that early embryos also have a right to life, or have an equally strong interest in remaining alive as you and I. They believe that embryos have the same moral status as an adult person – and should be treated accordingly. From this, it follows that it is normally unacceptable to kill an embryo for research purposes, just as it would normally be unacceptable to kill you or me for research purposes.[1]

Why do some people think that embryos have this moral status? Why do they think it is as wrong to kill an embryo for research purposes as it would be to kill you or me for the same purposes?

One common answer is this: embryos are human, and all human beings have full moral status simply in virtue of belonging to the species *homo sapiens*. This position has been criticised for being 'speciesist'.[2] The idea here is that, just as race or sex is a morally irrelevant factor when considering whether to protect someone's right to life, or her interest in remaining alive, so is species membership. It is very hard to think of a good argument for why the simple fact of belonging to the human species gives all humans equal moral status (and, it is usually asserted, a higher moral status than non-human animals). Some try to justify this by pointing out that humans have higher cognitive abilities than non-human animals, but this sort of argument runs into trouble since there are animals that have much higher cognitive abilities (e.g. great apes, dogs, and grey parrots) than some humans (e.g. humans with severe cognitive disabilities).

Others think early embryos have the same moral status as you and me because they have the potential to develop into people like you and me. Because they would – if all goes well – normally develop into a person, we should already treat them as such.[3]

This type of argument – often called the 'potentiality argument' – also runs into trouble. Acorns are not oak trees, nor are eggs chickens or, for that matter, omelettes. Just because something has the potential to become something different, it does not follow that we should treat it as if it had already realised that potential. Unless and until we achieve immortality, all of us share one important and inexorable potential: we are all potentially dead – but it does not follow that we must be treated as though we are already dead.[4]

Another problem with the potentiality argument is its scope. If the human embryo has the potential to become a human being and has full moral status as a result, then every other cell or group of cells with the same potential must be assigned equal moral status.[5] Since reproductive cloning in mammals became possible, every one of our skin cells could potentially develop into a person. (Cloning involves the reprogramming of a body cell to an embryonic state. The embryo-clone can then develop into a full-grown organism.) If we believe that anything with the potential to become a person should be treated as if it were already a person, then we are committing mass murder (or at least manslaughter) when we scratch our arm, as millions of potential human beings – our skin cells – will fall on the floor and never become children.

There's also a larger problem. Regardless of why some people might want to accord full moral status to early embryos, doing so has implausible implications, as illustrated by the following hypothetical scenario.

> Laboratory Fire: Scientists have created a thousand embryos in the laboratory to use for research. The embryos are being kept in a nitrogen freezer in a university research centre. One night, a fire breaks out there. This fire is threatening the lives of the embryos, but also that of an employee who is working late. As a firefighter, you are faced with a choice: either you can drag the freezer outside to rescue the thousand embryos, or you can rescue the employee. You cannot do both.

What would you do? Most people intuitively think you should rescue the employee. However, if embryos have the same moral status as you and me, you should drag the freezer outside as, all else being equal, it is better to save a thousand persons than to save one.

This thought experiment illustrates that the idea that embryos have full moral status is incompatible with commonly held intuitions.[6] Perhaps this is not in itself sufficient to show that embryos are not persons, but it does make the claim less credible.

Ascribing personhood to early embryos also has implausible implications in real-life cases. It has been estimated that miscarriage (between conception and the eighth week of pregnancy) kills 30 times more people (if embryos and foetuses are people) than cancer. If embryos have full moral status, then miscarriage is one of the greatest problems of our time and we should exert immense efforts to prevent it. But, though miscarriage is regrettable and often upsetting for the individuals who were expecting a baby, few believe that we should prioritise the prevention of miscarriage in early pregnancy over, say, the prevention and treatment of cancer.[7]

SOME EMBRYO RESEARCH IS ACCEPTABLE

Suppose we give up on the idea that early embryos have full moral status. We could still hold that they have *some* significant moral status. We would not have to hold that they have only instrumental value, like a toaster. Many believe that embryos have a moral status that lies somewhere between that of a person and that of, say, a toaster. They may believe that this moral status gradually increases during pregnancy – and perhaps infancy[8] – until full moral status is attained. Alternatively, they may think that there is some threshold, or a set of thresholds, at which moral status increases until full moral status is acquired; for example, when the foetus starts kicking, or when it is viable outside the womb. Those who hold these views accord what we could call an 'intermediate' moral status to the early embryo, between full moral status and no moral status.

Arguments in favour of the intermediate moral status view are similar to those expressed in defence of the view that embryos have full moral status: although the embryo does not have the same rights, or interests, as an ordinary adult human being, it has *some* moral status either because it is human, or because it has the potential to become a being with full moral status. According to the intermediate moral status view, deliberately destroying embryos for research is always problematic, but sometimes can be justified if the reasons for doing so are strong enough. For example, destroying an embryo may be justified if this is required to produce certain benefits. Animal experiments are sometimes defended in this way. Many people accord an intermediate moral status to monkeys. If monkeys have an intermediate moral status, then there are moral reasons not to kill them deliberately. These reasons can, however, be outweighed by other reasons. Killing monkeys in medical experiments may be defensible if doing so prevents significant harm to a very large number of people and if there are no other, less problematic, ways of conducting the research. However, the development of cosmetics may not provide a sufficient reason to outweigh the deliberate killing of monkeys.

So those who accord an intermediate moral status to early embryos may approve of embryo research when the expected benefits are significant enough, and when there are no other means to achieve the same goals within a reasonable amount of time. But they typically impose other restrictions on embryo research. For example, they often hold that embryo

Katrien Devolder

research should only be done on unwanted embryos that are 'left over' following fertility treatments such as IVF.

UNWANTED IVF EMBRYOS

A woman undergoing IVF receives hormone therapy to stimulate the development and maturation of multiple eggs. After retrieval, the eggs are fertilised with sperm in a petri dish in the laboratory. In most countries where IVF is practised, on average five to ten embryos are produced, one or two of which are transferred to the woman's womb in an attempt to initiate a pregnancy. The remaining embryos are frozen in nitrogen freezers. If an attempt to achieve a pregnancy fails, one or two embryos can be thawed for another attempt. Implanting only one or two embryos at a time reduces the risk of twin or triplet pregnancies. It also means that the woman may be able to try IVF multiple times without having to repeat the hormone therapy and egg retrieval procedure.

Typically individuals or couples embarking on an IVF treatment must indicate one of the following three options for the handling of any embryos that are left over once they have finished with IVF, usually because their wish for a child has been fulfilled: (1) anonymous donation to other infertile couples, (2) donation to scientific research, or (3) letting the embryos perish. The great majority of embryos used for research purposes are unwanted IVF embryos donated for research – as under option (2). I will refer to such embryos as unwanted IVF embryos.[9]

Many people who hold that embryos have intermediate moral status think that it can be acceptable to destroy these unwanted IVF embryos in the course of research. They do not, however, think it is acceptable to destroy embryos created especially for research.

In the remainder of this chapter, I discuss two possible arguments for drawing this distinction, and conclude that neither is convincing.

NOTHING IS LOST

One argument holds that research on unwanted IVF embryos is acceptable since these embryos are never going to be used for reproductive purposes even if not used in research. The thought is that destroying unwanted IVF embryos does not result in any loss that was not going to occur anyway.

Gene Outka, for example, writes that,

> embryos in appreciable numbers have now been discarded or frozen in perpetuity. They will die, unimplanted, in any case. Nothing more will be lost by their becoming subjects of research.[10]

It is then argued that because nothing is lost, and significant benefits are expected to come out of research with unwanted IVF embryos, it is acceptable to conduct such research. This is so, even if embryos have a significant moral status, so that it would normally be unacceptable to conduct destructive research on them. It is further argued that an equivalent argument cannot justify destructive research on embryos created especially for the purpose of research.

An analogue of this argument might work in some cases unrelated to embryo research. Suppose you like furniture made of tropical wood, but believe that it is unethical to fell endangered trees to construct such furniture. One day you discover that an endangered tropical tree in your garden has a terminal disease. After careful consideration, you fell the tree

Katrien Devolder

to make a table. Intuitively, this seems justifiable: though it is perhaps normally unacceptable to fell endangered trees to construct furniture, the tree in your garden was going to die soon in any case, and something good – a beautiful table – comes out of your felling.

But will unwanted IVF embryos die in the same way as the tree? Not really. The tree will die no matter what anyone does; no one can rescue it. But this is not true for unwanted IVF embryos. They are frozen, but still alive. Instead of being used for research, these embryos could remain frozen, or be given out for adoption and carried to term. Accepting destructive research with an unwanted IVF embryo on the grounds that it will die anyway would be like accepting that a researcher who stumbles across an abandoned baby may use this baby in lethal medical research on the basis that it would have died anyway. The correct response in this situation is to care for the baby. Likewise, the alternative to destroying unwanted IVF embryos is to keep them alive and frozen or to give them to others for implantation.[11]

RESPECT

Some argue that using unwanted IVF embryos for research is part of a practice – IVF – that treats the embryo, over the course of its whole life, with respect, whereas using research embryos to obtain stem cells is part of a practice that treats the embryo disrespectfully. The obvious questions that arise are: what is meant by respectful treatment in this context, and how it could be the case that research embryos are not treated with respect, whereas embryos created in the context of IVF but subsequently destroyed in research are?

Some think that embryos created in the course of IVF and then destroyed in the course of research are treated with respect because each embryo, at the time of its creation, had a 'a prospect of implantation'. Each had a chance of being implanted in the woman's womb to create a pregnancy, even those that end up being discarded and perhaps used in research.[12] By contrast, research embryos never had this prospect. From the moment a research embryo comes into existence, it is virtually guaranteed that it will be destroyed in research. After all, that is why it was brought into existence in the first place.

But does this prospect of further development really make a difference? Consider the following scenario. Suppose each time we create a batch of embryos for the purpose of research, we randomly select some for donation to infertile couples who can use it to fulfil their wish for a child. At the time of their creation, each embryo would, then, have the prospect of developing into a baby. This would be true even if we randomly selected only one embryo for use in a reproductive project. If we adopted such a scheme, would we then be treating research embryos with respect? If so, then the only thing we need to do to make the creation and use of embryos for research acceptable is to adopt something like this lottery scheme.[13]

Many think, however, that embryos in the proposed lottery scheme wouldn't be treated with respect. They argue that treating an embryo with respect requires that it is created with the intention to have a child. They reason that the intention with which embryos are created in the course of an IVF treatment is the creation of a child. At the time of the creation of the embryos, it is not known which, if any, of the embryos will become that child. By contrast, embryos created for research are not created with the intention to produce a child.

Even if we organised a lottery like the one just suggested, the intention would not be to create a child, but to advance the field of stem cell research.

But now consider this hypothetical scenario:

> Frozen Babies: Sonya and Steve want a child. Making use of IVF, they produce eight viable embryos, one of which is randomly chosen for transfer to Sonya's uterus. The remaining seven embryos, instead of being cryopreserved, are carried to term by surrogate mothers. After birth, the seven babies are (painlessly) frozen. The reason is that, should something bad happen to Sonya's baby at birth or shortly afterwards, one of the frozen babies can be thawed and given to her. Sonya would thereby be spared from having to undergo the IVF procedure and the pregnancy again. Fortunately, nothing goes wrong. Sonya and Steve do not want more than one baby, and decide to donate the frozen babies to scientific research that involves a process that will kill the babies.

This obviously seems wrong. Though the intention of Sonya and Steve is to have a child, there are two reasons why we would want to say the frozen babies are not treated respectfully. First, Sonya and Steve decide to donate the frozen babies to research instead of giving them a chance to live (for example, by having them adopted). Perhaps Sonya and Steve do not have a choice because, say, there is not enough demand for adoption. But even then, it seems intuitively clear that their actions are disrespectful. Imposing such grave risks on the babies (by creating many more than will likely be needed) is out of proportion to the good effect – preventing or reducing harm to Sonya from the IVF procedure, the pregnancy, and the delivery. Since Frozen Babies is analogous to standard IVF practices, we can conclude that embryos are not treated with respect in these practices either, even though they were created with the intention to bring a child into the world.[14]

Of course, there might be some important differences between Frozen Babies and the case of embryo research using discarded IVF embryos. One difference may be that babies have higher moral status than embryos. Perhaps babies have full moral status. Or perhaps they have an intermediate moral status, but still a higher intermediate moral status than embryos. However, this presents the proponent of the respect argument with a dilemma. On the one hand, she can say that early embryos have high enough moral status that – like babies, and unlike toasters – they should be treated with respect. In that case, discarding IVF embryos seems analogous to Frozen Babies. On the other hand, she can say that early embryos don't need to be treated with respect. But in that case, it's not clear what's wrong with creating embryos for the purposes of research.

CONCLUSION

Embryo research could lead to the development of therapies that will lengthen lives, alleviate suffering, and allow people to better achieve their reproductive goals. Some oppose all embryo research because they believe embryos have full moral status, i.e. the same status as you and me. However, it is difficult to find a good argument in support of this view. Appeals to the fact that embryos are human seem speciesist. Appeals to the potential of the embryo to become a person with full moral status are not sufficient to show that we should already treat the embryo as if it had achieved that potential. Reflecting on the fire in the laboratory example and the real-life case of miscarriage casts further doubt on the position that embryos have full moral status by showing its counter-intuitive implications.

Those who think that the early embryo has an intermediate moral status accept some types of embryo research depending on the origin of the embryo, and the expected research benefit. A common view is that embryo research is acceptable when done on unwanted IVF embryos, but not when done on embryos created especially for research. However, it is very difficult to explain why it is acceptable to destroy unwanted IVF embryos for research but not embryos created for research. The idea that nothing is lost when using unwanted IVF embryos is unconvincing, as something is lost (the life of the embryo that could perhaps have been 'adopted out'). Nor is it clear why using unwanted IVF embryos for research treats embryos more respectfully than embryos created for the purpose of research.

Opponents of (some types of) embryo research need to come up with better arguments to support their position. Alternatively, they could accord no moral status to early embryos. But in that case, embryo research is no more problematic than research on other kinds of simple organisms or cells.

NOTES

1 Nicholas Tonti-Filippini, 'The Catholic Church and Reproductive Technology', in *Bioethics: An Anthology*, edited by H. Kuhse and P. Singer (Oxford: Blackwell, 1999), 93–95.

2 Peter Singer, 'Speciesism and Moral Status', *Metaphilosophy*, 40, 3–4 (2009): 567–581.

3 Helen Watt, 'Potential and the Early Human', *Journal of Medical Ethics*, 22 (1996), 222–226.

4 Katrien Devolder and John Harris, 'The Ambiguity of the Embryo: Ethical Inconsistency in the Human Embryonic Stem Cell Debate', *Metaphilosophy*, 28, 2–3 (2007), 153–169.

5 David B. Annis, 'Abortion and the Potentiality Principle', *Southern Journal of Philosophy*, 22 (1984), 155–163.

6 George J. Annas, 'A French Homunculus in a Tennessee Court', *Hastings Center Report*, 19 (1989), 20–22; Matthew S. Liao, 'The Embryo Rescue Case', *Theoretical Medicine and Bioethics*, 27 (2006), 141–147.

7 Leonard M. Fleck, 'Abortion, Deformed Fetuses, and the Omega Pill', *Philosophical Studies*, 36 (1979), 271–283; Toby Ord, 'The Scourge: Moral Implications of Natural Embryo Loss', *American Journal of Bioethics*, 8 (2008), 12–19.

8 Alberto Giubilini and Francesca Minerva, 'After-Birth Abortion: Why Should the Baby Live?', *Journal of Medical Ethics*, 39, 5 (2013): 261–263.

9 Tom Douglas and Julian Savulescu, 'Destroying Unwanted Embryos in Research. Talking Point on Morality and Human Embryo Research', *EMBO Reports*, 10, 4 (2009), 307–312.

10 Gene Outka, 'The Ethics of Embryonic Stem Cell Research and the Principle of Nothing Is Lost', *Yale Journal of Health Policy Law & Ethics*, 9 (2009), 585–602, 596.

11 Dan W. Brock, 'Creating Embryos for Use in Stem Cell Research', *Journal of Law and Medical Ethics*, 38 (2010), 229–237.

12 The House of Lords, *Select Committee on Stem Cell Research. Stem Cell Research – Report*. (London: The House of Lords, 2002), Ch. 4, S. 4.27.

13 John Harris and Julian Savulescu have referred to similar lotteries. John Harris, 'Survival Lottery', in *Bioethics*, edited by John Harris (New York: Oxford University Press, 2001), 300–315; Julian Savulescu, 'The Embryonic Stem Cell Lottery and The Cannibalization of Human Beings', *Bioethics*, 16 (2002), 508–529.

14 Katrien Devolder, *The Ethics of Embryonic Stem Cell Research* (Oxford: Oxford University Press, 2015), Ch. 2.

Twenty

Francesca Minerva

AN UNEXPECTED CALL FROM THE GOOD
SAMARITAN HOSPITAL

One day you receive a call from a number you don't recognise. You answer the phone and from the other end of the phone a voice says:

> Good morning! I am calling from the Good Samaritan Hospital. We selected you among hundreds of thousands of people on the basis of a complicated algorithmic analysis combining information about your DNA, medical history, height, weight, age, and numerous other factors. We now need you in order to save the life of one of our patients.

You are taken by surprise. Of course you're happy to help, you say; you've been a blood donor for a decade and have even considered becoming a bone marrow donor.
The voice replies:

> I'm glad to hear that, but actually, what we need is not a blood or bone marrow donation. We need something more unusual – to grow a new intestine from stem cells for a patient in a desperate situation. We will put the

stem cells in a sack made of human tissues and implant this sack in your body. With our advanced technology, the new intestine will develop over nine months. After that time, we will remove the sack and transfer the intestine into the body of our patient. The whole process is unlikely to cause you more than discomfort; the final weight won't be over 3 kilos. We need you to come to the hospital today. The intestine of our patient is deteriorating quickly. If you don't help, she will surely die.[1]

THE RIGHT TO LIFE AND THE RIGHT TO BODILY AUTONOMY

You're very unlikely ever to receive a call like this. However, some people would argue that this hypothetical case is not fundamentally different from the real and common one of women who get unwillingly pregnant. In both cases, there is a person who finds herself in the situation of having to decide whether to allow the use of her body for nine months, and at a certain personal cost, in order to save a life.

The imaginary Good Samaritan Hospital helps to test intuitions about the ethical conflict between a right to life and a right to bodily autonomy. Abortion is more complex than the Good Samaritan Hospital dilemma for several reasons. These include the differences between a human foetus and a grown-up person, some specific aspects of pregnancy, and the uniqueness of the relationship between a foetus and the woman who carries it. We will consider any moral implications that might derive from these differences shortly. But for the sake of argument, let's assume for now that such differences are not relevant. If these differences *are* irrelevant, would it be permissible to refuse to help the patient?

Some philosophers have argued that your right to bodily autonomy – the right to decide what can and cannot be done to or with your body – should trump the right to life of the hospital patient (and, presumably, that of the foetus in the womb). This view also implies that a right to life does not entail a corresponding duty to save someone, if this comes at the cost of bodily autonomy.[2]

Other philosophers have argued, on the contrary, that the right to life should trump a right to bodily autonomy. Hence it would be wrong for you to refuse to help the patient, and it is at least *prima facie* wrong for women to have an abortion.[3]

Those who think that abortion is not morally permissible claim that a human embryo/foetus has the same right to life as a fully developed person like you and me and the patient at the Good Samaritan Hospital. According to so-called pro-lifers, for example, abortion is impermissible because it is the killing of an innocent human being and, they argue, killing innocent human beings is allowed only in exceptional circumstances (in some cases of self-defence, or when it is the unavoidable and unintended side effect of an action aimed at a great good).[4]

On the other hand, people who think that abortion is permissible (so-called pro-choicers) argue in one of two main ways. First, there are those who argue that the foetus has a right to life, but this right is trumped by a right to bodily autonomy. If one thinks that the right to bodily autonomy always trumps a right to life, then abortion doesn't pose any particularly difficult issue. But, second, some pro-choicers argue that abortion is permissible because the embryo/foetus doesn't have a right to life. Indeed, central to the abortion debate is the moral status of the foetus.

HUMAN FOETUSES ARE HUMANS

Imagine that you receive that phone call from the Good Samaritan Hospital, with one difference. The patient who needs your help is a cow. How would the patient not being human affect your duty to help?

Some philosophers argue that humans, including the ones at the beginning of their development, such as the embryo and the foetus, have a right to life merely in virtue of their being human; that is, in virtue of being members of the human species. According to certain religious views, in particular, humans have a right to life from conception because they are made in the image of God and God has given them a special place among living creatures.[5] Even though this view provides people with a clear answer about the morality of abortion, it won't necessarily convince the non-religious. Critics of this view say it is "speciesist." Merely being human, they say, is not a sufficient condition for granting a right to life. Claiming that humans are morally special merely because they are human is arbitrary (as arbitrary as racists who claim one race is superior to another).[6]

HUMAN FOETUSES AND CAPACITIES

Another possible explanation for why human foetuses have a right to life is based on the idea that a right to life depends not on individuals being members of the human species *per se*, but on their having certain *capacities*. And indeed, humans are capable of performing many more complex cognitive tasks than other animals.

Which cognitive capacities are morally relevant for the right to life? That is not easy to answer – and experts disagree. Suggestions include consciousness, sentience, the presence of self-concepts (e.g. the capacity to understand oneself as the subject of experiences) and self-awareness (e.g. the capacity to understand oneself as an individual separated from the environment), the capacity to reason, to communicate, and to engage in self-motivated activity (e.g. the capacity to act coherently with one's goals),[7] and the capacity to understand oneself as a continuing object of experiences (that is, the capacity to understand that we are the same subject of our past, present, and future experiences).[8]

Among these capacities, that of feeling pain (being sentient) is the one that seems to attract most consensus. There is no scientific consensus as to when exactly foetuses develop the capacity to feel pain, although this is very unlikely to occur before the 23rd week. Many people have the intuition that inflicting pain is wrong, and also that killing is bad because it inflicts pain. However, killing someone and inflicting pain on them are not necessarily the same. If you can feel pain, you may have a *prima facie* right that others not inflict pain upon you. But it is not obvious that merely having the capacity to experience pain is sufficient for having a right to life.

Why not? Well, many people believe that animals can experience pain and yet that they have no right to life. The same people who think that abortion is immoral because it entails the (painless) killing of an entity capable of experiencing pain, namely the foetus, do not object to the painless killing of cows, and regularly buy pieces of dead cows at the supermarket (indeed, even when they know that the cows have not been killed painlessly). These people do not appear to think the capacity to feel pain is morally relevant when applied to animals. Perhaps they are ill-informed, and don't know that animals feel pain. Or perhaps they don't regard non-human suffering as equivalent to human suffering. That, however, would open them up to the charge of speciesism. So it would seem to follow that we cannot attribute to the foetus a right to life on account of it being able to feel pain, unless we're also willing to accept animals have a right to life, too, and it is immoral to kill them.

But what about the other capacities mentioned earlier? The capacity to reason, to communicate, to engage in self-motivated-activity, or to understand ourselves as a continuing object of experiences seem to do a better job at capturing what humans are and to explain why humans and not animals might have a right to life: after all, these are all peculiarly human capacities. However, there are problems with linking a right to life to these capacities, and even greater problems with linking a right to life of the foetus to such capacities.

First, there is the issue of when such capacities are sufficiently present in human development. All these capacities develop progressively; it is difficult to tell whether one has them at a low degree or not at all. We cannot tell, for instance, at which point children actually start reasoning.

Second, counter-intuitive conclusions follow from this view. There are humans who never develop certain capacities or who lose them at some point during their lives. These individuals lack certain relevant capacities in the same way as a crab, a dog, a foetus, and a new-born lack them. Must we therefore conclude that the severely mentally disabled, for example, have no right to life? This inference seems hard to swallow.

Third, to return to the abortion debate, at least some – if not all – of these capacities are developed *after* someone is born, an implication that would make not only abortion permissible at any point during the pregnancy, but also infanticide a few months *after* birth.[9]

One possible way to avoid these counter-intuitive conclusions is to attribute a right to life not only to individuals who have developed certain capacities, but also to ones who have the potential to develop them.

HUMAN FOETUSES AND POTENTIAL

Imagine now that the phone call from the Good Samaritan Hospital presents a different dilemma: you can choose whether to save a human foetus or a dog. Neither the foetus nor the dog has the capacity to, say, reason or communicate. However, there is an important difference: the foetus has the potential to develop those capacities that some consider essential in order to be attributed a right to life. On the other hand, dogs don't have nor will they develop some or even any of these capacities. Their cognitive development is way more limited than that of humans. Some philosophers argue that your choice should be to save the foetus, because of its *potential* to become someone with a right to life.[10]

However, there is arguably a morally relevant difference between having a capacity, property, or right, and having the potential to develop such a capacity, property, or right. Consider this example: ten years ago, Meghan Markle had the potential to become a Duchess (as she ended up becoming). However, had she shown up at Buckingham Palace asking to move in and be treated as a royal, her request would have not been considered reasonable. She didn't have the right to be treated as a royal just because she had the potential to become a royal. So just because a foetus has the potential to become the subject of a right to life by developing certain salient capacities, it is not clear that it already has a right to life.

HUMAN FOETUSES AND THEIR FUTURE LIFE

According to Don Marquis, what makes death bad to grown-ups is the loss of the future.[11] The reason it would be bad if the human patient at the Good Samaritan Hospital died is that she would miss the opportunity to enjoy many years of future life. According to Marquis, abortion is bad because foetuses have "a future like ours," in that, if they were not aborted, they would go on to experience things just like fully developed human beings. And even though foetuses do not have the cognitive skills to value their future life, they will nevertheless come to value such future life. Most people alive today probably think "I am glad I am alive, and that my life was not cut short at any point, including when I was a foetus." Marquis argues it would be wrong to deprive an embryo or a foetus of a future like ours by aborting them, just as it would be wrong to deprive me of my future by killing me.

The problem with this view is that there is no subject with the capacity to attribute a value to their own future, precisely because the embryo/foetus is insufficiently developed to value its future. It is difficult to make sense of the claim that you are harming a person by preventing her from coming into existence, because the thought "I am happy that I was not aborted as a foetus" is only available to those who do exist, while the thought "I wish I had not been aborted" is not available to anyone.[12]

THE SUBJECTIVE EXPERIENCE OF PREGNANCY

So far, we have discussed the alleged right to life of foetuses. However, some argue that other considerations ought to be taken into account when assessing the ethics of abortion.

Pregnancy, they say, is relevantly different from the Good Samaritan Hospital case. The issue is not only whether a foetus has a right to life, but whether the burden imposed on the woman to carry the foetus is reasonable.

One problem with pregnancy is that it is difficult to establish how onerous it is. People evaluate the same experience in very different ways (think of the last time you went to the cinema and loved the movie, while your friend, sitting next to you and watching the exact same movie, found it insufferably dull). Different past experiences, different genetic predispositions and the circumstances we find ourselves in at a given moment can alter how we perceive something.

Moreover, a pregnancy might affect the body and the psychological wellbeing of the pregnant woman in completely different ways. For some women, it might be an overall positive experience, and for others an extremely fraught and painful one. There are psychological, social, and individual elements that make each pregnancy a unique journey, a journey which, according to some, each woman should be entitled to decide whether to embark upon or not.[13]

THE FOETUS-WOMAN RELATIONSHIP

Some philosophers have argued that pregnancy is a unique condition, and the relationship between a pregnant woman and the foetus cannot be exhaustively described as the relationship between a person who needs support to live and a person who is in the position to provide such support. In other words, it is not analogous to the Good Samaritan Hospital.

In particular, many women feel more responsible towards a foetus (and the child that could develop from it) than they could possibly feel toward a stranger. Bringing someone into existence entails a whole new level of responsibility. A woman might want to have an abortion because she fears the prospective child won't have a good enough life, or because she lacks economic resources, or because the foetus is affected by a congenital abnormality. Of course, one could always give up the prospective child for adoption, but a woman might be worried about the possible negative outcomes of relinquishing her own child to strangers;[14] she might therefore consider that abortion is a better option than adoption. If one thinks that life is always better than not existing at all, then such concerns are not good reasons to have an abortion. But if a woman believes quality of life should be above a certain threshold, then it makes sense for her to consider whether it would be better to bring a prospective child into existence or to have an abortion.

CONCLUSION

Disagreements about the ethics of abortion partly revolve around empirical matters, and partly around philosophical ones. Some empirical disagreements might one day be resolved – for example, if we find a way to measure levels of self-awareness in foetuses. But the main disagreements are philosophical. Whether a foetus should have a right to life, which cognitive capacities are linked to the right to life, and whether a right to life should entail a duty to sacrifice one's bodily autonomy, are not questions we can hope to determine with science. These are questions that philosophers are called upon to answer. We need to keep thinking about abortion with an open mind, including when we discuss abortion with people with an opposing opinion. The more we reflect upon possible arguments and counter-arguments, the more likely we are finally to find the truth.

NOTES

1 This hypothetical case is inspired by another famous hypothetical case, which was developed by J. J. Thomson in 1971. She described a woman who is asked to stay connected to a famous pianist for nine months in order to keep him alive until he recovers from an illness.
2 Thomson (1971).
3 Fischer (2013).
4 Pope John Paul II (1995).
5 Pope John Paul II (1995).
6 Singer (1975).
7 Warren (1973).
8 Tooley (1972).
9 Giubilini and Minerva (2013).
10 Reichlin (2007).
11 Marquis (1989).
12 Giubilini (2012).
13 Sherwin (1991).
14 Reader (2008).

REFERENCES

Fischer, J. M. 2013. Abortion and ownership. *The Journal of Ethics*, 17(4), pp. 275–304.

Giubilini, A. 2012. Abortion and the argument from potential: What we owe to the ones who might exist. *Journal of Medicine and Philosophy*, 37(1), pp. 49–59.

Giubilini, A. and Minerva, F. 2013. After-birth abortion: Why should the baby live? *Journal of Medical Ethics*, 39(5), pp. 261–263.

Marquis, D. 1989. Why abortion is immoral. *Journal of Philosophy*, 86, pp. 183–202.

Pope John Paul II (1978–2005: John Paul II) and Paul II, P.J., 1995. Evangelium vitae (p. 60). St. Louis Review.

Reader, S. 2008. Abortion, killing, and maternal moral authority. *Hypatia*, 23, pp. 132–149.

Reichlin, M. 2007. *Aborto. La morale oltre il diritto*. Rome: Carocci Editore.

Sherwin, S. 1991. *No Longer Patient*. Philadelphia: Temple University Press.

Singer, P. 1975. *Animal Liberation*. Sydney: Random House.

Thomson, J. J. 1971. A defense of abortion. *Philosophy and Public Affairs*, 1, pp. 47–66.

Tooley, M. 1972. Abortion and infanticide. *Philosophy and Public Affairs*, 2, pp. 37–65.

Warren, M. A. 1973. On the moral and legal status of abortion. *The Monist*, 57, pp. 43–61.

FURTHER READINGS

Boonin, D. 2003. *A Defense of Abortion*. Cambridge: Cambridge University Press.

Twenty One

Dominic Wilkinson

CASE

Jacob has lived a long and happy life.

He has had general good health, and has been active, and energetic, enjoying outdoor activities and long walks in the countryside near his home. He has several children and grandchildren and has always been very close to his family, with whom he lives. In recent months, though, Jacob's health has been in decline. His eyesight is failing and he has arthritis that makes it difficult for him to walk. Last week, concerned about weight loss, confusion, and fatigue, Jacob's family took him to see a specialist. To their sadness and shock, Jacob was diagnosed with metastatic cancer. Scans revealed that he had cancer in his liver, bones, and brain. The specialist performed some further tests, but she was not optimistic that treatment would help Jacob. This week, Jacob has been unable to walk, he has become incontinent and jaundiced. The specialist informs Jacob's family that he does not have long to live. They are devastated by this news, but resolve immediately that they do not wish him to suffer. It is impossible to know what Jacob would want, but the family feel that, since he is in pain and no longer able to appreciate and enjoy the things that he loved, it would be wrong to prolong his dying. With their agreement, the specialist draws up and administers a large intravenous dose of barbiturate. Jacob loses consciousness quickly, stops breathing, and is certified as dead a few minutes later.

Euthanasia in cases like that of Jacob occurs commonly, is seen as good practice, and is generally thought to be uncontroversial.

But of course, Jacob is not human. He is a much-loved Labrador. If he were human, the actions described above would be illegal, and viewed by many as morally outrageous.

Why is it that animal euthanasia is regarded as the epitome of compassion and mercy, but human euthanasia is seen as dangerous and unethical?

LANGUAGE

Before we analyse the ethical arguments, it is important to be clear about terminology. There are various terms that are used to refer to different practices around the end of life (see Box 21.1). Understanding the definitions is important to prevent misunderstanding. It is also important to recognise that some of the key terms contain implicit value judgements. For example, "putting to sleep" (often used for animal euthanasia) implies that it is kind to end a life, while "murder" implies wrongful or illegal killing (and is usually reserved for humans). If we want to debate whether ending someone's life could be either a good thing, or alternatively would be wrong, it would be ideal to use a neutral term. In fact, even the word "euthanasia" could be seen as loaded since it literally means a "good death," from Greek eu- (good, or happy) and thanatos (death). The box includes various different subtypes. In this chapter, for the most part, I am going to consider Euthanasia/Assisted Suicide together (and use the acronym EAS for short).

Box 21.1 Key terms

Killing: To intentionally cause the death of someone.
Euthanasia: To intentionally cause or permit the death of someone, for their sake.

> *Passive euthanasia*: To withhold or stop medical treatment that could prolong someone's life. (Other terms: letting die, allowing to die). For example, stopping life support.
>
> *Active euthanasia*: To take active steps with the intention of causing someone to die. (Other terms: deliberate ending of life, mercy killing). For example, giving a lethal injection.
>
> *Voluntary euthanasia*: Euthanasia at the request of a conscious and mentally competent patient (subtypes: voluntary active euthanasia, voluntary passive euthanasia).
>
> *Non-voluntary euthanasia*: Euthanasia performed for a patient who is not conscious or mentally competent.
>
> *Involuntary euthanasia*: Euthanasia performed for a conscious and mentally competent patient despite their request to continue to live. (Many people would not classify this as "euthanasia" – rather as a form of wrongful killing.)

Suicide: To intentionally cause your own death.

> *Assisted suicide*: To help someone to end their own life.
>
> *Physician-assisted suicide*: A doctor provides medical assistance to a patient to take their own life. (Other terms: medically assisted dying.) For example, prescribing a drug, which the patient administers to themselves.

EAS for humans is hotly debated. Many countries (e.g., UK, USA, Canada, Australia) have had active public and political debates about this practice. Do the usual arguments around euthanasia help us to understand why this would be ethically unproblematic in animals but contentious or forbidden in humans?

ARGUMENTS IN FAVOUR OF EUTHANASIA/ASSISTED SUICIDE

Autonomy

One of the strongest arguments in favour of allowing EAS is that this would respect someone's freedom. In medical ethics, the concept or principle of "autonomy" refers to the importance of allowing mentally competent adults to make decisions about their own lives. It is usually thought to be a problem if doctors claim that they know what would be best and perform medical interventions without a patient's consent or against their wishes (this is a form of "paternalism"). What is best for the individual will depend on their own values, on what is most important to them. It isn't going to be the same for everyone, so there is good reason to think that doctors don't always know what would be best for individual patients. Moreover, even if doctors are correct that a patient is making a poor choice, we usually think that they have a right to do so. People are free to make mistakes and bad choices – that is what freedom entails. It is reasonable for the doctor to try to persuade a patient, but it would be wrong to coerce, or force, a choice on the patient.

More broadly, it is seen to be wrong for the state to interfere in an individual's life for their own benefit. (It would be justified to limit individual freedom to prevent harm to others, but we will return to that later.)

Arguably, the decision about whether to continue to live, about whether life still has value, is the most important decision that anyone could make. It is, correspondingly, the most important freedom.

However, the autonomy argument in favour of EAS seems to favour euthanasia in humans rather than animals. It might be important to respect animals' freedom or autonomy (for example, by not caging them, restricting their habitat, or forcing them to perform demeaning or unpleasant acts). However, even if we accept that this is important, it doesn't apply to ending animal lives. Animals do not appear to choose to end their own lives, or decide that their life is no longer worth living.[1]

Finally, it is often thought that if EAS is to be permitted, the safest forms would be voluntary active euthanasia or assisted suicide. Non-voluntary euthanasia is usually thought to be more ethically challenging. Yet, non-voluntary euthanasia is the only form of EAS that is an option in non-human animals.

Beneficence

The second argument that is usually cited in favour of euthanasia is that in some circumstances, someone's remaining life would be so unpleasant, so distressing, that it would be bad for them to continue to live. It would be better for them to die sooner rather than later. Instances of severe physical and mental suffering appear to provide a powerful case in favour of ending life. Discussions about the ethics of EAS often include examples of patients with severe illness and overwhelming symptoms despite best available medical treatment.

This is the type of concern that motivated the specialist in Jacob's case to recommend euthanasia. But in some ways, the argument is even stronger for human euthanasia. First, it can be difficult to know how much an animal is suffering. That can be a problem, too, for humans with advanced illness (if they are no longer able to communicate). However, in many cases, it will be possible for them to tell doctors what they are experiencing. They can explain whether they are in pain, where they are in pain, how bad it is, in a way that animals can't. Second, humans will usually be able to communicate whether their negative experiences outweigh the positives. It was impossible to know how Jacob's pain compared with any pleasure or comfort he was experiencing from the presence and care of family members. Third, humans may anticipate and fear future suffering in a way that animals do not. A human with advanced malignancy may know that they are dying. They may have reason to fear continued unpleasant and distressing experiences until the end of their life. Greater understanding of illness and mortality might lead to more distress in a terminally ill human. (Though, in other circumstances, greater understanding might reduce someone's fear and lead to less psychological anguish than an animal with a similar illness.)

Some people deny that it could be a benefit to die. They might, for example, claim that it is not possible to compare a state of non-existence to existence. Death could not be better for someone than living, since, once they are dead, they will no longer exist. Or alternatively, they might argue that life itself has intrinsic value, which means that it is always better to live than to die. However, both of these arguments could apply equally to animal life and death. They would seem to rule out euthanasia for the Labrador Jacob as well as for humans with advanced illness. Someone might claim that only human life is intrinsically valuable – perhaps because it is a gift from God. However, such religious arguments do not appear to provide a reason to stop someone with a different religion, or no religion, from choosing euthanasia. They also seem to rule out passive euthanasia – stopping or withholding forms of life support, which is widely accepted and practised throughout the world.

Consistency

There are several different forms of a consistency argument in favour of EAS.

One consistency argument draws an analogy between passive and active forms of euthanasia. If Jacob were human, it is widely accepted that doctors could decide not to resuscitate him if his heart were to stop. If he had ended up in life support in hospital, it would be deemed ethical for doctors to switch off the breathing machines keeping him alive. It seems to many that it would be at least equally ethical to give him an injection to end his life. Whether he dies from injection or from having his breathing machine turned off can make no difference to Jacob. (Active euthanasia might, in fact, be preferable, since it could significantly reduce his suffering.)

Doctors already make decisions to provide passive euthanasia in gravely ill patients. To be ethically consistent, they should arguably also be prepared to provide active euthanasia in similar circumstances. But this argument applies equally to animals and humans. Passive euthanasia is accepted in both. There isn't any obvious reason to think that we should distinguish active from passive euthanasia in humans, but not in animals.

Another consistency argument is that in many countries around the world, suicide is legal. There are good reasons to try to prevent suicide, and to treat those who are suicidal as a result of mental illness. However, we no longer think that individuals should be prosecuted or imprisoned if they attempt to end their lives. It seems unfair, though, to have a situation where some people with severe physical disability (who cannot kill themselves) are effectively denied this choice. It may also be preferable and safer for some patients to have access to medical assistance in dying. This could prevent them from using techniques that are traumatic to themselves or family members, as well as potentially allowing health professionals to identify and treat physical or psychological symptoms that were contributing to the desire to die.

As with autonomy earlier, this consistency argument applies only to humans, and so strengthens the case for EAS in humans, but not animals.

So the principal arguments in support of EAS are actually more compelling for human than animal euthanasia. But what about the opposing arguments?

ARGUMENTS AGAINST EUTHANASIA/ASSISTED SUICIDE

Palliative care

It is sometimes claimed that modern palliative care makes EAS unnecessary. Palliative care is a medical specialty that provides holistic care and symptom relief for patients whose illnesses are not able to be cured. It can substantially relieve distressing symptoms and improve the quality of life of patients with chronic and terminal illnesses. If patients have access to this sort of treatment, they may no longer desire to die.[2]

However, if it were true that palliative care could relieve all unpleasant symptoms of dying patients, there would be no need for animal euthanasia. The techniques and expertise of palliative specialists could be used for animals, too. Imagine, for example, that Jacob's specialist offered to connect him to a morphine pump and provide a nurse to come and check on him each day. Jacob's family might decide to decline the option of euthanasia in that case. Alternatively, they might feel that this would be the wrong thing to do. Jacob might still have some discomfort at times, and would seem to gain little benefit from staying alive. Many people would, I suspect, feel that it should at least be an option to actively euthanise a dying animal, even if palliative care were available.

Incompatible with professional role

One common argument against EAS in humans is that actively ending life is contrary to the core ethical values and norms of being a doctor. In the words of 19th-century physician Edward Trudeau (founder of a tuberculosis sanatorium), doctors should "cure sometimes, relieve often, comfort always"; some would add to this: "but kill never."

However, it is unclear why those core values apply to doctors and not to veterinarians. It seems curious that ending life could be compatible with the profession of animal doctors, but not with the profession of human doctors. Even if as a matter of history, doctors have traditionally refrained from actively ending life, the norms of a profession can change. (After all, the original Hippocratic oath contained an injunction against surgery – forbidding "cutting for stone.")

Harming the vulnerable

Perhaps the most compelling arguments against EAS are those that express concern for patients who are vulnerable. One concern is that if EAS is permitted, patients who are disabled, elderly or chronically ill may be coerced into requesting assistance in dying. Alternatively, such patients may feel that the availability of EAS expresses a view that their lives are not worth living and suffer psychological distress as a result. Or they may be led to request EAS because they do not wish to be a burden on others.

These sorts of concern would not apply to animal euthanasia. Animals do not request aid in dying and cannot be coerced. Nor do they decide to die because they are worried about being a burden on others. Nor would they understand that other animals were being euthanised and be distressed as a result.

A related concern is that even if EAS were defensible in some circumstances (for example, at the request of a suffering competent patient with a terminal illness), in practice it would lead to EAS in other, much more troubling, situations. For example, voluntary active euthanasia in adults might be extended to adolescents or children. Allowing voluntary euthanasia now might lead later to laws permitting non-voluntary euthanasia.

These slippery slope concerns are relevant for humans, but do not obviously apply to animal euthanasia. For one thing, non-human animals are already killed for a wide range of reasons. Some animals are killed for entertainment, food, or medical research. Even companion animals like Labradors may be killed if they have bitten a child, are unwanted, or their medical care is deemed too expensive.[3]

Where does this leave us? Most of the arguments in the debates around EAS do not support the view that animal euthanasia is ethically less of a problem than human euthanasia. The arguments either apply *equally* to human and animal euthanasia, or they suggest that human euthanasia (at least the voluntary active form) may be easier to defend than animal euthanasia. Concerns about harm to others (particularly those who are vulnerable) *do* seem to apply more forcefully against human euthanasia. However, this does not necessarily mean that human euthanasia should be prohibited. That will depend on how likely these harms are, how severe they are, and how we weigh those harms against the harms of continued suffering, or restricted liberty for people who do not wish to live. It will depend on whether we think that safeguards that could be built in to policy are enough to mitigate or prevent those harms.

MORAL DIFFERENCE BETWEEN ANIMALS AND HUMANS

However, to return to the case of Jacob, one argument that we haven't considered is whether there is an inherent moral difference between a Labrador and a human. Maybe killing is a much bigger deal for a human than for a dog. Indeed, for many people, that is obviously true. Human beings have a strong right to life, which means that it is a serious moral wrong to kill them. Humans also, typically, have a strong interest in their future life – they have plans for their future, goals or dreams, relationships with others, a desire to go on living. All of these mean that it is a serious harm to them to die.

Those considerations do not necessarily apply to non-human animals. As a matter of law (though not necessarily of ethics), animals are usually thought not to have a strong right to life.[4] They may not have plans, goals, relationships, or desires that would be curtailed if they died. Correspondingly, it may not be a harm, or at least it may be less of a harm, for them to die.

However, at least when we think about the situation of a terminally ill human or a beloved companion animal like Jacob, it isn't clear that there is such a great moral difference between them. Jacob is a central part of a loving family. Their attachment to him may be just as strong as (or possibly even stronger than) their attachment to other family members.[5] If Jacob isn't really dying (imagine, for example, that the vet has negligently mixed up his test results), it would be, I suggest, a serious moral wrong for Jacob to be euthanised. That would be a terrible thing, both for Jacob and his family. On the other hand, a human with a terminal illness who has only a short time to live, and who is suffering substantially, may not have a strong interest in continuing to live. Indeed, in some circumstances, it could be a lesser harm for them to die.

It just isn't clear that if their medical condition were the same it would be worse for a doctor to provide active euthanasia to a human than to Jacob. Indeed, as I have argued, given that a human could express their own views, communicate how much (or how little) they are suffering, and understand the nature and outcome of their illness, the opposite may be true. There may be a stronger ethical argument for allowing EAS for a human with terminal illness than an animal with the same condition.

Ethicists and philosophers have often pointed to the worrying ways in which non-human animals are treated much worse than they should – they are regularly abused, and exploited. There are strong ethical arguments in favour of radically changing and improving the way that we treat animals.

However, whether or not animals are accorded rights previously reserved for humans, one question worth asking is whether humans might one day be granted a right currently usually reserved for non-humans. For people who are dying and suffering (and particularly if they have indicated that this is their wish), why are they denied the option of a rapid peaceful end to their life? After all (in the words of a famous Depression-era novel, and later film), "They shoot horses, don't they?"[6]

NOTES

1 Hogenboom (2016).
2 It isn't clear that provision of good palliative care does relieve all symptoms (Quill 1998). Some (human) patients request assistance in dying even with provision of high quality palliative care (Al-Awamer 2015).
3 Some might be tempted to argue in the other direction – that animal killing for these other reasons shows what might happen if human euthanasia is permitted. However, that would be a mistake. There is no reason to think that the modern practice of animal euthanasia has contributed to acceptance of other forms of animal killing.
4 A number of philosophers have argued that at least some non-human animals have a right to life, e.g. Regan (1983).
5 Reisbig et al. (2017).
6 The novel by this name, by Horace McCoy, was published in 1935. The film of the same name was released in 1969.

REFERENCES

Al-Awamer, A. 2015. "Physician-assisted suicide is not a failure of palliative care." *Can Fam Physician* 61(12): 1045–1047.
Hogenboom, M. 2016. "Many animals seem to kill themselves but it is not suicide." *BBC Earth*, 6 July 2016. www.bbc.co.uk/earth/story/20160705-many-animals-seem-to-kill-themselves-but-it-is-not-suicide

Quill, T. E. 1998. "Principle of double effect and end-of-life pain management: Additional myths and a limited role." *J Palliat Med* 1(4): 333–336. doi:10.1089/jpm.1998.1.333.

Regan, T. 1983. *The case for animal rights.* London: Routledge, 1988.

Reisbig, A. M. J., M. Hafen, Jr., A. A. Siqueira Drake, D. Girard, and Z. B. Breunig. 2017. "Companion animal death." *Omega (Westport)* 75(2): 124–150. doi:10.1177/0030222815612607.

Twenty Two

Jeff McMahan

When I was a child, I ate whatever food my mother served me. My only concern was whether I liked it; I was incurious about what it was or where it came from. I lived in the American South. When I was 12, my family moved to a rural area and I was given a shotgun. Over the next four years, until I resolved to stop, I killed as many game birds as I could. I would decapitate, pluck, and gut those I killed, and give the little parcels of flesh to my mother to cook for the family. When I shot a dove, duck, or quail, it would usually be dead when it plummeted to earth with a thud. But occasionally it would still be alive, perhaps having suffered only a broken wing, and would flap and flutter across the ground in a futile effort to evade me. I assume there must have been instances in which one or two pellets hit a bird that was nevertheless able to continue to fly and thus escaped me, though perhaps only to die later from the wound I had inflicted.

When I reflect on this, it is scarcely credible to me that I took pleasure in sending metal pellets ripping through the bodies of sentient beings going harmlessly about their own lives. Yet this was a morally less bad way of obtaining meat than that which is usual for the vast majority of meat eaters. The birds I ate had lived their lives in the wild and, with rare exceptions, suffered only briefly, if at all.

Most of the meat consumed in economically developed societies is from animals raised in factory farms. In these 'farms', the animals are tightly packed into filthy, stifling, indoor spaces, and thus suffer more or less continuous physical and psychological torment throughout their entire lives. When they reach full size, pumped with antibiotics because of the unsanitary conditions in which they are kept, they suffer a final period of panic and terror as they are mass-slaughtered, often in mechanized, assembly-line fashion.

Still, factory farming and hunting both inflict suffering and premature death on beings capable of having lives worth living. Neither the infliction of suffering nor the killing of a conscious being is morally neutral; both require moral justification. It should, indeed, be impossible for anyone who has suffered physically or psychologically to believe that such an experience could ever not matter at all, even when the victim is only a lower animal such as a chicken. Suffering is always intrinsically bad (though *pain* is not; a masochist may enjoy pain rather than suffer from it).

But it is possible that, while the suffering of an animal matters, it matters less than the equivalent suffering of a person. The suffering of a person may, for example, prevent that person from engaging in activities of greater value than any that an animal is capable of. And suffering can have psychological effects throughout the subsequent life of a person that are more damaging than any such effects could be in the shorter and psychologically more rudimentary life of an animal. It also seems that there are depths or intensities of psychological suffering to which persons are vulnerable but to which the simpler minds of animals are immune.

There are also, however, reasons why the suffering of an animal might be morally *worse* than the equivalent suffering of a person. Many people believe that persons can deserve to suffer (for example, as punishment for a crime), whereas few believe that animals can. (If an animal could deserve to suffer, it would have to be a morally responsible agent, and as such would be a morally higher kind of being than it is assumed to be.) If these beliefs are correct, the suffering of an animal is morally worse than the equivalent *deserved* suffering of a person. The suffering of a person can, moreover, sometimes be compensated for by a deepened understanding of life – an effect that cannot occur in most animals.

Most of these considerations, however, concern the possible *consequences* of suffering and, as such, do not affect the badness of suffering itself. The one exception is desert. *Deserved* suffering – if there is such a thing – may be extremely bad for the sufferer and yet not be *morally* bad at all. Some philosophers believe that something analogous is true of animal suffering. They believe that, although an animal cannot deserve to suffer, its suffering may nevertheless matter less *morally* because the animal itself matters less, or has a lower moral status.

It must be shown, however, that animals in fact have a lower moral status than we have. And this requires that we identify what it is that supposedly distinguishes us from animals and grounds our higher moral status. I have sometimes asked a class of students on what basis they think that we have a higher status, or matter more, than animals. Almost invariably, they cite certain psychological capacities, such as self-consciousness, rationality, free will, or the ability to distinguish right from wrong. I then point out that these claims are true and plausible if 'we' refers to people like those of us in the classroom but not if it includes young children. They then realize that they should have said, for example, 'self-consciousness or the *potential* to develop it'. I then point out that even this leaves out profoundly demented adults and adult human beings who from the beginning of their existence have lacked the potential to develop the relevant capacities. Demented adults can perhaps be accommodated by claiming that higher moral status can be grounded in the possession, *potential* possession, or *past* possession of the relevant capacities. But if the basis of our higher status is some function of psychological capacity, congenitally severely cognitively impaired human adults seem to be excluded. Yet no student of mine has been willing to accept that the suffering of these human beings matters less.

No one, in my view, has succeeded in identifying a morally significant intrinsic difference between these human beings and *all* nonhuman animals. We may, of course, be *related* to these human beings in morally significant ways, but only *intrinsic* properties – features of an individual itself and not its relations to others – affect moral status. If there is no relevant difference in intrinsic properties, and if the suffering of these human beings does not matter less, then the suffering of animals, or at least those animals with psychological capacities comparable to those of these human beings, also does not matter less.

But suppose that I am mistaken and the suffering of animals does matter less. It nevertheless remains true that their suffering matters and that causing it requires justification and is subject to certain moral constraints. Even the infliction of suffering on blameworthy *wrongdoers* is governed by moral constraints. Suppose, for example, that you are fighting in a just war and a particularly malevolent soldier on the unjust side is attempting to kill you. You can incapacitate him in either of two ways. One would cause him only a minor injury; the other would be more disabling and cause him great suffering. Both morality and the law require that you inflict only the minor injury, even if that would be more burdensome to you – because, for example, the more disabling option would render him more manageable as a prisoner of war.

This constraint is called the *requirement of necessity*: one must choose the least harmful means of achieving one's end, even when that would be somewhat more burdensome than a more harmful alternative. This requirement, which has been virtually universally accepted for centuries, is most often invoked in discussions of self-defence and war, but it applies to all acts of harming. It therefore implies not only that it is wrong to cause unnecessary harm in defending oneself from an aggressor, but also that it is wrong to eat meat from factory farms when one could obtain comparable pleasure and nutrition from foods produced without causing animals to suffer.[1] And it is well established that a vegetarian or, with some minor supplementation, vegan diet can provide all that is necessary for optimal human health.

Some people will say that they simply cannot get the same pleasure from plant foods that they get from meat. I suspect that in most cases this is a result of insufficient experience. I have known hundreds of vegetarians and vegans but only a few have thought, after months or years without eating meat, that their pleasure in food had been diminished.

But suppose it is true that in general you cannot get as much pleasure from a meal without meat. Even if that means that your eating meat satisfies the necessity requirement, there is still another requirement that you must satisfy: *proportionality*, which forbids acts that cause bad effects that are excessive in relation to their good effects. In a just war, for example, an attack that is necessary to save the life of one innocent civilian but would kill two other civilians as a side effect is ruled out as disproportionate.

Like the requirement of necessity, the requirement of pro-portionality applies to all acts that cause suffering or harm, including harm to animals. One pig can provide meat for about 100 meals. It could thus, on 100 occasions, provide you with the difference in pleasure between a meal with meat and a meal without meat. Yet for you to have those increases in enjoyment, a factory farmed pig must live in misery for between 6 and 12 months. Even if its suffering matters less because it has a lower moral status, it is hard to believe that the infliction of so much suffering could be proportionate in relation to your 100 momentary increases in minor pleasures. To make this vivid, ask yourself whether the *difference in pleasure* you would get from one brief meal with meat rather than one without it could offset or outweigh the suffering a pig endures over several days of stressful confinement (roughly 1/100th of its life).

It seems that eating meat from factory farmed animals is usually unnecessary for whatever benefits one gets, and that the suffering that factory farming inflicts is disproportionate in relation to those benefits. But factory farming is, of course, not the only way of producing meat. Animals intended for consumption can be raised without cramming them into densely packed, airless indoor spaces, hacking off their beaks or tails (to prevent the injuries that animals maddened by such conditions become prone to inflict on one another), and stuffing them with foods that are unnatural for them. Indeed, during most of the time since animal agriculture began, animals were raised in relatively open spaces in which they could be at least moderately content. Even now, humane rearing is practised on a small scale in various countries.

We can use the term *humane omnivorism* to refer to the prac-tice of eating meat only from animals that have been raised without being caused to suffer, and killed with as little pain and fear as possible. Although it does not involve the infliction of suffering, this practice standardly involves killing the animals when they reach full size, about 1/10th of the way through their natural life span. And killing, like inflicting suffering, requires moral justification. Again, if enhanced enjoyment by meat eaters can justify the killing, it must be proportionate. In this case, proportionality weighs the difference in pleasure for meat eaters against the future pleasures of which an animal is deprived by being killed.

Returning briefly to factory farming, one might claim that the killing of factory farmed animals is not morally objectionable because instead of depriving them of pleasure, it spares them further misery. But that claim parallels the obviously false claim that the Nazis' gassing of concentration camp prisoners was permissible euthanasia because the prisoners' continued lives in the camps would not have been worth living. What this shows is that we must compare death with what individuals' lives would be like if we were to treat them permissibly.

Those who believe that an animal's suffering matters less because the animal has a lower moral status presumably believe that its pleasure matters less as well (though recall that they must explain why the suffering and pleasure of human beings with psychological capacities comparable to those of an animal do not matter less). Many people also think that killing animals is easier to justify than causing them to suffer. It is, however, hard to see why this should be so. After all, killing a person need not cause her to suffer, but merely deprives her of good things her life would otherwise have contained. But killing a person is no less serious morally than causing her to suffer.

Consider, then, whether the increase in enjoyment that some people get from eating meat can justify the killing of animals raised humanely. Suppose a pig has lived contentedly for a year. It is now as large as it can get, so allowing it to live longer is economically wasteful. Killing it would provide each of 100 people with enhanced pleasure for one meal. Those benefits must be weighed against the pleasure the pig would be deprived of in losing the remaining five years of its natural life span.

Pigs, too, enjoy eating. (Recall which animal we compare a person to when he is bolting his feed with relish.) And they enjoy companionship with other pigs, as well as solitary pleasures such as lying in the sun. Pigs also concentrate on their eating, whereas we are normally distracted by conversation or, increasingly, electronic screens and are often only partially aware of what we are eating. Thus, even if the moral significance of a pig's pleasure is heavily discounted for lower moral status, it is implausible to suppose that 100 instances of the enhancement of mild human pleasure for a brief period – a total period of well under 100 hours – could matter more than, or outweigh, all the pleasures that a pig could have over five years. The killing required by humane omnivorism is therefore disproportionate in relation to the benefits the practice offers.

There are other problems with humane omnivorism. Factory farms evolved through efforts to increase the profits from producing meat by reducing the costs. The costs of humane rearing are much greater, so the cost to consumers must be correspondingly higher as well. If humane rearing were to replace factory farming, meat would become a luxury regularly available only to the rich. Although this would greatly benefit the health of the poor, it would still be inegalitarian. Another problem is that, in part because it would produce far fewer animals, humane rearing would be less bad for the environment than factory farming, which is a major cause of climate change. But it would still be significantly worse than purely plant-based agriculture.

There is, however, one interesting argument in favour of humane omnivorism. Consider the generations of animals raised and killed on a farm that practises humane rearing. These animals have lives that are worth living, though short. And they would never have existed had this farm not existed for the purpose of producing meat. (Animals born on other farms, including factory farms, would be different animals.) These animals, in other words, owe their good lives to the practice of humane omnivorism. Although they are harmed by being killed prematurely, the practice of humane omnivorism is overall not bad for them, and is perhaps even good for them.

This argument raises deep issues that there is no space to discuss here.[2] But it faces one obvious objection. There is a chronic shortage of donor organs for transplantation. Suppose that we could create embryos in vitro that would be genetically programmed to be congenitally severely cognitively impaired, with psychological capacities no higher than those of an animal. These individuals could be given contented lives until their organs could be used to save the lives of several people with psychological capacities in the normal range. At that point, they would be painlessly killed. If their lives would be worth living, overall the practice would not be bad for them and might even be good for them. Yet intuitively, this would not be morally acceptable. This suggests that humane omnivorism is not morally acceptable either.

The arguments I have advanced here challenge the moral permissibility of most people's eating practices. But they are of wider relevance. They raise questions, for example, about the permissibility of experimentation on animals. It is worth saying, however, that at least some experiments that kill animals or cause them to suffer are substantially more likely to be both necessary and proportionate than eating meat is. This is because the results of these experiments, particularly in the advancement of medicine, could prevent great harms, or provide great benefits, to many people.

My claims have other implications. Even if animal suffering does not matter as much as the equivalent suffering of persons, it still matters very much. And it is ubiquitous. Animals greatly outnumber human beings and their lives in the natural world are everywhere precarious. They suffer from disease, starvation, dehydration, predation, parasites, adverse weather, and other threats to their lives and well-being. If suffering and death are bad for animals when we cause them, they are also bad when they derive from other sources. While our moral reason not to inflict these harms is arguably stronger than our reason to prevent them, we ought not to be indifferent to the great suffering that many billions of animals endure every day. When our science becomes sufficiently advanced to enable us to ameliorate their suffering without doing more harm than good, it will become our duty to do that.

NOTES

1 See Rae Langton and Richard Holton, 'Animals and Alternatives', The Philosopher's Magazine 81 (2018): 14–15.
2 For a more thorough discussion, see Jeff McMahan, 'Eating Animals the Nice Way', Daedalus 137 (2008): 66–76.

Science and technology

Part Eight

Part Eight

Twenty Three

Thomas Douglas

THE RUBELLA CASE

Suppose that a woman would like to have a child but is currently suffering from rubella. If she conceives now, the rubella virus will likely cause her child to have a serious intellectual disability. If she waits three months to conceive, this risk will have passed.[1]

Most people think that this woman should defer conception, at least if she can do so at little cost. They accept that she has *a moral reason* to defer conception. She may also have reasons pushing in the other direction. For example, if it would be very risky for the woman's own health to defer conception, she may have a self-interested reason to conceive now rather than later. Perhaps those other reasons could even be stronger than her reason to defer conception. But the reason to defer conception is a reason nonetheless. It counts in favour of waiting three months before conceiving.

In this chapter, I explore some implications of the view that the woman in the rubella case has a reason to defer conception. In particular, I consider its implications for the ethics of *genetic selection*. Genetic selection involves choosing to bring one child into existence rather than another, based in part on the genetic characteristics of the alternative possible children. I will argue that, if the woman in the rubella case indeed has a reason to defer conception, then potential parents also have reasons to pursue some highly contentious forms of genetic selection.

FROM THE RUBELLA CASE TO GENETIC SELECTION

Why does the woman in the rubella case have a reason to defer conception? It cannot be because conceiving now would harm the future child – at least, not in the ordinary sense of harm. We normally say that something harms a person if it makes that person worse off than she would otherwise have been. Conceiving now rather than later would not make the resulting child worse off than he would otherwise have been, for he would not otherwise have existed. Had the woman deferred conception, a different sperm would have fertilised a different egg, and a different child would have come into existence.

Instead, it seems that the woman has a reason to defer conception because she has a reason to bring one kind of person into existence rather than another. Here's one way of characterising the reason: if she is going to bring a child into existence, she has a reason to ensure that the child will not be disposed to disability or disease. She has a reason to bring into existence a child not disposed to disability or disease rather than creating a child who is disposed to disability or disease.

This sort of reason could, however, be relevant in many cases besides the rubella case. This is because there are many ways in which potential parents could influence whether they have a child disposed to disease or disability.

For example, a woman could choose to have a child in her early thirties rather than in her late thirties in order to reduce the risk of having a child with Down's syndrome. Or a couple might choose to use an egg or sperm donor rather than conceiving with their own egg and sperm in cases where they know that they are at risk of passing on a genetic disease or disability. Suppose a man and woman would like to have a child together but they are both carriers of the cystic fibrosis gene. This means that, if they conceive in the usual way, there is a one in four chance that their child will go on to develop cystic fibrosis, a severe genetic disease that primarily affects the lungs and typically causes death before the age of 50. To avoid this risk, the couple might choose to conceive with the aid of an egg or sperm from a person who is not a carrier of cystic fibrosis.

There are also more high-tech ways in which potential parents can influence whether they have a child genetically disposed to disability or disease. One of these is *prenatal diagnosis and selective abortion*: a pregnant woman could have the foetus developing in her uterus genetically tested and could then decide to abort the pregnancy and try again for another child if the test revealed a genetic disposition to disease or disability. There are different ways in which this genetic testing could be done – different forms of 'prenatal diagnosis' – but one possibility would be to use a recently developed technique known as non-invasive prenatal diagnosis (NIPD). This takes advantage of the fact that small fragments of DNA from the foetus can be found circulating in a pregnant woman's blood. A sample of blood is taken from the mother, and laboratory technicians then study these fragments in order to 'read' the genetic code of the foetus.[2]

Another possibility is that prospective potential parents could employ *preimplantation genetic diagnosis* as part of in vitro fertilisation. In vitro fertilisation (IVF) is a fertility treatment that normally involves creating multiple embryos in the laboratory, and then deciding which of these to implant into the woman's womb to create a pregnancy. Suppose a couple are pursuing IVF as treatment for a fertility problem. They have produced four embryos and wish to implant one of these into the woman's womb. Prior to making their decision about which embryo to implant, the potential parents could have the embryos genetically tested via a procedure called *preimplantation genetic diagnosis*. Suppose this reveals that two of the embryos are genetically predisposed to develop Huntington's disease, a genetic condition characterised by brain damage that develops in mid-life. The other two embryos do not have this disposition. The couple might then choose to have one of the unaffected embryos implanted.

All of the methods that I have described involve choosing to bring one child into existence rather than another based in part on the genetic characteristics of those possible children. This is commonly referred to as *genetic selection*.[3] Moreover, in all cases, the choice could, as in the rubella case, affect whether the potential parents will have a child who will suffer from a disease or disability. It might seem that, if we think the mother in the rubella case has a reason to delay conception in order to have a child not disposed to disease or disability, then, likewise, potential parents have a reason to use techniques like prenatal diagnosis, preimplantation genetic diagnosis, and sperm or egg donation to reduce their chances of having a child disposed to disease or disability. After all, in all of these cases, the basic structure of the choice is the same: the potential parents must choose which, among different possible future children, to bring into existence, and one of the factors that could inform their choice is the likelihood that these future children will be disposed to develop a disability or disease.

EXTENDING THE ARGUMENT TO NON-MEDICAL TRAITS

In fact, accepting that there is a reason to delay conception in the rubella case may have even more radical implications. It may suggest that potential parents have reason to use genetic selection to avoid having a child with disadvantageous traits *even if those traits are not diseases or disabilities, or symptoms thereof.*[4]

I suggested earlier that the mother in the rubella case has a reason to delay conception because she has a reason not to have a child disposed to disease or disability. But this was a crude and misleading way of putting it; after all, there is nothing wrong with disability in itself. Disability is problematic only if and when it tends to reduce a person's wellbeing – that is, if and when it tends to result in a person's life going less well. The same goes for disease. Cystic fibrosis is not bad in itself; it's bad if and when it reduces wellbeing; for example, by causing pain and suffering, or by shortening what would otherwise have been a longer and good life.

This suggests that the reason at play in the rubella case, and in cases of genetic selection, is not ultimately a reason to avoid having children predisposed to diseases or disabilities. Rather, it is a reason to have children who will have good lives – lives containing much wellbeing. It just so happens that, in some cases, disability and especially disease tend to limit wellbeing. In those cases, the reason to have children with good lives will give rise to a reason to have children free from disease or disability. Ultimately, though, it's wellbeing that matters. Disease and disability matter only insofar as they detract from wellbeing.

This revision to how we understand the reasons in play here is significant because disease and disability aren't the only things that predictably reduce wellbeing. For example, there are also psychological characteristics like personality traits that tend to reduce a person's wellbeing.

Consider the trait of poor impulse control. This trait is very common and is not normally thought to be a disability or a disease, or a symptom of a disability or disease. But it's plausible that it tends to reduce wellbeing. In the 1970s, Walter Mischel performed a now famous series of experiments on young children in order to test their impulse control.[5] In the most well-known of these, 4-year-old children were left in a room with a single marshmallow and told that, if they could resist eating the marshmallow until the researcher returned, they would receive two marshmallows.

Some children ate the marshmallow as soon as the researcher left. Others used a range of strategies to distract themselves from the marshmallow and thus override their impulse to eat it. Mischel then followed up these two groups of children as they developed into adults. He found that, on average, those in the second group – those who had overridden their impulse to eat the marshmallow – had more friends, achieved better academic results, had more motivation, had healthier body weight, and committed crimes at lower rates.

Recent research suggests that these differences had relatively little to do with impulse control, and more to do with differences in socio-economic status: it may be that being from a better off family tends to cause both better impulse control, and the better life outcomes that Mischel observed.[6] But let's suppose that the different life outcomes found by Mischel were at least in part due to differences in impulse control; it does not seem too controversial to say that poor impulse control tends to diminish wellbeing. If a medical condition tended to cause criminality, worse academic performance, and less healthy weight, we would probably regard it as a barrier to wellbeing. So, it might seem that, if potential parents have reasons to have children with good lives, then they would have reasons to employ genetic selection to try to have children with good rather than poor impulse control, if this were possible. (At present, we do not understand the genetic influences on impulse control well enough to enable this, but in the future, perhaps we will.)

A variant of the rubella case provides some support to this conclusion. Suppose that, rather than causing serious intellectual disability, rubella infection during pregnancy caused poor impulse control and the negative outcomes that Mischel found to be associated with this. Would we, in that case, think that a woman affected with rubella has a reason to defer conception until the infection had resolved? It seems to me that we would. This suggests that we should think the same about cases involving genetic selection.

EXTENDING THE ARGUMENT TO THIRD-PARTY EFFECTS

The argument can be taken further still. I've been suggesting that potential parents have reasons to have children who will have good lives – lives containing much wellbeing. But decisions about what kind of child to have can also affect the wellbeing of others. Most obviously, they can affect the wellbeing of the parents themselves, of their other existing children, and of further children that they will go on to have in the future. They can also affect the wellbeing of strangers. Having a child with an expensive-to-treat genetic disease or risk factors for criminality can, for example, impose significant costs on others. If potential parents have reasons to have children with good lives, then might not they also have reasons to have children whose existence will contribute more to the wellbeing of others?[7] It seems arbitrary to consider only the wellbeing of the future child, and not that of others, when making reproductive decisions.

The thought that the wellbeing of others is relevant to reproductive decision-making can again be supported by considering a variant of the rubella case. Suppose that, rather than causing intellectual disability or poor impulse control, rubella infection during pregnancy causes emotional callousness. This callousness does not reduce the wellbeing of those who have it; indeed, these individuals tend to enjoy relatively good lives, because they are not much troubled by how others think of them or by the suffering they see around them. However, these callous individuals do tend to inflict significant harm on others. For example, they are inclined to exploit, defraud, and otherwise harm others whenever this suits them.

Were rubella associated with callousness of this sort, we would, I think, be inclined to say that a woman with rubella has a reason to defer conception until after such time as the infection has resolved. She would have a reason to avoid having a child whose existence can be expected to harm others. The same reason would apply to potential parents faced with the possibility of using genetic selection to select against emotional callousness. (Again, this is not currently technically possible, but it could become so in the future.)

OBJECTIONS

Starting from the rubella case, I have argued that potential parents have reason to pursue genetic selection to avoid having a child with (1) a disposition to a wellbeing-reducing disease or disability, (2) a disposition to other wellbeing-reducing traits, and (3) dispositions that tend to reduce the wellbeing of others.[8]

These are quite radical implications. Many people would find them unacceptable. Certainly, they are out of line with the laws and regulations regarding genetic selection in most countries. Even the United Kingdom, which has a relatively liberal policy on genetic selection, allows genetic selection via preimplantation genetic diagnosis only in very restricted cases. Potential parents pursuing IVF may employ preimplantation genetic diagnoses in order to avoid having a child with a strong disposition to certain serious genetic diseases or disabilities. But, with only very rare exceptions, they may not employ it to select against weak dispositions to genetic disease or disability, or against dispositions to non-medical traits.

To some extent, these regulations may simply reflect the current state of the science. For example, there is currently no known effective way to select against most non-medical personality traits, like poor impulse control or emotional callousness. However, existing regulations in the United Kingdom and elsewhere probably also reflect a widely accepted *moral* view: that, except where pursued to select against a strong disposition to a serious disability or disease, there is a decisive *moral objection* to genetic selection – any moral reasons in favour of selection in such cases are *outweighed* by competing reasons *against* genetic selection.

In the remainder of this chapter, I briefly consider three objections that might be raised against genetic selection. Some people would advance these objections only against the more controversial forms of genetic selection mentioned earlier: selection against non-medical traits, and selection for the benefit of third parties. Others would advance these objections even against the least controversial kind of genetic selection: selection to avoid disease or disability. I will argue that the objections fail in relation to all three kinds of genetic selection.

Objection 1: it's eugenics!

One objection often raised against genetic selection, especially when used to select against non-medical traits, holds that it is a kind of eugenics. 'Eugenics' is normally taken to refer to attempts to improve the quality of the genes of future people. It is frequently associated with attempts to eliminate the genetic bases of homosexuality, criminality, 'moral depravity', and intellectual disability in several North American and European jurisdictions in the late nineteenth and early twentieth centuries. The Nazi eugenics programme is the most notorious example. Nazi doctors, scientists, and ideologues encouraged 'Aryans' to reproduce, while sterilising or murdering people whom they regarded as carriers of defective genes, such as people with intellectual limitations or mental health problems. Even the Final Solution – the attempt to exterminate Jews – can be regarded as a part of the Nazi eugenics programme, since it was motivated in part by the mistaken belief that Jews were genetically inferior and were contaminating the European gene pool.

In assessing this objection, it's important to be clear about what exactly 'eugenics' means. If it means simply 'attempting to improve the genes of future people', then genetic selection certainly does amount to eugenics, but this doesn't seem to constitute an *objection* to it; it's not obvious what's wrong with seeking genetic improvement. On the other hand, if 'eugenics' means something like 'practices that are morally similar to the genetic selection practices of the nineteenth and twentieth centuries', then it is doubtful that genetic selection must involve eugenics. I believe that historical genetic selection practices were objectionable because they were informed by mistaken views about the value of different genetic traits, because they were grounded on bad science, because they were too often mandatory, and, most importantly, because they frequently involved killing or seriously harming existing people. There is no reason to suppose that future genetic selection practices would necessarily involve any of these objectionable features.

Objection 2: the expressivist objection

Another common concern about genetic selection is that it expresses an objectionable attitude. For example, it is sometimes said that using genetic selection to avoid having a child with Down's syndrome expresses the view that people with this syndrome have lives not worth living or the view that they do not deserve to live. Expressing such views might be said to wrong those people currently living with Down's syndrome.

One problem with this objection, which is normally known as the expressivist objection, is that, at least as I have just presented it, it exaggerates the attitudes of those who employ genetic selection. Potential parents who employ genetic selection to avoid having a child with Down's syndrome need not believe that people with that syndrome have lives not worth living or that they don't deserve to live. They may, for example, simply believe that people without Down's syndrome tend, other things being equal, to have better lives – lives containing more wellbeing. Given that many potential parents may hold only this weaker view, it's not clear why we should think that genetic selection invariably expresses a stronger view – such as the view that lives with Down's syndrome are not worth living. Nor is it clear why the weaker view is objectionable – after all, it may well be true that lives without Down's syndrome tend, other things being equal, to contain more wellbeing than lives with Down's syndrome. Certainly, this seems to be a view that potential parents could reasonably hold.

Objection 3: maintaining objectionable norms

Yet another worry about genetic selection is that it helps to maintain objectionable forms of discrimination. Suppose a mixed-race couple choose to implant an embryo predisposed to lighter skin rather than darker skin knowing that they live in a racist society in which those with darker skin are subjected to discrimination. Though the lighter skinned child might well enjoy more wellbeing than the alternative possible children, there seems to be something highly problematic about this selection decision. It implicitly encourages the maintenance of racist norms.

Note, though, that not all cases of selection support the maintenance of *objectionable* norms. Consider the example I gave of selecting against emotional callousness. Perhaps society *should* adopt norms against emotional callousness, given that such a trait may cause harm to other people.

Where a selection decision does help to maintain an objectionable norm, this will, I think, constitute an objection to the decision. But this objection may not be decisive. We may be faced here with a trade-off between helping to maintain the objectionable norm and bringing a person with lower wellbeing into existence. In some cases, maintaining the objectionable norm may be the lesser evil. For example, suppose that our societies currently, and wrongly, adopt norms of beauty according to which people with extremely asymmetric faces are less attractive than those with more symmetric faces. And suppose that selecting against a highly asymmetric face in one's child encourages the maintenance of these norms. But suppose also that having a highly asymmetric face *does* seriously limit a person's wellbeing; for example, because people with such faces are less likely to find a good job or romantic partner. In this sort of case, perhaps potential parents *should* select against asymmetric faces. To do otherwise would be to sacrifice the wellbeing of one's future child in order to fight for a worthy social cause. Arguably, this would be the wrong decision, at least if a great deal of wellbeing would be sacrificed for a very minor weakening of objectionable norms.

CONCLUSION

Many people think that a woman infected with rubella has a reason to defer conception if this would avoid intellectual disability in the woman's future child. I have argued that, if we accept this, then we should also accept that potential parents have reason to engage in genetic selection in order to avoid having children with:

1   diseases or disabilities (where these limit wellbeing);
2   other characteristics that would tend to limit the wellbeing of the child; and
3   characteristics that would tend to diminish the wellbeing of others.

I also surveyed three possible objections to genetic selection and argued that none of them is decisive in all cases.

One possible response to my argument would be to reject the common intuition about the rubella case. Perhaps the woman in the rubella case really has no reason to defer conception. But this seems hard to accept.

Another response would be to look further for a decisive objection to all forms of genetic selection, or at least to genetic selection that does not seek to avoid disease or disability.

But suppose that no such objection can be found. What then? Would it follow that reasons to engage in genetic selection are always decisive?

It would not. In many cases there are reasons both for and against genetic selection, and I have said nothing to show that the reasons against are *never* decisive. For example, if selecting for paler skin helps to maintain seriously objectionable racist norms, it seems to me plausible that the reasons against engaging in such selection will outweigh any reasons in favour. Most likely, the reasons in favour will be stronger in some cases, and the reasons against will be stronger in others.

What *would* follow from my argument is that there is no reason to rule out genetic selection – even in its more controversial forms – from the outset. What we need to do, I think, is to balance the reasons for and against selection on a case-by-case basis.

NOTES

1 I have taken this case from Derek Parfit, 'Rights, Interests and Possible People', in S. Gorovitz et al., eds., *Moral Problems in Medicine* (Englewood Cliffs: Prentice Hall, 1976). See also Derek Parfit, *Reasons and Persons* (Oxford: Oxford University Press, 1986), part IV.

2 NIPD is a new technology, but there have long been more invasive and riskier ways of genetically testing a developing foetus. For example, in amniocentesis technicians take a sample of the fluid that surrounds the foetus in the womb, and in chorionic villus sampling, they remove a small fragment of the placenta.

3 For excellent book-length treatments of the ethics of genetic selection, see Jonathan Glover, *Choosing Children: Genes, Disability, and Design* (Oxford: Oxford University Press, 2006); and Stephen Wilkinson, *Choosing Tomorrow's Children: The Ethics of Selective Reproduction* (Oxford: Oxford University Press, 2010).

4 For a more in-depth defence of this view, see Julian Savulescu, 'Procreative Beneficence: Why We Should Select the Best Children', *Bioethics* 15, 5–6 (2001): 413–426; and J. Savulescu and G. Kahane, 'The Moral Obligation to Create Children With the Best Chance of the Best Life', *Bioethics* 23, 5 (2009): 274–290.

5 See, for a description of these, Walter Mischel, *The Marshmallow Test: Understanding Self-Control and How to Master It* (London: Random House, 2014), esp. pp. 3–5.

6 Tyler W. Watts, Greg J. Duncan and Haonan Quan, 'Revisiting the Marshmallow Test: A Conceptual Replication Investigating Links Between Early Delay of Gratification and Later Outcomes', *Psychological Science* (2018): 0956797618761661.

7 For two articles that give a positive answer to this question, see Jakob Elster, 'Procreative Beneficence – Cui Bono?', *Bioethics* 25, 9 (2011): 482–488; and Thomas Douglas and Katrien Devolder, 'Procreative Altruism: Beyond Individualism in Reproductive Selection', *Journal of Medicine and Philosophy* 38, 4 (2013): 400–419.

8 The argument could also be extended to cases in which potential parents could alter the genetic code of an embryo prior to implantation, for example, through gene editing. For discussion of such cases, see Christopher Gyngell, Thomas Douglas, and Julian Savulescu, 'The Ethics of Germline Gene Editing', *Journal of Applied Philosophy* 34, 4 (2017): 498–513.

Twenty Four

Julian Savulescu[1]

One of America's top universities, Duke University, has banned the use of cognitive enhancers on campus. Its code about academic dishonesty covers various forms of cheating. Cheating, it says, includes "the unauthorized use of prescription medication to enhance academic performance".[2] An implication of this code is that students cannot take substances like Ritalin or Adderall without having a medical diagnosis, such as Attention Deficit Hyperactivity Disorder (ADHD), and a prescription by a doctor.

In this chapter I will examine whether "enhancement" is objectionable and should be banned. Or rather, as I believe, it is an opportunity and even a moral imperative.

WHAT IS ENHANCEMENT?

Enhancement means to make better. Education and good diet are enhancements. But when we talk about enhancement, we typically mean "bioenhancement" – in which improvement is made by direct biological intervention. Biological interventions into human performance include drugs, genetic modification, surgery, electrical or magnetic stimulation, insertion of computer chips or interfaces, etc. Pretty much any aspect of human performance can be improved.

It is useful to distinguish various types of enhancement:

Cognitive: Many aspects of human cognition can be enhanced. For example, wakefulness, (with caffeine, modafinil, and stimulants in general), stress reduction (with beta blockers like propranolol), attention, and memory.

Physical: Testosterone and growth hormone, for example, can increase strength. The hormone erythropoietin increases the number of red blood cells and so improves endurance.

Mood: Mood can be altered by recreational drugs, antidepressants, and, of course, alcohol.

Love: Testosterone and flibanserin can increase sexual desire. Oxytocin can make people feel more bonded with one another.

Most people understand human enhancement to be the enhancement of some kind of function within the normal range. Typically, a distinction is drawn between disease and health, and between treatment and enhancement. For example, intellectual disability is defined as an IQ that is less than 70, where the average is 100. So an intervention which increased somebody's IQ from a starting point of below 70 would count as treatment, whilst an intervention to increase intelligence on someone who already had an IQ greater than 70, would count as enhancement.

Some bioethicists distinguish between two different categories of functional enhancements. One category contains increases within the normal range – so for example, increasing somebody's IQ from 80 to 120 – whilst the other contains increases beyond what human beings could ordinarily achieve, such as increasing somebody's IQ from 150 to 200.

Still other bioethicists prefer to talk not about function (like IQ) but about welfare. According to the Welfarist definition, enhancement is a change in our biology or psychology that improves our wellbeing. Whether increasing or decreasing some function is good depends on the circumstances, our values, and our concept of wellbeing. Improving a particular function may be useful in one society, but irrelevant in another.

WILL ENHANCEMENT MAKE US HAPPIER?

Philosophers disagree about what counts as happiness. I think of happiness in a narrow sense to mean pleasurable mental states. There's good evidence that people's level of happiness is set biologically – we have a more-or-less fixed hedonic level. We tend to hover around this particular level, which varies from individual to individual, regardless of how good or bad our circumstances are.

In theory, there's no reason why we couldn't change people's hedonic levels. I would rather be happy, more of the time. Of course, if we were just pressing a happy button to experience euphoric mental states, that wouldn't be a good life. But think back to the happiest day of your life. If you could achieve that sort of happiness more often, what reason would there be to say no? Drugs like Prozac are starting to get us there, but they have unwanted side effects. In the future, there may be drugs that change how happy we feel without these side effects.

Some people worry that this will turn us into zombies – as in the novel *Brave New World* by Aldous Huxley, in which people are administered with the drug Soma. So, in order to decide whether the use of a drug is good for us, we need a philosophical conception of wellbeing. I believe that this should include things that are objectively good for people –

certain accomplishments, say, or real human relationships and not just virtual or imaginary ones. The feeling of happiness is only one part of a good life – it is not all that matters. Relationships – like friendships – matter, too.

We should evaluate biological interventions and their impact on wellbeing within the range of circumstances we face in the modern world. In our world, having a better memory, or stronger impulse control, or enhanced ability to draw logical inferences, are properties that are likely to make our lives go better.

ETHICAL OBJECTIONS

A variety of ethical objections have been made to enhancement.

Safety

People say that enhancement has health risks and is worrying in particular because it trades health for non-health-related benefits. But this is an odd objection. Health is an instrumental good. That is to say, it is a means to wellbeing: we want to be healthy to live a good life. But we balance health against other considerations all the time, and in this respect the safety issues around bioenhancements are no different. People risk health when they drive a car or play rugby, or try to climb Mount Everest, or drink alcohol.

Inequality

One worry about enhancement is that it would be unfair if only some people get an advantage. That's a valid concern. The classic presentation of this is the film *Gattaca*, where a two-tiered society of the genetically privileged and the genetically oppressed has been created through genetic selection. However, this is not an overwhelming objection to enhancement. There is natural inequality; we start off very unequal. Some people are born with low IQ, some with high. The same is true for every human characteristic, from empathy to self-control to athletic ability.

Whether enhancement increases or reduces natural inequality depends on how we use it. If it is expensive and allocated according to market principles, it will no doubt increase inequality, just as inequality is increased by expensive education or costly technology, such as computers. However, a case could be made for treating enhancement like health care, especially if it is important to wellbeing. In other words, everyone would be able to access enhancement at least up to a certain threshold level. And if there were a social safety net, so that it was offered to all, bioenhancement could actually *reduce* natural inequality.

But suppose bioenhancement did exacerbate inequality. Would this then be a fatal criticism of it? There are three reasons why I think it would not be.

First, there seems no good reason to treat biological enhancements differently than any other form of enhancement. We don't think that we should limit the development of the internet, computers, smart phones, and so on because the rich will benefit from the best versions of these technologies.

Second, we should take a long view. Historically, enhancements like reading and writing were only available to a tiny fraction of humanity. And now, at least in developed countries, they're available to everyone. Mobile phones were initially available only to the very wealthy. Now they're ubiquitous on every continent.

Third, the idea that everything new must be available to everyone immediately is unrealistic. Our system of patents, for example, is not ideal, but patents exist only for a period of time and are designed to stimulate innovation. When it comes to enhancement, some level of inequality should be tolerated for the sake of other values.

Solidarity

The philosopher Michael Sandel worries that a society in which enhancement was widely available would undermine solidarity. This is because those who didn't choose to be enhanced would then be *responsible* for their own disadvantage. At the moment, we have insurance schemes and social welfare because we're all potential victims of chance and misfortune. Such safeguards protect us against the threat of bad luck. Sandel worries that if misfortune was optional, we would no longer feel it a matter of justice to structure our institutions to protect the least well off.

Like equality, this is an important concern but, again, not overwhelming. There will always be natural misfortune, and enhancement will never guarantee a perfect life. So we will continue to need solidarity and insurance in the same way as we do now.

Gift

Sandel has another concern. If bioenhancement becomes widespread, then, rather than accepting our lives and our capacities as gifts, we will start to think of ourselves as the masters of our destiny. At present, we tend to accept our strengths and limitations. We are, as Sandel puts it, "open to the unbidden" and to chance. When we adopt the attitude Sandel is worried about, there is a danger of instrumentalizing ourselves – particularly using our children as a means to achieving certain goals. For example, if an embryo is chosen with a musical gift, Sandel worries the parents will subject the child to hours of music practice early in life to produce a genius, the next Mozart. They are using the child to produce a great pianist, perhaps because of their own shortcomings.

This objection confuses enhancement with bad parenting. How we treat our children is independent of what gifts we bestow up on them. Many people already "hyperparent" their children in the quest to turn them into musicians or sports-people, and so on. Whether or not we enhance our children, we should give them freedom and an "open future". This is consistent with enhancement.

Life is about trying to improve ourselves. We do this through education, diet, psychological techniques. Enhancement technologies are part of the same pattern – of trying to enable society to flourish and to live good lives.

Free will and authenticity

It is sometimes said that enhancement renders people's achievements inauthentic. A related argument is present in doping debates in sport. People say sporting success following doping is not really the person's own achievement, it's due to the drug or device they used (or the achievement belongs to the pharmaceutical company that produced the drug or device). But not all cases should be lumped together. Bionic limbs, like those of RoboCop, could dominate performance. For that reason, I think it was a mistake to allow the South African runner Oscar Pistorius to compete in the able-bodied Olympics. At some point, blade technology will vastly outperform normal human anatomy. However, nobody thinks that the computer that enables me to manipulate text and information much more quickly than at the start of my academic career is robbing me of my achievements.

Certainly, technology could dominate us. If my computer started telling me what to write, as Google is starting to do, then we would have a legitimate concern about autonomy. In theory, enhancement could undermine our authenticity and free will. But it could also enhance it!

My view of freedom is that we're free when we're able to set our own rules according to our own values. Sometimes being free requires delaying gratification, constraining ourselves in a world where, given our human limitations and weaknesses, we're prone to deviate from what we most value. What people often do is set pre-commitment contracts: "So as not to gain weight, I'm not going to stock chocolate biscuits in the cupboard". At that point, although you're constraining your options, you've achieved a certain outcome that you value – not to gain weight through eating chocolate biscuits.

One way in which a substance could enhance our free will is by improving impulse control. Ritalin, for example, enables us to delay gratification. Another way is through motivational enhancement, with drugs like Modafinil. One hypothesis is that Modafinil works by improving task engagement and enjoyment, so doing what we want becomes more enjoyable. This allows us to put aside distracting temptations. Does that rob us of free will? If it's a part of an intentional, value-driven project still requiring large amounts of effort but for which we use Modafinil to aid us, it's no different to training that enables us to perform effortlessly or enter a "flow state" in a sporting event. In these cases, we're not exerting huge amounts of effort and control, but that's because of prior effort and training. Provided we had that background effort as part of a value-laden project, I think that enhancement substances could enable us to be, in a certain sense, more free.

Unintended consequences

Won't human enhancement reduce diversity, and isn't diversity necessary for the survival of our species?

It's true that our species has survived in part due to genetic diversity. There is a group of people who are naturally immune to HIV. Throughout most of human history, an epidemic of HIV would have resulted in many, perhaps most, people dying off. Then, the few people who happened to have innate immunity provided by their genetic variation would manage to survive and repopulate the species. But is that how we survive HIV today? No. We're developing drugs to treat the disease and strategies to prevent its spread. So the idea that we have to rely on brute diversity as a means of protecting ourselves or enabling progress is outdated.

Of course, if we wanted diversity for its own sake we could engineer it through genetic manipulation. But in any case, it's not clear that all kinds of diversity are welcome. One percent of the population are psychopaths. That's 70 million people! Is that a good thing? Arguably, through most of human history having a psychopath in your group helped your group survive against another group. But as our technological power increases so does the damage one individual can do. For example, biological weapons could wipe out millions. It's not necessarily good that there are psychopaths in charge of countries and corporations.

Diversity is interesting within the context of discussions about neurotypical children and autism spectrum disorders.

Very severe autism is just a bad thing. But as you travel along the spectrum to disorders like Asperger Syndrome, there may be advantages and disadvantages. Here I think we have to say that ethics is not black and white. It's black, white, and grey, and there will be cases where we just can't judge whether the changes made are overall good or bad.

MORAL BIOENHANCEMENT

One particularly controversial enhancement that we have not discussed much so far is moral: enhancing the capacity to act morally. Ingmar Persson and I have argued that cognitive enhancement alone is insufficient to make people act more morally.[3] After all, cognitive enhancement could just allow a psychopath to be more effective about harming others. So we believe that qualities like sympathy and empathy should also be enhanced.

Psychopaths lack sympathy and, on some accounts, empathy (they can imagine their victims' suffering, but take pleasure in it). This raises two key questions in the enhancement debate: what should we enhance, and who should decide what is "good"? Recently, psychologist Paul Bloom has argued against empathy's positive role in moral decision-making. Bloom believes that empathy can sometimes be an obstacle to thinking clearly and to responding effectively. For example, we are not good at empathizing when large numbers of people are involved – such as when thousands of people are killed in an earthquake. Our empathy is "numb to numbers": we typically empathize with single individuals, especially those near and dear to us.

But we should make a decision about whether we need more or less empathy. My view is that the current – "natural" –

state is highly unlikely to be optimal. A large meta-analysis of psychological research over decades recently examined how empathy has been changing over time in the US, concluding that it has been falling, especially since the year 2000. Now, Paul Bloom might argue that that's a good thing – that's progress! Others might say it's a bad thing, and we ought to do something about it. The point is that we have to come to a conclusion one way or the other – and then if it's in our power to increase or decrease it, we should do so.

With Ingmar Persson, I have argued that empathy is not solely good, but it's an important motivational kick-starter ("The Moral Importance of Reflective Empathy"[4]). If we want people to change their behaviour, harnessing empathy is the most likely way of getting them to act. We can know something is important rationally, but what kicks us into action is empathy. So I think we should be enhancing empathy, but to the right degree and in conjunction with cognitive enhancements. It's possible to have too much empathy, and then we might become paralyzed, too emotional to act.

ENHANCEMENT IS A MORAL IMPERATIVE

There are a number of ways in which enhancement could be a moral imperative. If we're talking about Welfarist enhancement – enhancing people's wellbeing – then surely we have the same moral imperative to develop human enhancements as to develop treatments for disease. Why should we be developing treatments for disease? Because disease undermines people's wellbeing. But it's not just disease that's bad for people. A low IQ might be bad. Indeed, it might not be just having an IQ below 70 that is bad. Perhaps being slightly lower than *average* is bad. Everyone ages and people get deafer as they get older, they lose their sexual potency and their memory. That's typical – that's completely normal. But even though 100% of people get it, it's still not conducive to wellbeing! And if you can change it, then you should change it if the change would be for the better.

So if enhancement can improve wellbeing, there's a moral imperative to take advantage of it. A second reason why enhancement may be considered a moral imperative is this. We can all agree that it would be good if people were more moral. Well, a part of our moral behaviour is determined by our biology. And we can change aspects of our biology to make it more likely that we will behave morally. For example, most people are implicitly racist. This is programmed into our biology, perhaps in part because we evolved in small groups of 150 on the African savannah and morality evolved to facilitate cooperation with small groups, not with globalized societies. So we're distrustful of out-groups. One of my PhD students, Sylvia Terbeck, ran a study of Propranolol, a beta blocker, which indicates that measured by a standard test, taking the drug may reduce implicit racism. Do we not have an obligation to do what we can to reduce racism?

WHAT ARE THE ETHICAL LIMITS ON ENHANCEMENT?

There ought to be limits to human enhancement. Safety could set one limit, although, again, the claim that something has to be perfectly safe in order for it to be ethical is too restrictive. The risks have to be reasonable and commensurate with other risks to which we expose ourselves. Enhancements do have risks, but so do other activities: what matters is whether the benefits are worth the risks.

The second limit is that enhancement should aim at something that is plausibly good. This is most important when we're talking about children, who can't give consent. For children, enhancement is acceptable only if it promotes their wellbeing, based on a plausible conception of wellbeing. We can't just say, "Well, I think my child will be better off with one leg rather than two".

Adults should be able to decide what they do with their own lives, provided they are competent and fully informed. People should be free to choose whatever they consider to be an enhancement for themselves, as long as they bear the costs and don't harm others. This is in line with the liberty principle of the nineteenth-century philosopher John Stuart Mill.

RATIONAL EVOLUTION

Where do these arguments leave us? I believe we should be pursuing rational evolution. Rational evolution goes beyond Darwinian evolution, where the focus was survival. Rational evolution asks in what ways it would be rational to evolve. I believe there should be two goals to rational evolution. First, to increase wellbeing (and autonomy), and second, to achieve some sort of moral ordering of society. Our choices should reflect our pursuit of those goals.

The biggest questions that we face as a society are: what is a good life, and how do we balance individual interests against those of society as a whole? How much should we promote some conception of justice at the cost of some aspects of individual wellbeing? These questions are relevant, whether we're talking about education policy, or immigration policy, or our approach to biological enhancement. Varieties of biological enhancement will increasingly become available – which will have the consequence that we will be forced to confront these ethical questions.

REGULATION: A SPORTING CASE STUDY[5]

How then should bioenhancement be regulated? We began with the case of cognitive enhancement in education. However, a much more developed issue is the regulation of performance enhancement in sport.

The war on drugs in sport will inevitably fail. It will fail because the substances used today are so difficult to detect. Growth hormone, used in training to build muscle strength, is a natural substance which has so far proved impossible to detect. Blood doping boosts the oxygen carrying capacity of blood – it uses the person's own blood, stored months before. Only the incompetent or poorly resourced dopers get caught. Couple this with enormous financial incentives attached to winning, and the pressures to dope are irresistible. Meanwhile, the resources for detection are limited.

So my view is that the ban on enhancement drugs should be lifted.

First, it is ruining the sporting spectacle. We don't know who is clean and who isn't.

Second, it risks harming the health of athletes who use undetectable substances and methods, but often with no medical supervision.

Third, it is unfair. Honest athletes can't access safe enhancement methods to whittle down the advantage of the cheaters.

Finally, it is against the spirit of sport. Throughout human history, athletes have used various substances to improve their performance. Some doping agents have been permitted – like caffeine, which increases the time until an athlete feels exhausted by 10%. It used to be banned and athletes were stripped of the medals. It is legal today because it is safe enough. It hasn't ruined the spirit of sport. To be human is to be better.

The solution is simple. Relax the ban on doping. Allow performance enhancers in adults (not children) which satisfy three criteria.

First, they should be safe enough. Safety should be judged relative to the risks of sport, which are often considerable. American football can cause quadriplegia. Medically supervised administration of steroids has nothing like that kind of risk. Blood doping could be allowed up to a level of 50% red blood cells in blood. This is safe, and it can be monitored with a cheap and reliable test.

Second, the drugs taken should be consistent with the spirit of the sport in question. Steroids do not add some magical ability that is not naturally present – they simply enhance the effects of hard training and accelerate recovery from injury. However, beta blockers to reduce tremor would compromise sports which test the athlete's nerve – such as archery, shooting, and snooker. Drugs which eliminated fear in boxing would be against the spirit of boxing.

Last, the intervention should not dominate or dehumanize performance. Robotic limbs would substantially remove the human element from running. But steroids, growth hormone, and blood doping merely mimic natural processes.

I believe that we should move away from a zero-tolerance approach to performance enhancement in sport to an approach which balances different values of safety, spectacle, consistent record keeping, tests of physical and mental talents, and so on. In sport, this would allow "physiological doping", or doping using substances which occur naturally in the body within limits of safe, normal human physiology.

This is consistent with my view that enhancement is not intrinsically objectionable. But the enhancement revolution will require us to rethink our laws, policies, and nature as human beings.

NOTES

1 This chapter is derived from an interview: www.rotman.uwo.ca/should-human-enhancement-be-a-moral-imperative-an-interview-with-julian-savulescu/.
2 The policy can be consulted here: https://studentaffairs.duke.edu/conduct/z-policies/academic-dishonesty.
3 See *Unfit for the Future: The Need for Moral Enhancement* (Oxford: OUP, 2012).
4 Persson, I., and Savulescu, J. (2018) "The Moral Importance of Reflective Empathy". *Neuroethics*, 11(2), 183–193.
5 This section on doping is derived from www.nytimes.com/roomfordebate/2012/08/07/should-doping-be-allowed-in-sports/permit-doping-so-we-can-monitor-it.

AI and robot ethics
Twenty Five

John Tasioulas

INTRODUCTION

For almost all of human history, robots existed only as imaginary beings with a Jekyll-and-Hyde nature. At one extreme, they promise to usher in a utopia free of illness, poverty, and the drudgery of work; at the other, they are intent on enslaving or destroying humankind. But only in the middle of the last century did robots become a significant real-world presence. This is sometimes dated from the time General Motors installed 'Unimate' in one of its plants to carry out manual tasks – such as welding and spraying – that were too hazardous for human workers.[1] Today, robots are so commonplace in manufacturing that they are a major cause of unemployment in that sector. But the use of robots in factories is only the beginning of a 'robot revolution' – itself part of a wider revolution in Artificial Intelligence (AI) – that has had, or promises to have, transformative effects on all aspects of our lives.

Robots are now being used, or being developed for use, in a vast array of settings. Driverless cars are expected to appear on our roads within a decade. Such cars have the potential to reduce traffic accidents, which currently claim more than a million lives each year worldwide, by up to 90%, and in addition to reduce pollution and traffic congestion.[2] Robots perform domestic chores, including vacuuming, ironing, and walking pets. In medicine and social care, robots are used to make diagnoses or perform surgery, as well as in therapy for children with autism or in the care of the elderly. Tutor robots already exist, as do social robots that provide companionship, or even sex. In the business world, AI figures heavily in the stock market, where computers make most decisions automatically, as well as in the insurance and mortgage industries. Even the recruitment of human workers is turning into a largely automated process, with many job applications being rejected without ever being read by a human decision-maker. AI-based technology, some of it robotic, also plays a role in the criminal justice system, assisting in policing and even sentencing. The development of autonomous weapons systems (AWSs), which select and attack military targets without human intervention, promises a new era in military defence.

In this chapter, I'll examine some of the ethical questions posed by robots and AI (or RAIs, as I shall call them). The overall challenge is to find ways to harness the benefits of RAIs while responding adequately to the risks we incur in doing so. But first we must clarify some key terms.[3]

WHAT IS A ROBOT? WHAT IS ARTIFICIAL INTELLIGENCE?

A recent UNESCO report describes robots as artificial beings with four characteristics:

- mobility, which is important for functioning in human environments like hospitals and offices;
- interactivity, made possible by sensors and actuators, which gather relevant information from the environment and enable a robot to act upon this environment;

- *communication*, made possible by computer interfaces or voice recognition and speech synthesis systems; and
- *autonomy*, in the sense of an ability to 'think' for themselves and make their own decisions to act upon the environment, without direct external control.[4]

The sophisticated robots that are our topic in this chapter operate on the basis of Artificial Intelligence (AI). This is 'the science of making machines do things that would require intelligence if done by men',[5] such as face recognition or language translation. In understanding AI, two distinctions are important: (a) general and narrow AI, and (b) top-down and bottom-up AI. The first distinction relates to the scope of AI capabilities, the other to AI's technical functioning.

General AI refers to an intelligent machine that is able to replicate a broad range of human intellectual capacities, and even to surpass them. These forms of AI, although familiar from science fiction characters such as *Star Wars'* C3PO, probably lie in the remote future. To the extent that there has been significant progress in AI in recent years, it has occurred in *narrow AI*. These are machines that replicate, or surpass, human capabilities with respect to a limited range of tasks, e.g. car driving, medical diagnosis, or language translation.

AI operates by means of algorithms, which are rules or instructions for the solution of various problems, embodied in computers. Algorithms are of two broad kinds, corresponding to two kinds of robots: deterministic and cognitive robots. *Top-down* (or deterministic) algorithms control a robot's behaviour by means of a pre-determined program, with the result that the deterministic robot's behaviour is highly predictable. *Bottom-up* algorithms, by contrast, enable a robot to 'learn' from past experience and revise its algorithm over time.

An example of this 'machine learning' is Google's DeepMind algorithm, which taught itself to play Atari games, such as Breakout, inventing successful new strategies that astonished its own programmers. Cognitive robots of this sort enjoy a level of 'autonomy' not only in the sense that their behaviour need not depend on human decision, or be subject to human intervention, but in the more radical sense that it may not even be predictable by human beings.

We should, of course, exercise caution when throwing around terms like 'intelligence', 'reasoning', 'decision', and 'autonomy' in relation to AI. These terms must not obscure the fact that a vast chasm still separates RAIs and human beings. AI systems process symbols, but they cannot (as yet) *understand* in any meaningful sense what these symbols stand for in the real world.[6] Moreover, even if RAIs can be successful in achieving complex goals – like recognizing a face in a crowd or translating a document from one language to another – they lack anything like the human capacity to deliberate about whether or not to adopt a given goal. For some philosophers, this power of rational autonomy is the source of the special dignity that attaches to human beings and differentiates them from non-human animals. No RAIs known to us are anywhere near exhibiting such rational autonomy.

ETHICAL QUESTIONS

RAIs generate a variety of ethical questions on at least three inter-connected levels. One level concerns the *laws* that should be enacted to govern RAI-related activities. Do we need special traffic laws for driverless cars, and how should the law on accident liability apply to them? In addition to domestic legislation, RAIs also raise pressing questions that require regional or international legal solutions, e.g. through treaties on AWSs.

A second level concerns the kind of *social morality* that we should cultivate in relation to RAIs. Not all of the socially accepted standards that properly govern our lives are, or should be, legal standards. We rely not only on the law to discourage people from wrongful behaviour, such as murder or theft, but also on moral standards that are instilled in us from childhood. Similarly, we need to reflect on the shape of a morally sound culture in relation to RAIs.

At a third level, there are questions that arise for *individuals and associations* (businesses, universities, professional bodies, etc.) regarding their engagement with RAIs. Whatever social modes of regulation exist on these matters, individuals and associations will still need to exercise their own moral judgement. This may be because law and social morality lag behind technical developments, or because they are deficient in some way, or because they confer on individuals the freedom to make their own decisions in certain areas.

These three levels interact in complex ways. For example, it may be that there are strong moral reasons against adults using a robot as a sexual partner (third level). But, out of respect for their individual autonomy, they should be free under the law to do so (first level). However, there may also be good reasons to cultivate a social morality that generally frowns upon such activities (second level), so that the sale and public display of sex robots is legally constrained in various ways (through, say, taxation or advertising restrictions) akin to the legal restrictions on tobacco (first level, again).

FIVE MAJOR MORAL ISSUES – A FIRST ANALYSIS

Many of the moral issues raised by RAIs can be arranged under five main headings – functionality, inherent significance, rights and responsibilities, side-effects, and threats – which generate the acronym 'FIRST'.

Functionality

The first issue is whether a proposed RAI is functional. Functionality concerns a RAI's ability to:

- achieve a *worthwhile* goal, e.g. transporting passengers to their desired destination, and to do so:
- *effectively*, i.e. with a reliable degree of success;
- *efficiently*, i.e. without undue expenditure of resources; and
- in a *morally appropriate way*, i.e. without violating moral norms as part of its operation, e.g. rights to privacy.

Let's focus on the last requirement, which throws up two large questions: (a) what are the moral standards that apply to RAIs, and (b) how can they be built into the operation of RAIs?

A famous attempt to address the first question is Isaac Asimov's 'Three Laws of Robotics':

1 A robot may not injure a human being or, through inaction, allow a human being to come to harm.
2 A robot must obey the orders given it by human beings, except where such orders would conflict with the First Law.

3   A robot must protect its own existence as long as such protection does not conflict with the First or Second Laws.[7]

But Asimov's laws have problems. For example, the first law underestimates the complexity of the dilemmas RAIs may confront.[8] A classic dilemma is how a driverless car should respond to situations where there is a choice between avoiding harm to its passenger – e.g. by swerving out of the path of an oncoming truck – versus avoiding harm to other humans (drivers, passengers or pedestrians) who are at risk of death or injury if the car swerves to save its passenger. This is the famous 'trolley problem', and it receives conflicting responses. Most people believe that passengers should be sacrificed in order to save a greater number of bystanders, yet most would also prefer to ride in a car that always saves its passenger.[9] That suggests not enough people would buy the first type of car to make it worth producing.

The second question, about how to build ethical norms into the workings of RAIs, is no less challenging. Many doubt whether algorithms can ever replicate the sophisticated moral reasoning of humans. Variations in the moral problems that confront us are too complex, they claim, for algorithms to register. And sound moral reasoning depends on certain emotional capacities – such as fear, empathy, guilt – that machines cannot possess. On the other hand, if the correct account of morality is given by a theory such as utilitarianism, requiring complex predictions of which action would maximize utility, the prospects for moral reasoning by RAIs may be much brighter.

But even if RAIs can't replicate human moral reasoning in general, can they at least abide by specific moral norms relevant to their functioning? One challenge to the ethical functioning of RAIs is that of algorithmic bias. RAIs are driven by algorithms that are trained on datasets. They operate by generalizing from these datasets to future scenarios. The problem arises from the fact that the training data may itself be defective. It may be statistically skewed, e.g. not representative of minority groups, or it may embody prejudices about certain classes of people. Recent examples of real-life algorithmic bias include an algorithm used by an English police force that discriminated against people from poorer areas in deciding whether to keep offenders in custody, job search tools that favoured men for high income jobs, and facial recognition algorithms, used in a range of applications from internet image searches to police enforcement, that have been shown to have much higher error rates for women and non-white people.[10]

Does it matter whether RAIs function as well as humans? That depends on the value of the goal in question and the risks we should be prepared to run in order to achieve it. For some tasks, such as housecleaning, it may be enough that a RAI performs adequately even if not quite as well as humans. In other tasks, such as driving, medical diagnosis, or the sentencing of criminals, what is at stake may be so important – life, health, liberty – that RAI functionality must be at least as good, or better, than that ordinarily achieved by human beings. Superior performance by RAIs is something that may also be needed to outweigh the unwelcome side-effects and threats that reliance on them may also generate, such as job losses or sabotage by malicious agents.

Inherent significance

Even if RAIs can achieve sufficient functionality in a given task, questions may arise about the inherent significance of assigning that task to RAIs. Sometimes, the elimination of the 'human factor' may be beneficial. In the case of an elderly person who needs assistance when bathing, for example, a robot carer can minimize the risk of embarrassment. But the elimination of the human factor can also be troubling. One context where this concern seems especially acute is that of RAIs making decisions that have serious consequences for human beings. What is mainly at issue here are decisions based on bottom-up, not top-down, algorithms which are therefore not necessarily predictable by the human manufacturer of the RAI.

Consider, for example, the sentencing of criminals by RAIs or the use of AWSs. Even if RAIs could achieve a level of functionality comparable, or superior, to human judges and soldiers, we might be troubled by the fact that RAIs' decisions impact so severely on human life and liberty.

Why? Well, one thought here is that decisions about the life and liberty of others are so significant that something valuable is lost if they are made by a being who cannot take *responsibility* for them as an autonomous rational agent. There is no decision-maker of whom one can demand *their* reasons for reaching the decision they did. There is a valuable human solidarity and reciprocity – human beings recognizing each other as fellow human beings and forming their attitudes and decisions on that basis – that disappears in the context of fully automated decision-making.

Another context in which the absence of the human factor is troubling is that in which RAIs enter into personal relationships. Here is John C. Havens' imaginary description of meeting his 16-year-old daughter's first date, Rob, who is a robot:

> But this robot was dating my daughter. This was my Melanie. I realized that Rob was a far cry from an iPhone or smart fridge in terms of his advanced technology,

but I couldn't stop feeling a sense of revulsion in his presence. As hard as I tried to be civil, I knew he was equipped with facial recognition and physiological sensor tracking and could tell I was freaking out. My pulse was racing and my pupils were dilated in ways Rob's technology would easily correlate with stress. Hopefully he wasn't live-streaming the data to his blog or other social channel. I could just picture the tweet: *Girlfriend's dad freaking out because I'm not 'human'. #robot_racism.*[11]

The narrator's revulsion arises from the introduction of a robot into a form of relationship that – up until now – we have reserved for humans. Ideally, in a romantic relationship, the parties value each other not simply as means, but as ends in themselves, partly in virtue of their ability to reciprocate feelings and emotions such as love and affection. Dating a robot with a human form may not be quite as weird as a romantic attachment to an iPhone, but it's arguably still problematic for the same sort of reasons. An instrument is being made to play a role that properly belongs to a person.

Rights and responsibilities

If a RAI is functional and there are no compelling inherent reasons against deploying it, the question arises as to whether it possesses a moral status that confers upon it rights and responsibilities. As an artifact, created to further our ends, it seems doubtful that a RAI can possess the inherent value required to ground such a status. If RAIs replicated our general capacity for rational autonomy, there would be a case for according them a comparable moral status to human beings, with corresponding rights (e.g. to self-defence) as well as responsibilities (e.g. to pay taxes). Indeed, it may be that in coming years, the human/machine divide itself will gradually blur and even disappear with the appearance of various hybrids or cyborgs (RAIs integrated with human beings). In the words of a proponent of 'transhumanism', Ray Kurzweil:

> Computers started out as large remote machines in air-conditioned rooms tended by white coated technicians. Subsequently they moved onto our desks, then under our arms, and now in our pockets. Soon, we'll routinely put them inside our bodies and brains. Ultimately we will become more non-biological than biological.[12]

Such developments could have radical implications for the content of the moral standards that apply to RAIs, such as a right to self-defence that could justify killing or harming humans who pose a threat to them. However, as we have already seen, general AI seems a very distant prospect, even if it cannot be totally ruled out as a logical possibility.

The more pressing question is whether a good case exists for attributing legal status, with corresponding legal rights and responsibilities, to RAIs alongside other 'artificial persons' recognized by law, such as corporations. Such a case seems more plausible for cognitive robots, given that their behaviour is not fully predictable, than deterministic robots. In the case of the latter, it makes sense to attribute legal responsibility to manufacturers, owners, or users. But in the case of the former, given the unpredictability of their behaviour, rights and responsibilities might be attributed to the robot itself. Along these lines, the European Parliament has entertained the possibility of creating a special legal status for robots, so that at least the more sophisticated autonomous robots have the status of electronic persons. As such, they would be responsible for making good any damage they may cause.[13] Critics say that this approach serves only to enable makers and users of RAIs to evade their responsibilities.

But even if this criticism is sound, it is arguable that cognitive robots are sufficiently different from most machines that existing law must be revised to take into account their capacity for autonomous behaviour. Underlying this issue will be the need to solve a technical problem: how to ensure the 'traceability' of RAIs in order to be able to assign moral or legal responsibility in relation to them. Traceability involves being able to determine the causes that led a RAI to behave in the way that it did, and securing it seems especially difficult in the case of RAIs that involve bottom-up, non-deterministic algorithms.

Side-effects

We also need to consider the side-effects, both good and bad, likely to result from the use of RAIs. One positive side-effect, for example, is that of affording people greater opportunities to develop their personal relationships or pursue leisure activities. On the other hand, many worry that RAIs will cause significant levels of unemployment and, ultimately, spark social deprivation and unrest. These are, properly speaking, side-effects, since even RAIs intended to replace human labour do not have as part of their goal to cause unemployment or its attendant societal problems. These are at most foreseen but unintended consequences.

Experts disagree about whether the widespread use of RAIs will significantly increase unemployment. One study claimed that up to 50% of American jobs, including jobs performed by lawyers, doctors, and accountants, are at risk of being automated.[14] In the United Kingdom, more than one in three jobs could be taken over by RAIs in the next 20 years, with the impact disproportionately affecting those in repetitive, low-paid jobs.[15] But this may not necessarily cause a significant rise in unemployment. The history of technological innovation suggests that new kinds of jobs, of which we currently have no inkling, might emerge, often responding to new wants that technological advances have helped generate.[16] Others take a pessimistic view, especially if they anticipate that RAIs will come to have superhuman capacities that will render pretty much all human workers obsolete.[17] Whatever the truth turns out to be, it is likely that many people will lose their jobs to RAIs and will face great difficulty in retraining for any new jobs that eventually emerge.

These possibilities force us to address the value of work. Partly its value has to do with earning income. But work also serves other values: it is a source of accomplishment and self-worth, it fosters virtues of responsibility and self-discipline, and it provides a focus for social engagement. Will we need to limit, in some way, the incursion of RAIs into our economic life in order to preserve adequate human access to these values? Perhaps we should use RAIs mainly as tools to assist, rather than replace, human workers. Or are there feasible, and perhaps even preferable, ways of realizing these values through other pursuits, such as family life, art, religious worship, or sport?

Unemployment is just one worrying potential side-effect of RAIs. A more diffuse worry is that over-reliance on RAIs may lead to the loss of valuable skills and to diminishing our sense of responsibility for our own lives. Doctors, drivers, and pilots, for example, may lose the skills they need to perform well in emergencies; ordinary people may become excessively dependent on RAIs for daily decisions about everything from the food they eat to the books they read. There are other serious worries, including corrosive effects on our relations with other humans. The more that our lives revolve around interactions with machines – often endowed with human-like forms and voices – that service our desires, the more we might slip into adopting the same instrumentalizing attitude towards our fellow humans.

Threats

Threats to our interests and values can arise from RAIs that are specifically designed to carry out bad goals, such as privacy-violating surveillance, financial fraud, or terrorist attacks. They may also arise from RAIs that were created to perform worthwhile ends being sabotaged or subverted, such as by having their algorithms fed with false or corrupted data or being hacked by malevolent agents. The prospect of a world in which your smart phone is spying on you or AWSs fall into the hands of terrorists is hardly far-fetched. And the threats come not only from criminals, terrorist groups, or corporations, but from governments, too, which may use RAIs as instruments of repression.[18]

One of the gravest threats posed by RAIs is to the proper functioning of democracy itself. Democracy not only requires that all citizens have a vote, but also that they are able to exercise their vote after free and informed deliberation and debate on the issues at stake. Concerns have arisen in recent years about the use of RAIs to distort these democratic processes. Methods used to this effect have included sending individuals personalized political advertisements based on data illicitly gleaned from social media platforms, such as Facebook, or using robot accounts – 'bots' – that masquerade as human in order to saturate Twitter and other platforms with propaganda. As to the magnitude of the threat to democracy, the moral philosopher Onora O'Neill has issued a stark warning:

> Not deceiving is one of the fundamental duties. When I think about technology, I wonder whether we will have democracy in 20 years because if we cannot find ways to solve this problem, we will not. People are receiving messages and content which is distributed by robots, not by other human beings, let alone by other fellow citizens. It is frightening.[19]

Ways of addressing this problem will include technology-specific measures such as enhanced privacy protection for personal data, greater transparency regarding the use of data by online platform providers, and more stringent registration processes for social media accounts. It will be important also to address structural deficiencies of our political systems. For example, the United States' lax campaign-financing laws arguably make it easier for resources to be funnelled into the large-scale dissemination of 'fake news'. More generally, we face a conundrum. What is needed to counter most of the societal threats posed by RAIs is to ensure decision-makers are held to account through democratic politics; but this involves us in a race against time, since one of the gravest of those threats is precisely to the functioning of democracy. We need democratic solutions to the problems posed by RAIs before they are used to destroy democracy itself.

However, according to some, the greatest threat posed by RAIs is the one from which this chapter began: that they become so much smarter than humans that they eventually subjugate or eradicate us in pursuit of their own ends. This doomsday scenario has been emphasized by prominent figures in the business of RAIs, such as Bill Gates and Elon Musk, as well as by leading scientists, such as the late Stephen Hawking, who observed towards the end of his life:

> A super-intelligent AI will be extremely good at accomplishing its goals, and if those goals aren't aligned with ours, we're in trouble. . . . You're probably not an evil ant-hater who steps on ants out of malice, but if you're in charge of a hydroelectric green energy project and there's an anthill in the region to be flooded, too bad for the ants. Let's not place humanity in the position of those ants.[20]

Some have dismissed such warnings as irresponsibly speculative, on the basis that general AI, let alone general AI of a superhuman form, is not a realistic prospect in the foreseeable future.[21] On this view, doomsday scenarios are fantasies that distract us from other, urgent RAI-related problems that we face. But another response focuses on the assumption that underlies Hawking's warning. Why assume that the goals of super intelligent RAIs will be troublingly unaligned with ours? If RAIs develop truly superhuman abilities, won't these include the abilities to reason about, and conform to, morality? Imagine, then, a world in which we are governed by just and benevolent RAIs that far surpass any human in intelligence and goodness. Would this scenario be the ultimate fulfilment of the promise of RAIs to serve humankind? Or would it, rather, be a deep betrayal of our interests and values?

1 http://my.ilstu.edu/~kldevin/Introduction_to_robotics2/Introduction_to_robotics6.html

2 J.-F. Bonnefon, A. Shariff, and I. Rahwan, 'The Social Dilemma of Autonomous Vehicles', *Science* 352 (2006), pp. 1573–1576. http://science.sciencemag.org/content/352/6293/1573

3 For helpful overviews of developments robotics and AI, and the ethical issues they raise, see D. Edmonds, 'Can We Teach Robots Ethics?', *BBC News*, October 15, 2017. www.bbc.co.uk/news/magazine-41504285 and M. Tegmark, *Life 3.0: Being Human in the Age of Artificial Intelligence* (London: Penguin, 2017), esp. ch.3.

4 UNESCO, *Report of COMEST on Robotics Ethics* (Paris, September 14, 2017), p. 4. http://unesdoc.unesco.org/images/0025/002539/253952E.pdf

5 M. Minsky, quoted in UNESCO, p. 17.

6 M. Tegmark, *Life 3.0: Being Human in the Age of Artificial Intelligence* (London: Penguin, 2017), esp. ch.3.

7 I. Asimov, "Runaround". *I, Robot* (hardcover) (The Isaac Asimov Collection ed.) (New York City: Doubleday, 1950), p. 40.

8 See the fifth framework ethical principle outlined in House of Lords AI Committee, *AI in the UK; Ready, Willing and Able?* April 16, 2018, HL Paper 100, p. 125: 'The autonomous power to hurt, destroy or deceive a human being should never be vested in artificial intelligence'. https://publications.parliament.uk/pa/ld201719/ldselect/ldai/100/10002.htm

9 J.-F. Bonnefon, A. Shariff, and I. Rahwan, 'The Social Dilemma of Autonomous Vehicles', *Science* 352 (2006), pp. 1573–1576. http://science.sciencemag.org/content/352/6293/1573

10 www.wired.co.uk/article/police-ai-uk-durham-hart-checkpoint-algorithm-edit. Also: www.wired.co.uk/article/machine-learning-bias-prejudice and C. O'Neil, *Weapons of Math Destruction: How Big Data Increases Inequality and Threatens Democracy* (Penguin, 2016). http://proceedings.mlr.press/v81/buolamwini18a/buolamwini18a.pdf

11 John C. Havens, *Heartificial Intelligence*, (London: Penguin, 2016), p. 4.

12 R. Kurzweil, 'We Are Becoming Cyborgs', March 15, 2002. www.kurzweilai.net/we-are-becoming-cyborgs. For a fuller discussion, see R. Kurzweil, *The Singularity Is Near: When Humans Transcend Biology* (London: Penguin, 2005).

13 European Parliament, Report with recommendations to the Commission on Civil Law Rules on Robotics, Jan 27, 2017, para 59(f). www.europarl.europa.eu/sides/getDoc.do?pubRef=-//EP//NONSGML+TA+P8-TA-2017-0051+0+DOC+PDF+V0//EN

14 C.B. Frey and M.A. Osborne, 'The Future of Employment: How Susceptible Are Jobs to Computerisation?', September 17, 2013. www.

oxfordmartin.ox.ac.uk/downloads/academic/The_Future_of_
Employment.pdf

15 A. Tovey, 'Ten Million Jobs at Risk from Advancing Technology', *Telegraph*,
November 10, 2014. www.telegraph.co.uk/finance/newsbysector/
industry/11219688/Ten-million-jobs-at-risk-from-advancing-technology.
html

16 B. Milanovic, 'Three Fallacies that Make You Fear a Robot Economy',
Evonomics, September 1, 2016. http://evonomics.com/three-fallacies-
robot-economy-branko/. For a different perspective, see C. Drury,
'Mark Carney Warns Robots Taking Jobs Could Lead to Rise of Marx-
ism', April 14, 2018. www.independent.co.uk/news/uk/home-news/
mark-carney-marxism-automation-bank-of-england-governor-job-
losses-capitalism-a8304706.html.

17 See the video 'Humans Need Not Apply', *Aeon*. https://aeon.co/videos/
the-robots-are-coming-for-our-jobs-why-the-human-workforce-is-at-
risk

18 J. Brown, 'Would You Choose a Partner Based on Their "Citizen Score"?',
March 13, 2018. www.bbc.co.uk/news/business-43335813

19 Onora O'Neill interview with Elena Cué, 'Onora O'Neill: 'I Wonder
Whether We Will Have Democracy in 20 Years', *Huffington Post*. www.
huffingtonpost.com/entry/onora-oneill-i-wonder-whether-we-will-
have-democracy_us_5a4f8a12e4b0cd114bdb324f (downloaded 1/5/
2018). See also D. Helbing et al., 'Will Democracy Survive Big Data
and Artificial Intelligence?', *Scientific American*, February 25, 2017.
https://www.scientificamerican/article/will-democracy-survive-big-
data-and-artificial-intelligence

20 A. Griffin, 'Stephen Hawking: Artificial Intelligence Could Wipe Out
Humanity When It Gets Too Clever as Humans Will Be Like Ants', October 8, 2015. www.independent.co.uk/life-style/gadgets-and-tech/
news/stephen-hawking-artificial-intelligence-could-wipe-out-
humanity-when-it-gets-too-clever-as-humans-a6686496.html

21 L. Floridi, 'Should we be Afraid of AI?', *Aeon*, May 9, 2016. https://aeon.
co/essays/true-ai-is-both-logically-possible-and-utterly-implausible

Index

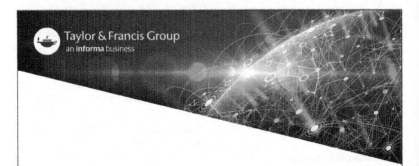